MOURNING DIANA

The death of Diana Princess of Wales, on 31 August 1997, prompted public demonstrations of grief on an almost unprecedented scale. Global media coverage of the events following Diana's death appeared to create an international 'community of mourning'. However, such scenes of 'mass grief' were shadowed by significant social and political tensions. The mourning (and not mourning) of Diana seemed to cross and yet confirm social divisions, to shift and at the same time redraw political boundaries.

Mourning Diana examines the events which followed the death of Diana as a series of cultural and political phenomena, mediated through popular narrative and social performance. It explores the distinctive ways that 'mass mourning' and the spectacle of public grief appeared to witness dramatic shifts in power relations, political affiliations, and cultural identities. Contributors investigate the complex iconic status of Diana as a 'spectral' figure able to sustain a host of alternative identifications. They trace the posthumous, highly gendered and racialized, romanticization of aspects of her life, such as her 'humanitarianism' and her relationship with Dodi Al Fayed, and examine the centrality of the Diana events to the New Labour project. The contributors argue that the mourning of Diana dramatized a complex set of cultural processes in which the borders dividing nationhood and citizenship, charity and activism, social dispossession and royal privilege, private feeling and public politics were sharply contested and yet ultimately reaffirmed.

Contributors: Jean Duruz, Susanne Greenhalgh, Valerie Hey, Carol Johnson, Richard Johnson, Adrian Kear, Joe Kelleher, Mica Nava, Arvind Rajagopal, William J. Spurlin, Deborah Lynn Steinberg, Diana Taylor, Jatinder Verma, Valerie Walkerdine.

Adrian Kear is a senior lecturer in drama and theatre studies at Roehampton Institute, London. **Deborah Lynn Steinberg** is a senior lecturer at the Department of Sociology at Warwick University.

MOURNING DIANA

Nation, culture and the performance of grief

*Edited by Adrian Kear and
Deborah Lynn Steinberg*

London and New York

First published 1999
by Routledge
11 New Fetter Lane, London EC4P 4EE

Simultaneously published in the USA and Canada
by Routledge
29 West 35th Street, New York, NY 10001

Routledge is an imprint of the Taylor & Francis Group

© 1999 Adrian Kear and Deborah Lynn Steinberg for selection and
editorial matter. Individual chapters © 1999 contributors

Typeset in Garamond by
J&L Composition Ltd, Filey, North Yorkshire
Printed and bound in Great Britain by Biddles Ltd, Guildford and
King's Lynn

British Library Cataloguing in Publication Data
A catalogue record for this book is available
from the British Library

Library of Congress Cataloging in Publication Data
Mourning Diana/edited by Adrian Kear and Deborah Lynn
Steinberg.
p.   cm.
Includes bibliographical references and index.
ISBN 0–415–19392–3 (hardbound: alk. paper).—
ISBN 0–415–19393–1 (pbk.: alk. paper)
1. Diana, Princess of Wales. 1961–   —Death and
burial. 2. Mourning customs—Great Britain—History—20th
century. 3. Monarchy—Great Britain—History—20th
century. 4. Mourning customs—History—20th
centiruy. I. Kear, Adrian, 1970–   . II. Steinberg, Deborah Lynn.
DA591.A45D5348 1999
941.085'092—dc21   99–25590
[B]   CIP

ISBN 0–415–19392–3 (hbk)
ISBN 0–415–19393–1 (pbk)

CONTENTS

CONTENTS

ACKNOWLEDGEMENTS

Adrian Kear would like to thank Peter Reynolds and Alan Read for supporting the writing of this book, and Joe Kelleher and Susanne Greenhalgh for their academic comradeship. Nancy Jenkins provided invaluable help at the hardest of times, and Deborah Lynn Steinberg showed exemplary care and clarity throughout the collaborative process. Deborah Lynn Steinberg would like to thank Debbie Epstein and Richard Johnson and the members of the narrative group for their intellectual support and assistance. Both editors would also like to thank the contributors to this book for their thoughtfulness, hard work and commitment to the collection.

Preface

MOURNING DIANA AND THE SCHOLARLY ETHIC

Adrian Kear and Deborah Lynn Steinberg

In the preface to the unusually rapidly produced academic collection *Planet Diana*, Ien Ang argues that:

> Academics are generally slow and late, often too late, in their response to public matters that matter now, not tomorrow. Beaten by the immediacy of journalism, their seriously theorised but nonetheless on-the-spot insights do not often get the opportunity to enter into the public arena until everyone else has moved on.
>
> (Re:Public 1997: v)

It seems beyond doubt that the reflective (as well as futural) orientation of scholarship demands a certain taking of time and that this time can appear to be out of sync with the temporal intensities and immediacies of everyday life. Journalism's rapid turnover of successions of 'significant moments', its trade in evaluative judgements – often cast as certainties or singularities – produced *in* the moment, seems to override scholarship's need to widen the moment and to think through its complexities. Ang's invocation of the need for academic responsivity to the responsibilities *of* the moment is a demand for a change in the scholary ethic that goes beyond a simple temporal shift. It is a requirement to inhabit a 'now time' of reading and analysis (Benjamin, cited in Diamond 1997: 146) that enables direct participation in the construction of the contemporary. At the same time, Ang's seeming dismissal, here, of the scholarly obligation to 'tomorrow' would appear to deny the *historicity* of the 'now' – the constitutive pasts and futural possibilities contained within a present moment and necessitating continuing critical reflection. Thus an exhortation to scholarship *of* the present *in* the present, without the anticipation of the long view back, might sacrifice the scholarly ethic it is trying to extend. It risks collusion with the 'maelstrom of ever more rapidly running time' (Re:Public 1997: vi) and submersion in the seamless sequences of a continuous present.

Mourning Diana is an attempt to respond to the critical imperatives and renewed perspectives of hindsight. The collection comprises a range of intersecting approaches and interdisciplinary frameworks (including those drawn from feminist, queer and cultural studies, peformance studies, studies of visual representation, sociological, literary and political theory) in order to unpack the complexities of the Diana events. The book aims to elucidate the seemingly dramatic cultural changes and subtextual recuperations emergent in the enactment of mourning Diana. It considers the distinctive ways in which loss, mourning and popular spectacle mediate the (re)formation of common senses and social relations. In particular, this collection of essays emphasizes the performativity of grief and loss in the (re)construction of cultural identities and political hegemony.[1]

The volume is structured around a number of interrelated thematic currents. The first is what might be termed *mobilized mourning* in which the Diana events are examined as cultural-political phenomena, emphasizing their role in the reconstitution of political affiliations and ideological formations. Here questions of 'mass movement' intersect with those concerning the theatricality of public spectacle. A second area of concern focuses on the complex dynamics of *identification* and the cultural construction of *iconicity*. Here the tools of psychoanalysis and the methods of semiology provide frameworks through which to consider mourning and visual representation as sites of phantasmatic investment. The third area concerns the question of boundaries: for example, between the personal and the political; the local and the global; the ontological and the spectral. In this context, competing discursive constructions of 'the people', 'the nation' and 'the international community' are examined as sites – embodied and ephemeral – in which political borders are constituted, transgressed and reconfirmed. A fourth theme foregrounds questions of *institutional privilege*, *social dispossession* and *cultural power*. Emphasis is placed on the apparent breaching yet silencing of classed, racialized and (hetero)sexist social divisions in the wake of the Diana events, and on the ways in which mainstreams appeared to be 'queered', margins moved and boundaries reinscribed.

Notes

1 As Tony Walters (1999) notes, his similarly entitled collection *The Mourning of Diana* can be differentiated from this book by its emphasis on empirical analysis and sociological record. Furthermore, Walters's own chapter provides an excellent summary of key academic and journalistic approaches to both Diana and the responses to her death.

References

Re:Public (Ien Ang, Ruth Barcan *et al.*) (eds) (1997) *Planet Diana: Cultural Studies and Global Mourning*, Kingswood, New South Wales: Research Centre in Intercommunal Studies, University of Western Sydney, Nepean.

Diamond, Elin (1997) *Unmaking Mimesis: Essays on Feminism and Theatre*, New York and London, Routledge.

Walters, Tony (1999) 'The Questions People Asked', in Tony Walters (ed.) *The Mourning of Diana*, London: Berg.

1

GHOST WRITING

Adrian Kear and Deborah Lynn Steinberg

In the early hours of 31 August 1997, the Mercedes Benz transporting Diana Princess of Wales, Dodi Al Fayed, Henri Paul and Trevor Rhys Jones crashed into the wall of a Paris underpass, killing the first three and seriously wounding the fourth. This fatal crash occurred during their high-speed flight from the paparazzi of the world press.

In the aftermath of this accident an escalating series of incidents cata-pulted the death of Diana into a worldwide event. For instance, regular broadcasting schedules were disrupted, and in Britain they were virtually suspended as the news of Diana's death was announced across the globe. The first flowers of mourning were laid to mark her death as initial steps toward what would become multiple and monumental shrines. Crowds began to assemble in public demonstrations of mourning outside royal palaces and in common spaces. The media, struggling to produce coherent accounts of these deaths and of the growing scale of response to them, focused on and thereby created mourning Diana as both public spectacle and spectacular media event.

Commentary upon the deaths became another facet of events. The frag-mentary and contested knowledge of 'what really happened' provided a fertile ground for spiralling interpretations. The first register of commentary was, perhaps inevitably, disbelief and blame. The role of the press in the deaths appeared to place the powers of the media under censure. Conspiracy theories of assassination implicated the royal family and the British estab-lishment (those who disapproved of Diana and of her 'miscegenation' with Dodi Al Fayed) in their deaths. The jammed speedometer and the leaked information about the driver's intoxication also pointed the blame towards Henri Paul. In a second register, a multitude of differing and differently emphasized Diana stories were told, which seemed to testify to her pervasive significance. A third register was commemoration: massive queues of people waited up to eight hours to sign the books of condolence provided for the inscription of popular and personal memorializations; media and publishing institutions mobilized an immense Diana industry of endlessly reproduced images, biography, music and documentary.

Through these events, a number of contestatory 'Dianas' appeared to emerge as the products of a process of cultural mythmaking. The oxymoronic phrase 'the People's Princess', coined by the Prime Minister in his public statement on the morning of her death, seemed to capture the multiple and contradictory investments in 'Diana'. These were elaborated both in 'the People' – an unusually multicultural assembly – 'taking to the streets' together in mourning, and in the marginalized resistances to this interpretation of this action. Similarly, contestations concerning the 'appropriate' protocols of the funeral were resolved into what was typically represented as a 'People's Funeral' that would combine the grandeur of royal pageantry with 'democratized' informality. The social drama of the Diana events, with their transgressive yet inevitably reinscriptive dynamics, seemed to reach their apogee in the funeral performance. Gigantic television screens were erected in Hyde Park and in various sites around central London to ensure a fully mediatized spectacle. A British military gun-carriage carried the body of a woman who famously campaigned against landmines through streets lined with 'common people' and imperial architecture. Images of the cultural geography of (post)imperial Britain were relayed via satellite to a global audience. The funeral oration of an hereditary aristocrat appeared to perform the function of an insurrectionary incitement against injustice. And the tumultuous applause that accompanied it echoed its demand for change through Westminster Abbey – the historical burial place of poets and kings.

The event of death

death calls me into question as if by my possible future indifference, I have become the accomplice of the death to which the other, who cannot see it, is exposed; and as if, even before vowing myself . . . I had to answer for this death of the other . . . The other becomes my neighbour precisely through the way the face summons me, calls for me, begs for me and in so doing recalls my responsibility.

(Levinas 1989: 83)

Simon Critchley has argued that the death of Diana Princess of Wales was 'possibly the biggest single *event* in world history' (Critchley 1997, original emphasis). This absurdly grandiloquent and clearly untenable claim nevertheless draws attention to the ways in which *eventness* is characterized by a certain economy of scale. Following Aristotelian precedent, the quality of an *event* is that it 'possesses magnitude' (Aristotle 1973: 9 [6]). The event happens in a contained space of time yet occupies a theatrical duration and intensity that appears to speak beyond its own temporal and locational boundaries. The almost prosaic manner of the death of Diana, in itself no more than an ordinary, everyday incident, nonetheless set in play a series of extraordinarily spectacular *Diana effects*. The monumental scale of mourning Diana, whilst not entirely without historical precedent, nevertheless constituted a dramatic and heavily dramatized phenomenon of seemingly epic proportion.

Scale implies *Meaning* (even if meaning might reside in apparent meaninglessness – the 'banality of evil' for example (Arendt 1977)). But the meanings inherent within even the holocaust, that absolute event of history (Blanchot 1995), can emerge in startlingly contradictory and, as suggested by Arendt's stark epigram, at times disturbingly understated ways. Similarly, the 'monumental event' may also be an effect of overstatement, an assumption of universal significance. Certainly this has been the substance of continuing critiques from both 'establishment' and left-academic commentators, who argue that the Diana events were essentially the cloyingly sentimental effects of media manipulation and populist reaction.[1] Ironically, given that the meanings of mourning Diana were so ubiquitously expressed, the significance of the events could only be further evidenced by an investment in refusing their meaningfulness. What is of interest then are not only the ambivalent economies of scale that characterized the mourning of Diana but the ambiguities of their effects. To take up Richard Johnson's productive formulation, mourning (and not mourning) Diana appeared to bear witness to sharply contrasting meanings and affects, in which the figure of 'Diana' became a projective touchstone for competing cultural values and political claims.

Monuments of scale

The monumental quality of mourning Diana was in many respects overdetermined by the colossal scale of the Diana industry prior to her death. The seemingly inexhaustible columns of newspaper coverage, the pervasive preoccupations of televisual time and space with the royal institutionalities that she appeared at once to embody and eschew, the endlessly recycled photographic effigies of that famous face, all enshrined Diana in a ritual economy of postmodern mediatization. The insistant fascination with the 'live' Diana, seemingly always-already entombed within the spiralling currency of media circulation, prefigured her staged Resurrection on the event of her actual death. In these circumstances, the resonance of 'Diana', which had been contained by 'that element of resistance her being alive provided',[2] was spectacularly amplified in the event of her sudden removal. It seemed that without the restriction of the living referent, these industries of reverence, revenance and remembrance were no longer held back by the demands of ontological presence. The 'Diana' that reappeared in the hauntological domain[3] provided a figure for a contemporary articulation of the *Quem Queritas* trope, in which the Diana sought in the space of her disappearance was precisely she 'who was here, but is risen'.[4] The resulting enactment of visible grief was both a mediatized epic production and an improvised grassroots performance.

The place of death

The Paris underpass became the mythical site of Diana's disappearance. The impossibility, however, of erecting a shrine to her there (the tunnel of an arterial road could not become a sacred grove[5] or house a mausoleum) contributed to the construction of multiple topographical monuments to her spectral presence. As Susanne Greenhalgh argues, the shrines of flowers, soft toys, poetry and photographs did not simply reference the lost body Diana but embodied wider cultural tensions. The diverse forms and the divergent communities of mourning attendant on these sites seemed to bear witness to both emergent political protest and residual ideological recuperation. The complex intersections of globality and locality figured the Diana events as forms of post-colonial cultural renewal as well as nostalgic imperialistic return. For example, a globalizing media made claims of national and global unification even as the imagined 'community of mourning' produced exclusionary closures and disunities. Joe Kelleher theorizes this manoeuvre as the effect of a complex *rhetoricality* through which discursive relations of power reorganized the Diana events into a powerfully persuasive spectacle. The spectral powers of the media apparatus appeared to provide the invisible *deus ex machina* through which the revenant Diana was staged as an almost godlike figure, capable of containing multiple, even contestatory identifications. This constructed Diana space seemed to offer a double-faced redemptive possibility of lost ground recovered, of community regained, of the possibility of the possible (and of its foreclosure) (Heidegger 1962: 307).

The time and space of mourning

In local British time, the particular longitudes of mourning Diana navigated currents of 'release' that followed the succession of New Labour in electoral victory – with its attendant sense (if not substance) of a turning of the political tide. As Valerie Hey elaborates, this moment – with its sense (if not substance) of imminent deliverance from the despairs and destructions of eighteen years of Conservative government, its sense (if not substance) of emergent possibilities for a 'stakeholding' society in which margins would be rearticulated to the centre, wealth redistributed, services saved, rights (re)asserted, and society restored – produced and contained a set of affective political movements that were already in play before the election. The Diana events emerged from and appeared to crystalize these political longings and social discontents and to catapult them into international significance. Diana's oft-perceived place in a constellation of anti-

conservative critique appeared to ally her with the New Labour project.[6]
Blair's coinage of the title 'the People's Princess' on the morning of her
death gave her transubstantiated body just such retrospective currency in
the construction of the New zeitgeist. This manoeuvre seemed not only to
capture but to instigate and invoke popular mourning, and to evoke 'the
people' as a New political entity. Diana, the disappeared, became the host
for the feints and counter-feints infusing the New body politic, with its
emergent hungers for change, with its defensive, resistant hegemonies and
with the latent portents of recuperation shadowing the languages of the
New and now.

These local temporalities of mourning Diana were inflected by and
informed global latitudinal formations. For example, the rush after her
death to forge comparisons, however awkward, with other iconic figures
in the 'global imaginary' (that quintessential effect of Western media
imperialism) – Marilyn Monroe, Princess Grace of Monaco, Eva Perón
and, following the coincidence of her death a few days later, Mother Teresa
– elaborated a contemporary discourse of stardom in which celebrity effectively functions as a global monarchy. At the same time, Diana's deliberate
association with international causes (for example, banning landmines or
securing justice for people living with AIDS) enabled her celebrity to
foreground what to some appeared to be an increasingly politicized 'humanitarian' activism and to others a trivial dalliance with issues beyond her
grasp. Upon the event of her death, however, Diana's investment in these
campaigns retroactively accrued the value of a reciprocal cultural capital
through which 'her' campaigns became beatified as *causes célèbres* and Diana
herself was recast in a performatively 'heroic' light as a 'tragic' figure – a lost
champion of the dispossessed and redressive righter of wrongs. Arvind
Rajagopal contrasts Diana's approach to charity activism to that of Mother
Teresa – the iconographic charity worker whose embodied asceticism
appeared to signify both 'Third World poverty' and the 'generous superiority' of the (Christian) West. Whilst Mother Teresa appeared to serve the
demands of regulative governmentality (the 'harmonious' organization of
the social), at a micro-level the place of Diana's campaigning work – as a
resistive space within international networks of cultural power – at times
seemed to disturb the seamless continuities of global economy and its
normalization of extreme privilege and poverty.

A similar, and perhaps starker, reconstruction in this context was the
mediatized *volte face* transformation of Diana's relationship with Dodi Al
Fayed from *mésalliance* to star-crossed romance. Here it seemed that only
the tragic *drive* towards death (Freud 1955) – now attributed the retroactively evaluative status as an anticipation of doom – could enable a
transformation of raced repudiation into apparent anti-racist rehabilitation. Mica Nava argues, furthermore, that this romanticization of 'Diana
and Dodi' provided a genre of projective imagining through which the

possibility of a differently constituted multicultural society could be represented by both those who feared and those who desired its emergence. Embedded within these narratological reconstructions were temporal markers of a wider ethical injunction to 'set the world to rights'. As Adrian Kear's chapter further suggests, the time of mourning seemed to signal a time in which to 'repair injustice . . . or more precisely to rearticulate *as must be* the disjointure of the present time' (Derrida 1994: 25, emphasis added).

Mourning's performance

> we are made all the more fragile . . . and all the more mobile when ambivalence and loss are given a dramatic language in which to do their acting out.
>
> (Butler 1997: 150)

Butler suggests an intimate and integral link between mourning and performance, in which mourning is featured *as* performance and plays a central role in the performative construction of identity. In many ways, theatre itself can be seen to be a place of mourning. In the Western classical formulation, for example, theatre evokes multiple losses, restaging past events and resuscitating the voices of those who are no longer there. At the same time, it enables an 'acting out' of projective losses, those phantasmatic griefs that remain unspoken within the performance of everyday life. The model of classical tragedy, moreover, provides an exposition of the performative structures of mourning. That is, the public performance of grief brings about the community it appears to represent precisely by invoking the ghosts of the past. The theatre of mourning, then, provides a key stage for the performative construction of the contemporary through the dramatic rearticulation of the past.

Correlatively, mourning can be understood as a theatricalized space. The performance of mourning in the everyday life of Western culture, for example, is a ritualized activity in which the orchestrated and ordered display of grief can be seen as an attempt to compensate for and contain the loss of the other. It enables the performers, like the tragic actor, to embody the dead within themselves and to conjure up the other's dramatic return. Diana Taylor explicates this 'hauntology of performance' as a framework through which globalizing forms such as tragedy appear to function as universalizing norms. These claimed 'universalities' are then strategically 'downloaded' and reconfigured on a local level as particular enactments of a wider social drama. Mourning appears to be just such an instance where the loss of an individual appears to parallel (and play out) a universal tragedy of loss. The funeral speech, for example, provides a telling space for the (dis)interment of the lost voice of the dead other, a performative enunciation of a life completed (even if prematurely)[7] and an evocation of their see-mingly still agentful presence. The transformational eulogy occupies that in-between space through which the dead departed re-enters the memory of the living in the guise of a tragic hero – as having lived a life replete with significance. Perhaps it is no accident, then, that *theories* of mourning are themselves similarly intrinsically theatricalized, often borrowing their forms and figures from the narrational structures of tragic drama.[8]

Many of the chapters in this book draw upon a range of psychological and psychoanalytic frameworks – including object relations theory (Hey, Johnson, Kear) and Lacanian–Zizekian analysis (Kear, Kelleher) – to consider the social relations of mourning as *psychically invested* processes (Walkerdine, Taylor). These frameworks illuminate many aspects of the performance of mourning. For example, Richard Johnson's elaboration of the concepts of 'splitting' and 'identification' provides insights not only into *mourning* but also *not mourning* as 'felt' imperatives. In this context, (dis)-identifications with Diana, the mourning of 'Diana', 'the people', 'the nation', the 'international community' and so on appeared to be experienced as psychically compelling social demands. Adrian Kear's chapter, further-more, extends the frame of mourning to encompass the question of *melanch-olia* – those losses that cannot be spoken or mourned. In this context he argues that mourning Diana seemed to provide the theatrical opportunity through which the unspeakable losses felt in the exigencies of everyday life could be 'acted out'. Thus, as intimated in William Spurlin's analysis, the queer calling of mourning was in part signalled by the ways in which Diana seemed to be a representative of the damage caused by the enforcement of compulsory heterosexuality. The loss of Diana appeared to resurrect the multiple losses experienced under heteronormative power – reinforced not least by her AIDS activism – and to reinforce resistance to its continuing stranglehold. Mourning Diana then, was a site for mourning multiple possibilities as well as multiple losses.

Mourning's visions

The complex social impact of Diana's image might be usefully elaborated by drawing a distinction between the role of the *icon* and the processes that produce *iconicity*. The icon can be understood as the formal construction of official culture – quintessentially, the religious icon on the wall of the church. It occupies a central function in organizing the repertoire of socially sanctioned images. In this sense, icons are embedded in the dominant ideological framework of a specific culture.[9] Iconicity, by contrast, can be described as the effect of a process through which particular individuals (or groups) are rewritten as culturally resonant social figures whose *iconic* status resides in the ways they provide expansive spaces of subjective identification. In this formulation, The Madonna is an icon; Madonna is an *iconographic* product. Diana herself occupied the powerful space between icon and iconicity. She began as the socially sanctioned icon of royal romance and the majesty of monarchy and was transformed into a figure able to sustain a host of alternative identifications.

Sandra Kemp (1998) draws attention to the ways in which media fascination with Diana's face was central to her construction as a multifaceted icon. In particular Kemp emphasizes the importance of photographic portraiture in the effigial imaging of Diana during the events of her death. Mourning Diana was both effected through and effectively comprised a mourning of her image – 'the public grieved not over a body but a face' (Kemp 1998: 45). William Spurlin notes the ways in which the metaphors underpinning the framing of Diana's face reveal the relations of power implicit within the photographic processes of 'capture' and 'containment' (Barthes 1977). It can be argued, for example, that the paparazzi's assaultive lexicon – of 'dicing Di', of 'slashing' and 'smashing' her – articulates a violatingly expropriative conflation of the ontological Diana with her hauntological double. Indeed, both her posed soft-focus portraits and the 'hard-hitting' news photographs taken of her appeared to frame Diana with a forensic intensity. In this iconographic process, the face of Diana appeared to be ripped from her body and transplanted into the image economy of the always-already dead.

Both William Spurlin's and Jean Duruz and Carol Johnson's chapters examine Diana's iconicity through the frame of the 'queer' or alternative identifications made with her. Duruz and Johnson argue that the mourning of Diana in Australia was the product of her media iconicity rather than her formal status as an icon of British royalty. Correspondingly, it was Diana's global iconicity rather than a local particularity – Australian debates about secession from British royalty – that engendered the mourning of Diana in the Australian context. The reverse side of this process became evident, Duruz and Johnson argue, in the ironic expropriation of the 'Diana effect' to incorporate 'local'/national politician Pauline Hanson, leader of the right-wing political movement Nation First. 'The press's dubbing of Hanson as "the People's Politician" and "the Princess of Wails" played upon Diana and Hanson's apparent vulnerability as well as Hanson's appeal to those unhappy with the current direction of Australian society' – the trend towards recognition of the rights of Aboriginal and Asian Australians. In other words, the attempted staging of Hanson through the iconography of Diana – specifically her currency as charity activist – euphemized a violently racist and exclusionary political movement as an inclusive 'supporter' of social diversity.

The iconographic 'Diana', then, appears to be an 'open text' that can sustain a variety of identifications, including those that appear to be diametrically opposed to the residual sense of 'what she stood for'. On the one hand, 'Diana' provides an emergent space of identification enabling expansive reinvention of social identities – 'what she could stand for'. On the other, 'Diana' provides an exhortative space for mobilizing the dynamics of iconicity to produce a dominant 'closed text' signifying 'what she should stand for'.

Mourning's genres

It can be argued that stories provide an ephemeral space, which is at the same time an organizing *performative* matrix for the regulation and deployment of material power. Stories inform power and its enforcement even as its capillary actions infuse particular narrational genres – as in the reciprocal centralities of romance to compulsory heterosexuality or of adventure to imperial domination. Epstein, Johnson and Steinberg (1999) have noted that jurisprudential and legislative processes are, for example, embedded in the praxis of storied eventness. Typically this praxis involves interplay between 'real-life' stories taken up as Meaningful events and metanarrational registers of allegory, fable and mythos. Contained within these subsequently aggrandized narratives are the *imperatives* of law and precedent – the 'little narrative' writ large demands a regulative or redressive action.

Moreover, as Ken Plummer (1995) has argued, there are moments in which particular dispersed 'little narratives' become transformed into a widely recognized *cultural narrative* – for example the 'coming out story' or the 'rape survival story'. In this convergent space, the act of telling shared stories reconfigures the dispersed place of the Benjaminian *storyteller*[10] whose repertoire contains the embedded knowledges and empirical understandings structuring cultural common sense. Storytelling provides a resource for the constitution of identities and an explanatory framework for particular experiences. More than this, stories can accrue the function of testimony in which collective identity or shared experience is both referenced and invented. Narration, in other words, both enables and embeds the performative construction of collective and individuated identities; it provides a structuring dialectic mediating the imaginary and the material. Correspondingly, a narrative analysis can illuminate the shifting ethos and power relations of a particular cultural context even as narrative itself enacts normalizing effects that may be simultaneously 'progressive' and recuperative.

The Diana events were both predicated on and provided a catalyst for a distinctly 'grand' narrational repertoire. Diana's extreme celebrity, from the moment of her association with Prince Charles, was constituted through multiple genres of folkloric tale: the fairytale princess who marries her prince; the virgin bride with the wicked stepmother whose love is betrayed; or, in Hollywood vein, the naive girl who is discovered, transformed and a star is born. On the event of her death, these narratives were reinvoked and reinflected in the context of a rapidly escalating discourse of 'Diana' in which even everyday occurrences were retold as epic tales. Furthermore, Diana stories occupied an expansive scale of narrational registers – from epic myth to grounded mythology, from fairytale to feminist fable.

The narrational dimensions of the Diana events constitute a central mode of performance analysis for many of the authors of this collection. Valerie Walkerdine, for example, mobilizes contemporary televisual and filmic narratives such as *The Missing Postman* and *The Full Monty* alongside the events of mourning Diana to account for shifts in the gender and class dynamics of post-industrial British subjectivities. Concomitantly, Jatinder Verma utilizes pre-colonial epic stories – for example the story of 'the beautiful, proud Heer, the jewel of the Punjab, poisoned by her own uncle on the eve of the wedding she desired with her cowherd-lover, Ranjha' – to account for the investment of post-colonial British Asian subjects in the mourning of Diana. These stories provide a framework through which to narrate the ambivalence of Asian Britons towards both the empirical experience of 'multi-racist Britain' (Cohen and Bains 1988) and a multiply imagined and experienced 'home'. In elaborating a similarly ambivalent post-colonial standpoint (Australian), Jean Duruz and Carol Johnson invoke another level of storying, in which personal testimonies of loss and mourning elaborate distinctly gendered forms of grieving and identity formation.

The narrational structures of Mourning Diana appear to gain their performative effectiveness from this powerful conjunction between ahistorical myth and historically grounded mythologies. The mythology 'Diana' in contradistinction to many of the parallel referents analysed in this book (Jackie O, Selena, Mother Teresa) appeared to be able to sublate the resonances of myth (fairytale princess, Artemis/Diana, Heer, the Lady of the Lake) into a peculiarly reverberating dramatic embodiment. Diana's status as a tragic figure was formed in a fusion of modern and anachronistic tragic forms. She inhabited both the 'elevated' status of royal protagonist (that quality central to Aristotle's understanding of the power of tragedy as deriving from the representation of the terrifying and pitiable end that befalls even the best of men (*sic*)) and the ubiquitous 'ordinariness' of the 'anti-hero' of modern tragedy whose terrible/pitiful existence could connect with any of us (Arthur Miller's tragedy of the 'little man' (*sic*)).[11] It was through these fused narrational structures that the storying of 'Diana' was able to incorporate mythic power into mythological form. That is 'Diana' invoked myth but remained Diana (a grounded mythology). There was therefore that 'something in Diana more than herself' that produced a powerful interpellative frame for contradictory effects: mourning Diana, actively resisting mourning and even the critical analysis of her mourning (and its resistances).

The significance of the narrative turns of both the Diana events and their theorization resides in the narrational remarking of the boundaries between the culturally central and the socially marginal. Indeed it is the very act of narrative enunciation which appears to provide a political performative through which cultural identities can be remade. The convergence of multiple narrations in the Diana events produced what seemed to be a 'collective' storyteller through whom fragmented, dispersed and differently told tales were rearticulated as new 'grand narratives' (Lyotard 1984). At the same time, the address of the 'collective storyteller' produced a 'collective addressee' – the speech-community-in-mourning (Bakhtin 1986). As Joe Kelleher argues, this speech 'community' was the performatively effected construct through which multicultural difference was re-produced as a reportedly 'common treasury'. The dialogical exchanges of mourning Diana appeared to open an inclusive intersubjectivity and with it, the possibility of counter-hegemonic utterance. And yet at the same time they effected multiple dispossessions and foreclosed the space of certain other dialogues.

Mourning's politics and poetics

In the dark paradise the other people
grope on an arduous road.
And the only brightness that sometimes lights
their nightly march like an ephemeral spark
is a brief impression of a chance
magnetic neighbourliness –
a brief nostalgia, a momentary shudder,
a dream of an hour of sunrise
a blameless joy suddenly flowing
into the heart and suddenly fleeting.[12]
(Cavafy 1976: 218)

The events attendant upon the death of Diana Princess of Wales appeared to dramatize a complex, contradictory set of cultural processes in which the borders dividing social categories and ideological norms were redrawn. The emergent possibilities of these events, with their seeming promise of a new cultural politics – of 'chance magnetic neighbourliness' – were also haunted by spectres of nostalgic reoccupation. The 'arduous road' to common ground lay strewn with the residue of claims and counter-claims to ownership of the place of 'the other people'. Diana's death, as 'ephemeral spark', seemed to ignite both dramatic unities and distinctive destabilizations, for example of the conventional boundaries of nationhood and citizenship, charity and activism, private feeling and public politics, social divisions and common cause. At the same time, these spaces of possibility enlightening 'the nightly march' of a mobilized mourning were contained places foreshadowed by the guarded movements and accommodating gestures of an entrenched status quo. The 'momentary shudder' of mourning Diana appeared to enunciate a common vernacular of cultural critique, for example of the powers of the media, of the destructive dispossessions of Thatcherite politics, and of the pervasiveness of social intolerance. But the perceptions of possibility emergent in this 'hour of sunrise' were also glimpses of the 'dark paradise' of hegemonic reconstitution.

> Like beautiful bodies of the dead who had not grown old
> and they shut them, with tears, in a magnificent mausoleum,
> with roses at the head and jasmine at the feet –
> That is how desires look that have passed . . .[13]

(Cavafy 1976: 3)

Notes

1 See for example, Mandy Merck's (1998) collection *After Diana: Irreverent Elegies*. An example of an 'establishment' critique was elaborated in Christopher Hitchens's (1998) documentary *Diana: The Mourning After*.

2 This phrase is taken from Marge Piercy's novel *Vida* (Piercy 1984/80: 402), in which the eponymous protagonist attempts to theorize the consuming and destructive desire of her former lover. She asks herself if his overpowering 'need' for her would have been better served had her body not been encumbered by her living being. Her conclusion that he needed the 'resistance her being alive provided' captures something of the ambivalence of the mediated hunger to capture Diana (dead or alive).

3 The phrase 'hauntological' is taken from Jacques Derrida's (1994) play upon the spectral transformation of the ontological into the ghostly. That is, it is the space of the living dead, the ghostly realm that disturbs the certainties of the living present. Kear's and Taylor's essays in this collection investigate and extend the implications of this formulation in the context of mourning Diana.

4 The *Quem Queritas* trope refers to the question asked of the women of Nazareth by the Roman guards at the tomb of Jesus. The guards ask the women, 'whom do you seek' and they answer 'Jesus of Nazareth, who was here and is risen'. In this theatrical trope, the sacred figure appears to disappear in order to reappear more powerfully prominent than before (Kubiak 1991: 4).

5 In Sophocles' play *Oedipus at Colonus*, the place of Oedipus' disappearance into death becomes a sacred grove in which the wounds of the nation will be healed.

6 Indeed, Diana's role in the campaign to ban landmines was taken by the Conservative party itself as well as by the Tory press, as a naive and improper anti-Conservative gesture that risked an inappropriate and irresponsible politicization of the monarchy by appearing to be pro-Labour.

7 Aristotle's definition of tragedy is 'the imitation of an action' in which the action is understood to be a complete and completed singular life (Aristotle 1973: 10).

8 Freud's metapsychology of mourning, for example (Freud 1957), refers back to the foundational premise of the Oedipus complex as 'the tragedy of destiny' (Freud 1958: 262). Similarly, Lacan, through a reading of Shakespeare's *Hamlet*, locates the circulation of desire within the structures of performing mourning (Lacan 1982).

9 Our use of the term 'dominant' in this context does not necessarily imply a
totalizing and inclusive framing of 'culture'. Neither does it exclude the
possibility that alternative counter-hegemonic 'cultures' also have 'dominant'
or normative ideological constructions. See for example Hebdige's theorization
of culture and subculture (1979) and his analysis of imagery and cultural
iconography (1988).
10 Benjamin's essay on 'The Storyteller' (1968: 83–109) argues that the power of
the event narrated through the live presence of the performer has been
dissipated and dispersed throughout modernity. Furthermore, he argues
that there is no longer a singular persona who serves the function of formally
narrating the culture.
11 For further elaboration of different tragic 'structures of feeling' see Williams
(1992).
12 This poem is entitled 'For Them Nature is a Familiar Garden' (Cavafy 1976:
218).
13 This poem is entitled simply 'Desires' (Cavafy 1976: 3).

References

Arendt, Hannah (1977) *Eichmann in Jerusalem: A Report on the Banality of Evil*,
Harmondsworth: Penguin.
Aristotle (1973) *The Poetics*, trans. G. Else, Ann Arbor: University of Michigan Press.
Bakhtin, Mikhail (1986) *Speech Genre and Other Late Essays*, trans. V. W. McGee,
ed. Caryl Emerson and Michael Holquist, Austin: University of Texas Press.
Barthes, Roland (1977) *Image-Music-Text*, ed. and trans. S. Heath, London: Fontana.
Benjamin, Walter (1968) *Illuminations*, trans. H. Zohn, New York: Schocken
Books.
Blanchot, Maurice (1995/80) *The Writing of the Disaster*, trans. A. Smock, Lincoln
and London: University of Nebraska Press.
Butler, Judith (1993) *Bodies that Matter: On the Discursive Limits of 'Sex'*, New York
and London: Routledge.
Butler, Judith (1997) *The Psychic Life of Power: Theories in Subjection*, Stanford:
Stanford University Press.
Cavafy, Constantine (1976) *The Complete Poems of Cavafy*, trans. R. Dalven, New
York and London: Harcourt Brace Jovanovich.
Cohen, Philip and Bains, Harwant S. (eds) (1988) *Multi-racist Britain*, London:
Macmillan.
Critchley, Simon (1997) 'Di and Dodi Die', *Theory and Event*, vol. 1, no. 4 (Johns
Hopkins Electronic Journal) http://128.220.50.88/journals/theory_&_event/
v001/1.4critchley.html
Derrida, Jacques (1994) *Specters of Marx: The State of the Debt, the Work of Mourning
and the New International*, trans. P. Kamuf, New York and London: Routledge.
Epstein, Debbie, Johnson, Richard and Steinberg, Deborah Lynn (forthcoming
1999) 'Twice Told Tales: Transformation, Recuperation and Emergence in the
Age of Consent Debates 1998', *Sexualities*.
Freud, Sigmund (1955) *Beyond the Pleasure Principle* in *The Standard Edition of the
Complete Psychological Works of Sigmund Freud, Volume XVIII (1920–22): Beyond
the Pleasure Principle, Group Psychology and Other Works*, trans. J. Strachey,
London: The Hogarth Press and The Institute of Psycho-Analysis: 7–64.

Freud, Sigmund (1957) *Mourning and Melancholia* in *The Standard Edition of the Complete Psychological Works of Sigmund Freud, Volume XIV (1914–16): On the History of the Psycho-Analytic Movement, Papers on Metapsychology, and Other Works*, trans. J. Strachey, London: The Hogarth Press and The Institute of Psycho-Analysis: 237–58.

Freud, Sigmund (1958) *The Standard Edition of the Complete Psychological Works of Sigmund Freud Volume IV (1900): The Interpretation of Dreams I*, trans. J. Strachey, London: The Hogarth Press and the Institute of Psycho-Analysis.

Hebdige, Dick (1979) *Subculture: The Meaning of Style*, London: Routledge.

Hebdige, Dick (1988) *Hiding in the Light: On Images and Things*, London: Routledge.

Heidegger, Martin (1962) *Being and Time*, trans. J. Macquarrie and E. Robinson, Oxford: Blackwell.

Hitchens, Christopher (1998) *Diana: The Mourning After*, Channel 4 (UK), 27 August 1998.

Kemp, Sandra (1998) 'Myra, Myra on the Wall: The Fascination of Faces', *Critical Quarterly*, vol. 40, no. 1, 38–69.

Kubiak, Anthony (1991) *Stages of Terror: Terrorism, Ideology and Coercion as Theatre History*, Bloomington and Indianapolis: Indiana University Press.

Lacan, Jacques (1982) 'Desire and the Interpretation of Desire in *Hamlet*', trans. J. Hulbert, in Shoshana Felman (ed.) *Literature and Psychoanalysis: The Question of Reading Otherwise*, Baltimore: Johns Hopkins University Press.

Levinas, Emmanuel (1989) *The Levinas Reader*, ed. Seán Hand, Oxford: Blackwell.

Lyotard, Jean-François (1984) *The Postmodern Condition: A Report on Knowledge*, trans. A. Bass, Manchester: Manchester University Press.

Merck, Mandy (ed.) (1998) *After Diana: Irreverent Elegies*, London: Verso.

Piercy, Marge (1984/80) *Vida*, Harmondsworth: Penguin.

Plummer, Ken (1995) *Telling Sexual Stories: Power Change and Social Worlds*, London: Routledge.

Williams, Raymond (1992) *Modern Tragedy*, London: The Hogarth Press.

2

EXEMPLARY DIFFERENCES

Mourning (and not mourning) a princess

Richard Johnson

This chapter looks at 'Mourning Diana', with the emphasis on the 'Mourning'. It addresses the puzzlement, expressed by many commentators, about the intensity of popular feelings around her death. My interest derives, in part, from personal experiences. The death of Jill, for thirty-three years my partner, lover and wife, in January 1992, thrust me into the turmoil and practices of grief, which became, in turn, objects of reflection. As often in cultural inquiry, personal experiences provide clues to wider investigations.[1]

In mourning Diana (and in not-mourning) many other issues were involved. The mythologies around her are hard to grasp without an awareness of the power of sudden death over those who live on; but the mourning patterns also depended on a life which was colossally, excessively, represented. This was a life in which sexual relations 'in private' were often public, in which death itself was in, or by, the camera's eye, and in which the scale and significance of happenings was grandiose – national at least, often international or global. I argue later that this episode – and the figure of Diana in general – was particularly rich in cultural themes and political issues.

How can we comprehend the peculiar intensity of this moment, organized through the dynamics of mourning? And how did mourning Diana, as a cultural and psychic process, interact with significant contemporary themes, especially the politics of the sexual and the dialectics of the national/international? In what follows I explore the mourning process first; then, working out from this centre, tease out the national–sexual themes.

Some emotional dynamics of mourning

When Jill died I was working with a group on the politics of sexuality. Grieving for Jill and thinking about the sexual went hand in hand, so that when the group published its book, *Border Patrols: Policing the*

15

Boundaries of Heterosexuality, the poems I wrote to grieve for Jill were published in it, alongside an autobiographical commentary. In the commentary I wrote:

> it seems to me that death is another kind of 'border' and that grieving and its accompanying activities are another kind of 'patrol'. Like all 'border patrols' grieving rituals and practices are there to police the boundaries. At the same time, even the best defended frontier guards may tremble at the perils of dwelling in the borderlands. They are dangerous places where new identities – neither One nor the Other – may arise . . . [So] From one point of view, grieving is a work of reassurance and boundary-maintenance against the shock of death and loss. But the reassurance is necessary – even though it may not succeed – because the death of someone close to us produces a 'madness': overwhelming emotions, that throw into giddy, vulnerable, high relief all our current identities.
>
> (Steinberg, Epstein and Johnson 1997: 234–5)

In my case, grieving destabilized my investments in heterosexuality and certain kinds of masculinity. We had struggled for a long time over gender power and domestic roles, over the greedy tyranny of my life over hers and of my professional occupation over our marriage, about monogamy and constancy, about intellectual equality and respect. When she died we had – in my opinion, I cannot speak for her – been taking on these issues with some success, made some crucial decisions anyway, including my early retirement. Her dying, and my sense that I was responsible for her death, brought out the old contradictions and put all the 'solutions' in doubt.

Grieving for Jill involved powerful feelings of love, sorrow, guilt and personal disorganization; it also involved attempts to control these feelings, and to recompose myself. I tried, in vain, to contain overwhelming feelings to the hours around 4.30 a.m. when I always awoke, in unconscious fear of my own death or, perhaps, in hope of saving Jill. I kept a diary which became the space for writing poems. I made a photographic record of Jill's life. I went to bed in or with her clothes. I haunted her spaces, searched out her things, her creations, and used them, assumed her roles, became more like her – tidier, more 'careful' about money, more practical, more domestic, more 'caring', you could say more 'feminine'. Much of this was done out of necessity and in desperation, but many activities were also intensely pleasurable. Doing what Jill did was getting, staying closer to her. I was also doing what I should have done before or should have done better. I was showing her I could. In a way, I was appropriating her things, her job, her roles – her very Self? Mourning activity was fiercely concentrated, wholly

16

engrossing, 'obsessive'. In speaking and writing about Jill in public, I felt I was 'doing her justice' in ways I had failed to do in life.

Later I started to read about death, loving and mourning, especially psychoanalytic works. I found Melanie Klein's accounts moving and illuminating (especially Mitchell 1986). Her discussion of 'the depressive position' (a 'normal' psychic state, a key moment of infantile experience, but available to adults too) shows the closest of associations between feelings of loss and mourning on one side and love and reparation on the other. Klein sees 'inner chaos', intense activity and infantile feelings as key features of mourning (*ibid.*: 146–74). She understands this as a loss of identity – more precisely 'the loss of *internal* "good" objects'. 'Objects' here are the images or versions of 'real' others we have introjected. In this intensely relational version of psychoanalysis, developed further by the school called 'Object Relations', we internalize a version of significant others, and this becomes the site of the working out, the splitting off, and at best the reconciliation, of our emotional ambivalences, our loving and our hating. When a loved one dies, we try to recreate and re-embody the lost one, more or less consciously, as an object we can love (again) as a 'good' object. This repeats struggles in our earlier life, especially our struggle to save our internal good objects from our own destructive feelings towards carers in infancy. In my grief I too was 'setting up the lost loved object inside himself'. I was constructing and embodying, including 'becoming like', my 'best Jill', a perfected, idealized version. The emotional complexity of this process was the complexity of our turbulent relationship relived in the mo(u)rning. Ethically, politically, mourning was complicated too: it involved deepening attempts at reparation, and acts of appropriation, possession, even 'triumph'. My grief could also function as a more general catharsis – as a focus for other griefs. When I cried for Jill, part of the torrent came out of an eight-year-old who was sent away to boarding school and put up with abandonment in dutiful silence. The restoration of 'good objects' associated with loving Jill worked on the older damage too. Not surprisingly, I emerged from the most intense period of grieving without the undertow of constitutional melancholy that had been habitual. Mourning was a last inequality between us. Not only did she die and I live, I lived to benefit from her dying, or, to see it rather differently, she left me this as a possibility.

Talking to other mourners showed the importance of the precise circumstances of dying. Patterns of mourning follow from our lives together but also from the *how* of dying itself. Jill awoke early one morning with pains in her chest and died in an ambulance on her way to hospital. She had no chance to reflect upon her own death. The rest of us carried the burden of comprehending the impossible.

Clues to mourning Diana:
emotional dynamics and critical differences

I was moved by Diana's death and by the actions of other mourners. I was caught by surprise by my own tears. Partly, I thought, this was because I had learned to cry, perhaps to cry too easily. I realized there were convergencies between the two situations that might have aided a process of transference: Jill's second name was 'Diana', a name resonating with some of the same mythological references noted for her namesake; she was 'elegant', liked clothes and was full of energy and life; like Diana, she lived through a major crisis in her marriage (though not a divorce); our marriage was not aristocratic or royal, but it was (or had been?) patriarchal; Jill struggled for and achieved a large measure of independence and a 'project' of her own; they were both courageous, risk-taking, resourceful women. These parallels, and my 'feminism', put me in the pro-Diana camp, though I had some countervailing feelings: why should this woman receive so much attention when women like Jill or women much poorer and living more difficult lives, achieving so much, were forgotten?

None of these feelings was intense or lasting. And I was not unaware of the possible transferences – and their inappropriateness. Many people seemed more deeply moved than I was by events, though I noted a measuredness, a certain 'good sense', in their mourning too. We watched the funeral on television, but I never thought of joining the crowds in London or going to one of the local 'shrines' – Leicester Town Hall Square in our case. But in two clear ways the stories do converge: first, my own grief made me sympathetic to 'mourning Diana', especially to its 'madness' or excess, more sympathetic, perhaps, than many 'intellectual' contemporaries; second, reflection on my personal grieving does provide clues, I think, to the public occasion.

Of course, it will not do to neglect differences, including the massively mediated nature of the royal Diana figure. Yet I disagree with critics of the mourning who make an in-principle distinction between 'face-to-face' and more 'mediated' mourning, between for instance, 'the death of someone who was actually a friend and the more ethereal loss of someone known only as a media figure' (Wilson 1997: 136). It is not clear why mourning with a mediated aspect must be 'more ethereal', less real. For many Diana mourners, and not only for those who had met her face-to-face, mourning was 'real' enough to produce significant actions and discussions within everyday spaces. Similarly, Diana's celebrity, even her privilege, does not in itself inauthenticate the feelings woven around her. It is often argued that there was a surplus of 'fantasy' in people's relationships with her, fantasies heightened by media representation.[2] Yet fantasy accompanies all our relationships: we idealize, install as 'good objects', the living and the dead, our companions and our public hero/ines. We also seek to ground

18

our imaginings, to test them against reality. This may be easier when we can meet face-to-face, but contemporary citizens are probing, sceptical readers of media representations and have ways of checking them out. Moreover death itself, as both Freud and Klein argued, is the decisive 'reality test' – mourning involves coming to terms with the real absence of the loved one (Mitchell 1986: 147).

Clues to the mourning process are needed because so much of the commentary has been incomprehending. Acute observers were surprised and shaken by the public response (e.g. Mckibbin in Merck 1998: 15). There was a widespread sense of a popular initiative which was out of everyone's control (e.g. *The Independent* in MacArthur 1997: 39). This is the best evidence against the argument that the grieving was merely a media event.

More sympathetic interpreters focus on the thematics of Diana's life, her struggle with royal and patriarchal institutions including an exploitative relationship with an unloving husband, and her search for a personal and royal role (See many of the accounts in MacArthur 1997, especially Moore: 33–5; Burchill 1998; Campbell 1998.) Less sympathetic accounts show an angry impatience, even a disbelief, towards pro-Diana popular reactions and most media coverage. Elizabeth Wilson, for example, 'could neither understand nor share the apparent outpouring of grief'. She was 'baffled and deeply alienated by the public response' (Wilson 1997: 136). Several critics make a sharp distinction between Diana's strategies and public admiration for her on one side and a rational politics on the other. As Linda Holt put it, feminist columnists who praised Diana's emotional authenticity 'cleared a blank space where myriad fantasies could be projected and ring-fenced against reason'. It followed that 'Diana's death and suffering had no political consequences' (Holt in Merck 1998: 190 and 196). Similarly, John Pilger has published an angry denunciation of 'women's writing' and 'feminist journalism' for wasting time, opportunistically, in 'the Diana Supermarket' and ignoring more important issues (Pilger 1998: 19).

Neither side deals self-reflexively with the fact that the debate itself was part of a process of mourning (and not mourning) Diana's death. The strong and contradictory feelings – Elizabeth Wilson's or John Pilger's political passion as much as Julie Burchill's or Suzanne Moore's – were the feelings associated with mourning. 'Inner chaos' was painted large in collective public acts which I found strangely reminiscent. Many popular actions were dramatic, passionate, 'mad' or unusually expressive. There was lots of poetry again. The lost one's spaces were occupied – Kensington Palace, royal places, Spencer places, Al Fayed places. Most places had their shrines. Familiar boundaries were broken by gestures that seemed melodramatic, operatic – flower throwing, clapping a funeral procession, besieging royal buildings, criticizing commemorative practices, or the lack of them, even watching television on a Saturday morning! There was emotional language and weeping in public. When people in London left their television sets to walk towards Westminster Abbey, it was to experience 'the atmosphere, the silence, the emptiness of the city, the strangeness of it all' (Silverstone in *Screen* 1998: 82). There was concentrated, 'obsessive' activity: queuing for condolence books, buying or picking flowers, writing cards and messages, choosing memorabilia, placing them. The crowd was possessive: they claimed 'ownership of an event' by performances 'for the self' and performances 'for the other' (*Screen* 1998: 84). Mourning was a collective social action fuelled by private but shared feelings and meanings: a particular alliance was activated. Nor is there a good enough reason to exclude the colossal media coverage, as much a social response, from all this: press, television, radio phone-ins, magazines, and, later, the commemorative objects from books to porcelain figures. Some of the most interesting material was 'local' or communal – the coverage in the gay monthly magazine *Gay Times* ('Diana: A Tribute', October 1997), or the depiction of Diana as an eight-armed Goddess by Asian artists (*Eastern Eye*, 25 September 1998), or the Special Debate in the academic film magazine *Screen*, part critical commentary, part 'an act of mourning in the classic sense' (1998: 67).

To argue that these forms broke from 'reality' – to dismiss them as 'manufactured' and 'fantasy' – is to neglect the way they referenced the familiar, used existing codes and repertoires. There was little new about poems or flowers, especially when we take into account the growing popular practice of creating little shrines at sites of fatal car accidents.[3] The sources of inspiration were sometimes surprising but none the less everyday – of course, because we live in an intricately inter-discursive and intertextual culture where media moments are mixed up with unmediated ones, where this distinction remains but shifts about. The connection between royal representation and soap opera narratives, familiar since Ros Coward's comments in *Female Desire*, is a case in point (Coward 1984: 164–71). As Christine Geraghty shows, soap opera was a main form of narrative by which the Diana story was written and understood, especially among women. But values drawn from soap opera, among other sources, also set the dominant terms of popular mourning:

> what is striking . . . is the dominance of soap opera values in the way that people spoke about Diana's death. Talk about private feelings – the staple of soap opera – was valued as the best way of expressing grief, and indeed as a sign of grief itself.
>
> (*Screen* 1998: 73)

'Soap' is not used dismissively here. It is understood that 'soap' forms arise from ordinary living, are appropriated and changed by media production and return to us as audience members. They influence our sensibilities, responses and outcomes – including our face-to-face encounters, without however, determining them. In this case, soap-opera-like sensitivities acquired a kind of dominance:

> In this discourse the refusal of the Queen and Charles to speak was taken to signify a lack of grief, and was harshly criticized . . . For those outside this 'feminine' discourse, there was very little space in which to speak.
>
> (*Screen* 1998: 73)

Geraghty also suggests that mourners sought ways of checking out the reality of the meanings of Diana's death. Popular scepticism about the media image fed an appetite for direct witness from those who had met Diana, hence the movement from television set to street. Witnesses emphasized physical proximity and touch against 'the media's endless use of photographs'. Physical presence at sites of mourning seemed the fuller experience: 'television offered a better view, but not the smell of the flowers, the touch of the crowds'. Even then, mediated and unmediated truths chased each other in endless circles: 'the crowds at the palaces became a media event in which those present used the media to tell those who relied on the media what they were missing' (*Screen* 1998: 73). Yet as Jenny Kitzinger puts it in the same edition of *Screen*, 'public response, though choreographed by the media, sometimes exceeded its mediation' (78).

Both sides of mourning – chaos, policing – were there in August 1997. Diana's sudden, accidental, initially inexplicable death shook existing identities, erased borderlines. Royal power and conventions of grieving were thrown into crisis; media struggled to find appropriate rhetorics. Death's diminution of the human was unusually strong and pervasive. If someone so hugely present and protected could suddenly disappear – 'no more photographs' – what chance of survival for me? Is the death line so fine? From the beginning, however, there were also 'border patrols', regulating and containing panic. Denial was offered, or solace. How often it was said that she could 'live on through our memories', had 'gone to heaven' or was an 'angel' or 'saint'? More rationalistically, the cognitive challenge of a sudden 'accidental' death was taken up: why did Diana die? In hostile accounts, for example, much easier to articulate a year later, Diana's last month was presented as 'a hurtling towards chaos', as though the chaos had belonged to exclusively to her and not at all to us (Flett 1998).

As this example suggests, the more analytical, 'political' responses, feminist or left-wing for example, were not immune from instability. There was a marked splitting into 'good' and 'bad' Dianas. She was much idealized. In a beautifully designed book full of fascinating photos, she is Julie Burchill's 'sweet princess' – a 'spirited, compassionate and beautiful Englishwoman' (Burchill 1998: 9 and 236) For Andrew Morton, she was 'flag-bearer for a new generation, a new order and a new future' no less (Morton 1997: 9). For both these popular journalists, feelings about their exploitation of an icon may well accompany their unreserved praise. As Klein puts it: 'The ego feels impelled . . . (by its identification with the good object) to make restitution for all the sadistic attacks that it has launched on that object' (Mitchell 1986: 120). Idealization is expressed in a hyperbolic style which no one could mistake for measured judgement.

On first reading, the anti-Diana writing seems to invert all this. It presents a sternly super-egotistical damming up of emotions that threaten to spill out, drowning out a thoughtful politics. The Other here is the tyranny of 'feelings': emotional self-indulgence in Diana's own life but public mourning and pro-Diana writing is implicated too. Reviewing Beatrix Campbell and others, John Pilger spits out the familiar epithets with reiterative disgust: 'agony aunts', 'the therapists couch', 'self-pitying' and 'emotional grandstanding'. Such indulgence contrasts with 'real feminism' that connects with the issues of a global class politics. Clearly the boundaries of 'real politics' are being patrolled here.

Yet the mounting of these patrols suggest another kind of madness going on. By expostulating about *not* mourning Diana, critics add to the attention they so much deplore. Reason sits oddly with heavy, angry satire or plain disgust. Pilger, for instance, reads Beatrix Campbell's committed but analytical and explanatory book on royal and aristocratic patriarchy as 'a rant against Charles the Wicked Prince' and constructs his own intra-feminist opposition between feminist writers tricked by 'celebrity consumerism' and his 'honourable exceptions' who are treated as heroines, who celebrate heroines (Pilger 1998). His own passion in and for a politics is unacknowledged: a passionate polemic in which good and bad are starkly defined, much too starkly in this case. What is problematic in the attack on mourning is the (impossible) splitting off of thought and feeling, all too familiar in 'science', 'intellectual seriousness' and in the political left.

The differences between pro- and anti-Diana camps illustrate variant psychic dynamics in mourning and refusing to mourn, different ways in which political identities are constructed. But they are also important 'in their own terms'. They are one of the ways in which the figure of Diana condensed an extraordinary clustering of cultural meanings and political issues: here, differences over reason and emotion in politics, over modern and postmodern political styles, between a puritan or purist choice of issues and a certain opportunism or 'strategy' about 'interventions'.

These differences run through both feminist and left-wing politics. They also divide cultural researchers. One strand has been preoccupied with uncovering Diana's 'popularity' by unwrapping the political and cultural contents of support for her, drawing on different frameworks, materialist, poststructuralist, psychoanalytic (e.g. *Screen* 1998; Campbell 1998; this book). Another has been concerned to interpret events according to a theory about 'celebrity', 'sainthood', 'glamour', 'paranoia', 'the operatic', emotion-ality or soap opera – pushing these categories as far as they will go, and often applying them rather dismissively (e.g. many but not all contributions in Merck 1998). The debate about Diana is an example of the continued tension between a 'mass culture' perspective, ultimately contemptuous of popular forms and idols, and an identification with the popular, sometimes criticized as an unthinking 'cultural populism' (e.g. McGuigan 1992). Diana's privilege obscures her popularity or encourages critics to override it; but the debate shows how active the mass culture framework remains and how important it is to keep contradictory political spaces open by critiquing it.

Other issues that clustered around 'Diana' included the future and (un)popularity of the monarchy, the media's role in the lives of public persons, many questions of 'sexual politics' including patriarchy and class, marriage, sexual morality, monogamy, 'adultery', and what constitutes feminine 'independence', the politics of HIV, AIDS and homophobia, the production and use of landmines (and so the long-term consequences of warfare), the politics of royal representation in Britain and abroad, the political role of 'charities' and the differences between 'humanitarianism' and 'politics'. Within the last two issues nestle many of the concerns – about the global class system predominantly – that animate the politics of the sharpest materialist critics.

If mourning Diana was a hugely over-determined event, its ruptural character was secured by two main eventualities. The first – which we have discussed – was simply her dying – her dying as she did, when she did. The second, to which we now turn, was Diana's extraordinary avail-ability as a figure or 'object' in the identity work of others.

Diana represents the nation: the emotional and the global

Diana was unusually 'available' in two main ways. Most obviously she was extensively represented in public media throughout the world; she was 'the most famous woman in the world'. But she was also available 'subjectively', in that so much of her personal story, sometimes in her own words, was reported and discussed. Areas usually regarded as private – family relations, sexual relationships, food problems and visits to the gym for instance – were in her case made conspicuously, selectively public. Her fame was matched by her evident vulnerability. She was vulnerable as an inexperienced young woman cheated and scorned by her husband, as a bulimic, as someone who damaged her own body and attempted to kill herself, as what she called 'a media toy', as a 'outsider' (of a kind) in the royal circles. Even her points of strength, her motherhood for example, were points of danger: would she be allowed to bring up William and Harry, to be gentle princes, as she wished?

Popular availability was also part of a survival strategy. She appealed to her publics for love and for support in a difficult life, most evidently in the wounded, wooing looks and sensational personal disclosures of the interview she gave to the prestigious BBC current affairs programme *Panorama* in 1995 and in the tapes that informed Andrew Morton's biography (Morton 1997: 23–69).

So Diana, or the Diana figure, was available to a vast and differentiated public. This made her a rich resource for the cultural and psychic work of others. I want to draw attention, here, to four main forms of attachment. All four categories are relational or dialogic: they express relationships between Diana and her publics.

First, she related to others as a representative. She represented 'us' to others, especially people in Britain to others 'abroad'. This was inscribed in her official role as a royal, but also in her self-ascribed identities as 'a Queen of Hearts' and as 'an ambassador for this country' (*Panorama* interview, quoted Morton 1997: 257–8) and in her posthumous title as 'the People's Princess'. The *Panorama* interview typically combined vulnerability and strategy:

> As I have all this media interest, let's not just sit in this country and be battered by it. Let's take them, these people, out to represent this country and the good qualities of it abroad.
>
> (Morton 1997: 258)

How, then did Diana's strategy or being a new kind of national representative effect the work of identity of others around her, processes both global and national?

One important moment in national identity as a process is its production 'as against' others, especially as against other national identities. In the most literal versions of this argument, the relation with national others is seen as external: Englishness is defined against Frenchness, Irishness, Americanness etc. Contemporary theories of cultural identity, especially when they extend to psychic dynamics, show how little 'external' these relations actually are.[4] Defining yourself against an other, itself only one of the psychic dynamics of identity, involves several different operations. The other must first occupy the same psychic or cultural space as the self. A version of the other is internalized or introjected; it becomes an image or 'object' – the Other.[5] But the image of the Other must also, in this paranoid pattern of self-production, be disavowed, expelled, projected 'outside'. Such processes are imaginary but have literal, spatial accompaniments and consequences: internal others are thrust 'beyond the pale', outside the bourgeois spaces, or the all-white spaces, or the men-only spaces. These spaces must in turn be policed. The tortured history of war, conquest, pogroms, genocide, lynchings, 'ethnic cleansing' and forced exclusion shows the consequences for groups who figure as Others in powerful collective imaginaries. Yet for the most powerful categories even physical expulsion is self-defeating or self-depleting. External boundaries are, as Slovaj Zizek argues, also internal limits (Zizek 1991). An identity that holds itself in place by expelling others is doomed to the constant repetition of similar processes. Its relation to Others remains peculiarly intimate or proximate; the struggle for purity is a struggle with itself. Given the porosity of boundaries – social, cultural and psychic – in the modern period, such paranoid externalization has to be repeated unendingly.

Paranoid patterns were certainly present in the representation of Diana's life and death. On the side of pro-Diana sentiment they flourish in the elaborate conspiracy theories around her death (e.g. Benton in Merck 1998). They are especially evident in anti-Diana representations. We have already noted the splitting and projection which accompanies the sometimes justifiable arguments about emotionality. In the weeks before they both died, the British press was also starting to issue public warnings around the relationship with Dodi Al Fayed. As the tabloid newspaper *The Sun* put it: 'Please tread carefully Di. A new love affair can be as dangerous as the Bosnian minefield' (quoted in Flett 1998). Had the couple lived and their relationship continued, the press's narrative might well have swung much further in an anti-Diana, anti-Muslim, nationalist direction. The possibilities of a racist–nationalist closure here were strong. It is important to remember too that another Diana had loomed large in the public myths of the early 1980s, the heyday of Thatcherite nationalism, the era of the heightened fantasies of Wars and Weddings, of the Falklands adventure and Charles-an'-Di.

The later Diana was not, however, a nationalist icon of this kind, opposed to foreign others. Her liberation from royal wifedom was accompanied by a redefinition of her national significance. 'Dianaized' versions of the nation were not typically nationalistic, militaristic or paranoid; if anything they were 'depressive' or introjective. They involved taking in, or 'taking on', versions of the other or versions of the self seen through the other's eyes. This shift can be elaborated both negatively and positively.

Attempts to produce the later Diana as exclusively British or English were often forced or confused. There was the obvious anomaly that the 'English Rose' of the Elton John song was also the Princess of Wales. This was confusing when, in the historical semiology of the nations, 'Englishness' works best in its domestic oppositions to Welshness, Scottishness and Irishness(es). Christine Gledhill has analysed a larger confusion or transition in the mourning speeches of Tony Blair. Sometimes he claimed Diana as British, implicitly underlining an opposition to others. Sometimes he included, in 'the People's Princess', the rest of the globe: 'the people everywhere, not just here in Britain but everywhere' (Gledhill in *Screen* 1998: 79).

Nor could the later Diana be recruited very effectively to serve Conservative political mythologies. This was mainly because of her ambiguous relation to monarchy, a central nationalist definer. She shifted from being a queen-in-waiting to being the ex-wife of a prince (whose own claim to succeed was not unquestioned). Despite attempts to disguise the fact, their divorce meant more than a change of titles. Diana's strongest claim to royalty was as mother of a future king. Even this claim was being attacked, morally, in her last months, when some journalists dubbed her 'a trash icon for our times', 'the Queen of England manqué' (Nigel Fountain quoted Flett 1998) and, in classically sexualized language, a 'fast woman' (*Sunday Telegraph* quoted in Flett 1998). I agree that Diana was never a plausible republican heroine, but also with those that argue that her painful struggle for recognition and for a liveable place in a bizarre world highlighted many of contradictions of royal institutions, especially its particular and oppressive forms of aristocratic patriarchy (Campbell 1998). For one royalist section of pro-Diana opinion, she came to represent not what monarchy was but what it might be. She was a kind of royal promise. The promise was offered first through herself, by performance as much as vows; but a promise was also made through or on behalf of her children, in her own lived fantasy of William as a 'once and future king' of a new kind. To another kind of pro-Diana sentiment, her life and struggles showed up the oppressive roles of royalty, strengthening a preference for republican solutions.

It was hard, anyway, for such a figure to represent the 'historic' nation, replete with its residual themes. It was hard to use Diana for the anti-Europeanism of the popular Conservative press, for example. The figure of the Queen (or better still the Queen Mother?) can still be recruited to British Euro-phobia, as in panics over whether the royal portrait can appear on the new Euro currency, or rows about attempted reconciliation with Germany in the commemoration of the Second World War. As a fully postwar figure, Diana was more distant from British Germano phobia and the safe, un-self-critically affirmative version of 'the War We Won'. Moreover, as a divorced woman and a single mother and as the socially compassionate 'Queen of Hearts', she was in tension with key themes in Thatcherite nationalism, especially the reckless stress on 'enterprise' and the moral traditionalism of 'the family'. Even Douglas Hurd, a 'moderate' Conservative ex-foreign-secretary and a pro-European, had to work hard to 'nationalize' Diana through her royalty:

> Diana, Princess of Wales used to the full the traditional manners and methods of the Royal Family. She spoke and carried herself like an English girl from the background that was in fact hers, adding the particular personal flair that made her a star.
>
> (Hurd in MacArthur 1997: 98)

Hurd must expunge the massively publicized antagonisms between Diana and Charles and the struggles with royal institutions. He must represent everything in her life which is out of the (royal) ordinary as purely personal – including her 'bitterness' for example. His national ascriptions ('an English girl') work best where they are personal, implicit, feminine and bodily ('carried herself') not projected outwards into the public or registered against an Other.

Positively, this meant that grieving for Diana was, for many liberal royalists, a mourning, as Dorothy Thompson put it, 'for a better monarchy' (Merck 1998: 33–40). Grief accumulated around lost possibilities, or possibilities not recognized in Diana's lifetime, or not properly credited to her as her contribution. The forms of mourning brought this out. The ceremonial trappings of war (gun-carriage, soldiers, pacing male mourners) seemed inappropriate contrasted with her own disassociation from the royal culture of soldiering and of 'hunting, shooting and fishing', and the implied pacifism of the mines campaign. Yet other Dianas were present too in the card to 'Mummy', in the obviously civilian charity workers, the marked gay presence, the multi-ethnic composition of crowds, the clapping and the flowers. It was as though Diana was being recognized for what she had done, for what she was, in 'national' terms – but, in that characteristic depressive regret of grief, too late. So there was much in the official mourning not only to feel with (as the critics have it) but also to think on. It was hard to articulate these weirdly coexisting elements at the time. Yet the new, as carried by Diana, had died. What did it all mean?

Some concluded that a chance for reform was lost; others that Diana had shown the limits of royal institutions, their historical redundancy. Most commonly, perhaps, in the absence of an explicit answer, the meanings, were performed, acted out. A large part of the popular emotional drive to mourn Diana was expressed in copying her, not in an abject dependency but out of respect. Just as Diana had opposed traditional royalty with her more democratic princely or knightly promise, so we, the mourners, reproached Queen and Establishment for unjust neglect, and acted out our different way of mourning. We represented the representative. We recognized the recognizer.

But the central difficulty of a nationalist appropriation of Diana's symbolic value lay in her standing as an international celebrity. Her celebrity has been discussed as a limit to her political significance, involving those who loved her, apparently, in self-defeating narcissism (e.g. Mark Cousins in Merck 1998: 77–86). Less often appreciated is the way celebrity blocked nationalism and fuelled an internationalism. She was internationally famous, it is true, as a British royal, but she carried her royal ambiguities into this international domain. She was famous also as a media celebrity, a worker for international charities, a campaigner on landmines, AIDS and other issues and, latterly, as the lover of an international playboy from a wealthy (would-be) British-Muslim dynasty. She was, according to her brother's tribute, 'a very British girl who transcended nationality' (Earl Spencer in MacArthur 1997: 179). She also 'talked endlessly of getting away from England mainly because of the treatment that she received at the hands of the newspapers'.

The discovery of Diana's fame abroad, sometimes by surprising routes, was a common theme in the aftermath of her death. On visits to Amsterdam, in 1998, for instance, a friend told me about a regular newspaper series called 'Dianarama' – a series that continues today. Later she sent me a Dianarama clipping, with a photograph taken in Aleppo, Syria, by a Dutch photographer, of an advertisement for Muslim women's headwear, featuring Diana's face (Dianarama 60, *de Volkskrant*, 16 June 1998).[6] Mary Dejevsky's round-up of US and French responses for *The Independent* showed the extent of the impact of her death on other close cultural neighbours. Reassuringly perhaps, similar patterns were observed as in Britain: the queues (!) to sign books of condolences at embassies, the high proportions of gay men and lesbians and 'people of colour' in the crowds, the sense that Diana was on the side of 'ordinary people'. Her conclusion was less reassuring:

> This creates for Britain abroad a problem similar to the one that now faces the Royal Family at home. The monarchy has lost at a tragic stroke all that was young, beautiful, sympathetic, accessible and even relevant about British Royalty.
>
> That is also what Britain has lost in the world. For millions of people who knew or cared little for international diplomacy, Diana was the lively, modern and humane face of Britain.
>
> She was a global Ambassador on a scale that is only now apparent.
>
> (Mary Dejevsky in MacArthur 1997: 43)

While 'Britain' is yet again produced as a unity in this account 'we' are also invited – through Diana's international celebrity – to adopt an unfamiliar gaze. We are not looking outward at the Other, or even boasting about our Queen of Hearts. Our subjective position is more 'depressive' than paranoid, self-doubting not self-aggrandizing. Diana's death invites us to look at ourselves through Other eyes, eyes rather like our own, that recognize our loss, but judge it according to our ability to be seen and heard. In this gaze the self is relativized, seen as changeful and historical. The conclusion is decidedly melancholy. Consider how our 'face' must now appear outside, now that our best self, according to outside observers, is eclipsed: as 'all that is' ugly, insensitive, inaccessible, dull, archaic, inhumane and irrelevant! Again, the loss of Diana bears on national identity but in a self-reflexive, thought-inducing way. Again the mourners' response is to remember, to hold on to this 'good-object-in-the-eyes-of-others', to make it part of our new self. The whole pattern suggests a very different relation to the other than in the usual nationalistic excess.

It is important too that Diana's representative function was not limited to the national frame, even when her royal repertoire was mobilized. Diana could also represent *sections* of 'the people' to the rest. Both 'the sections' (the represented subject) and 'the rest' (the addressee) could be transnational as well as national. Some of her most dramatic representational acts were performed in the United States, and later in the anti-mines campaigns in Angola and Bosnia. In her more sectional representational acts, there was a definite pattern. She typically represented groups that had been othered or marginalized in power relations and in representational processes. When she concentrated her charitable activity after her divorce, she focused on The Leprosy Mission, Centrepoint (a London-based charity for the homeless), The National AIDS Trust, the Royal Marsden National Health Service Trust (a cancer hospital) and the Great Ormond Street Children's Hospital (Morton 1997: 252–3). Later she took a leading role in the Red Cross's campaign against landmines.

From a left political perspective, her 'charitable' relations were deeply problematic because of the inequalities between her and her 'subjects' and because of the proximity of the relationships to royal and aristocratic condescension. It was in this context, however, that she developed her personal styles of interaction – touching and, more important, being touched, concentrating hard on listening to others, approaching people through shared 'human' territory (through her fanship of soaps, for instance!), using humour and a general informality to break the royal distance – but still use it. Her own self-ascriptions – ' I am a humanitarian. I always have been and I always will be' (quoted Katharine Graham in MacArthur 1997: 95) – and her wishes for her royal boys – 'I want them to grow up knowing there are poor people as well as palaces' (quoted W. F. Deedes in MacArthur 1997: 69) – were hardly socialist or republican (palaces and poverty it seems will remain). But she was a representative who sought out the hidden and tragic sides of those she represented, authenticating them to her own publics. This, once more, made her available for other kinds of relationship, real and imaginary. Especially important were the intersections of her role as a representative with her role as a recognizer of the other.

Diana and the other: recognition

Our second relational category is recognition. It is one peculiarly appropriate to Diana. A main theme of sympathetic commentary – and of most of those who speak of actually meeting her – is her ability to recognize others, to say and do things related to their needs. Christopher Spence, founder of the AIDS charity The London Lighthouse, called her 'a natural counsellor':

She knew how to pay attention, the most dignifying thing that one person can do for another. Time after time over a ten-year period I watched her intuitively knowing what to do and say in order to come close to another person – often people very near to death. She knew how to make a real connection, enabling people to talk to her from their hearts about what really mattered. She could sense what someone, or even a whole group of people, might need with unfailing accuracy.

She would usually ask a simple question: 'Hello, how are *you?*'

(MacArthur 1997: 101)

Perhaps the source of this gift, or of the intensity and generosity of its employment, is that the woman who was often a 'good object' in the minds of others so badly needed to restore the 'good objects' inside herself. The urgency of this need was not directly articulated, often. It was expressed, practically, as risk, in the 'lengths she was prepared to go'. It is interesting how much of her charitable work explored the borderlands of dying: from AIDS and other dangerous diseases to the sudden immolation or death from explosive charges to the work in children's hospices. It is interesting too how often she dealt in 'social death' – in recognizing the unrecognized or unrecognizable, in touching the untouchable. It is quite wrong to imply that everything this celebrity did was self-seeking in a narcissistic way, not least because much of her charitable work was, when the media would allow, private and hidden. It was also often beyond the call of duty. In these dangerous places, she seems to have sought recognition too, not least for her 'professionalism'. Her own descriptions of such moments – when she connects with people and they cling to her and cry – stress her own comfort too, her unwillingness, even, to leave:

He was crying his eyes out and clung on to my hand and I felt so comfortable in there. I just hated being taken away.

('In Her Own Words', published in Morton 1997: 65)

Even in more public encounters where she seems 'like a pop star', the word 'comfortable' returns, if discomfortingly:

People thanking me for bringing happiness in their lives; little sentences that put together make a very wonderful, very special day. Thanking for coming; thank-you for making the effort; thank-you for being you and all those things, [I] never used to believe. Now I'm more comfortable receiving that sort of information whether or not it's true. I can now digest that sort of thing whereas I used to throw it back.

(Morton 1997: 67)

That Diana was intensely needy, but expressed her need by recognizing the needs of others, was part of a popular common sense about her, especially among women familiar with this psychic economy. More technically, we could say that she projected her needs on to others and tried to meet her own needs by caring for them. Such a strategy, which is central to conventional gender relations in our culture, is posited in risk – the risk of one-sidedness for the carer, who is usually a woman. She risks exploitation of her emotional labour and a personal depletion. This unrequited pattern is also clear in Diana's own account:

> No-one has ever said to me 'Well done'. Because I had a smile on my face everyone thought I was having a wonderful time. That's what they chose to think – it made them happier thinking that.
>
> (Morton 1997: 67)

On the other hand, where recognition *is* returned by the object of caring it can create powerful bonds of love. Recognition, then, has some measure of mutuality in it. Diana's plentiful self-revelations were surely bids for mutual recognitions of this kind. Were they often responded to? Did she think they were? Does the deficit here explain something of why she was so loved and mourned, or loved-in-the-mourning? Did we try to make some reparation for her desperate giving, often one-sided, when she died? I believe that all these moments were active in the mourning process.

Identification, dis-identification and transference

Though representation and recognition have emotional and psychic dimensions, they also express social relations in quite a direct way. Our third and fourth relationships – identification and transference – often operate, by contrast, quite unconsciously. It was clear, however, that the figure of Diana was the object of a continuous play of *identification* and *dis-identification*. Many members of her public defined their own identities in relation to her, sometimes as very different, sometimes as like her in some way. Identification of this kind is never total, or fixed or without ambivalences. It can also cross social categories – including rich and poor, royal and not-royal – in surprising ways. We will return in a moment to the concrete pattern of these identifications or dis-identifications in considering the version of nation which mourning Diana produced.

Finally, in terms of forms of attachment, Diana was clearly the object of many *transferred feelings*, feelings that had little to do with her own life and death, and everything to do with the lives of members of her public. Many people told television interviewers or radio chat-show hosts how they had cried for Diana, but also at the same time for some other loss, unmourned at the time, rather as I cried for my own (parental) loss in mourning Jill.

Such transferences are aided by relations of representation, recognition and/or identification in very complex interactions. Diana's relationships with gay men and with gay community organization is a striking example here. According to Jonathan Grimshaw, founder of the Landmark Centre in London, Diana's HIV/AIDS interventions were crucial:

> When society rejects you, the symbolic importance of having a member of the Royal Family, a representative of the nation, talking to you and saying 'I want to hear what you have to say' is enormous.
>
> (quoted in *Gay Times 1997: 51*)

For Susie Parsons, current chief executive of the London Lighthouse, Diana was not only a representative but also a 'champion for people with HIV' and 'a friend' to them too (*Gay Times* 1997: 51). Her recognitions – listening, holding hands, hugging and joking – were crucial in breaking the massive non-recognitions, the active homophobia that was rampant in the mid-1980s. In a fascinated and fascinating essay, Richard Coles, formerly of the Communards and now a Radio 3 broadcaster, critiques and satirizes dependence on 'feelin's', but also does justice to her gay alliances. It was not just that she managed to be royal and not-royal at the same time, but that she keyed into, used and lived indeed, a gay style and repertoire. 'Diana', writes Coles, 'was a gay man,' (Coles in Merck 1998: 176). This element can be seen in Diana's 'coming out' on television, in her narration of her life as 'redemption' from oppression, and in her fascination with glamour and the 'fabulousness' of gay men in show business and the arts. Coles stresses how Diana identified with gay men, but it must also be the case that many gay men found in her life, too, grounds for identification and for a transference of feelings. Again this connection was particularly poignant in her dying, since gay culture was perforce so expert in the dying game. No wonder that Diana was mourned with a special intensity within the gay community and that there was so marked a gay presence and flavour in the rituals of mourning. As the playwright, actor and director Neil Bartlett put it, 'We were being included in Diana's funeral not as spokespersons for a cause, but as honoured guests' (quoted in *Gay Times* 1997: 52).

It is important to end the discussion of 'attachments' by stressing the political power of Diana's strategies. Her life and the mourning of her death do *not* collapse down into 'feelin's', important – in politics – though feelings are. By recognizing the unrecognizable, she extended the boundaries of effective citizenship. She could bring marginalized groups into a centre of concern and self-activity. In single acts – touching and being touched by men and children with AIDS for example – she could shift the relations of force in public representations, re-establish a sense of worth in those she recognized and challenge her publics, individually and collectively, to do likewise. Her strategies certainly stemmed from a particular psychic economy, but one within which a definite politics was embedded.

Diana's Britain: (not) one nation, (more) the differences among Us

I want to end this chapter by pulling together some themes around the 'Dianaized' nation.

Most accounts of national identity have stressed the production of the nation as a unity, emphasizing cultural homogeneity and cohesion. This goes for traditional Conservative cultural theory, of course, but for critical writing on national identity too. Homogeneity is constructed but it is still a distinctive feature of nations. It is produced by social networks or by 'complementarity of social communication' (Mackenzie 1978, Deutsch 1966) or by common symbolic imagining through modern media (Anderson 1983), or by nationalist movements, political intellectuals and educational institutions (Gellner 1983) or by the political working up of pre-existing cultural commonalties or 'ethnicities' (Smith 1979). In many accounts it is also a rather top-down construction. For Gellner, for example, national identity is produced through the diffusion and imposition of a universal 'high culture' – a 'school-mediated, academy-supervised idiom, codified for the requirements of reasonably precise bureaucratic and technological communication' (Gellner 1983: 57).

The language of national unity suffuses accounts of the Diana phenomenon and not only in tabloid newspapers: 'the emotions which overwhelmed the country' (Ignatieff in MacArthur 1997: 187); 'a nation in a state of shock' (Tony Blair in MacArthur 1997: 17); Diana as 'our common creation and national possession' (*Independent*, MacArthur 1997: 21). The forms of mourning – especially their expressivity – are seen as marking a shift in national character, dubbed 'American' or 'Neapolitan' or perhaps a pre-Victorian recovery. For John Gray, the mourning is 'a revelation of the country we have become . . . already more modern than its politicians have yet understood' (MacArthur 1997: 187). 'The British', with or without a hint of parody, conform to type, or break from stereotype, as a 'country' or a 'people' as a whole:

> Uncertain what to do next, the British followed their instincts and began to queue . . . By lunchtime the official waiting time was two hours . . . By 9pm the wait was seven hours, and many prepared to wait all night. Foreign tourists did not seem enthused by this prospect. The British, however, reacted differently.
>
> (Matthew Engel, in MacArthur 1997: 26)

Most accounts of the mourning crowd stressed its inclusiveness. Engel again:

> The waiting crowd seemed as near as it was possible to get to a cross-section of the country: young and old, men and women, rich and poor, black and white. Many of them were carrying flowers. Only the time-pressed and the hyper-sophisticated were missing.

Even those who recognized the specificity of the crowds – as *The Daily Mail* characteristically recognized its femininity for instance – felt the pressure to include everyone: 'Who were they? Anyone or everyone probably a better cross-section of the British people than you could find at any comparable event' (MacArthur 1997: 30). It was only really those commentators – on left and right – who felt excluded from the mourning process who doubted the 'unities' it was supposed to produce. As Elizabeth Wilson put it. 'I [did not] believe that the tragic event had in any real or permanent sense "united the nation" as we were being told' (Wilson 1997: 136).

It is doubtful if national identities are *ever* fully formed and entire in 'a real or permanent sense'. I agree with Beth Edginton who concludes that 'the nation really is an extremely delicate construct' (*Screen* 1998: 81). Even moments of national unity passed down as 'historic' – Britain in the Second World War for instance – reveal fractures when explored more closely. Given the actual diversity of ways of living within any space marked out as national, such descriptions are bound to be selective and partial. They ignore those who stay away. They flatten contradictions and coexisting differences. They may be insensitive to what is hidden but emergent or subversively 'supplementary' in national formations. Alternatively, as often the case in Diana representations, picking on one feature, they exaggerate the import of the 'new' by representing it as the whole future.

In this chapter I have pursued a different strategy and I have found it valuably explanatory. I have focused not on *unity as a product* but on the *processes of the production* of identity *in and through social difference*. This process involves psychic dimensions, particular forms of emotional investment that flow between persons and between persons and public representations. The construction of the nation on the basis of difference was not a unique feature of 'Dianaization'. In unequal societies all cultural renderings of nationality work in and through difference in this way. Some social categories are always rendered central or exemplary; others are pushed to the social margin; others still are treated as Other, different from Us. The citizens, in other words, are put in their places. In Thatcherite Britain the preferred sexual categories, for instance, were heterosexual, monogamous and married, the preferred gender and child–adult social ordering was a traditional (and strongly wishful) version of 'the family'. The splitting off and political exclusion of homosexualities, as viable alternative ways of living, were crucial to this formation. In a long historical perspective, this may represent the last phase of a particular modern articulation of the heterosexual procreative couple to the modern nation-state (Epstein and Johnson 1998).

What finally fascinates me about the story of mourning Diana is not that differences were made, but that the nation was composed in such a different pattern. This overall difference, a difference from a very oppressive 'norm', is everywhere in our analysis.

It can be seen first in the chagrin of marginalized intellectuals of the left, unable to identify with Diana and therefore unable to see the democratic underside of her politics beneath the privilege and the hype. Left-wing rationalism is often accompanied by a righteous anger on behalf of the unrepresented poor of the world, yet many critics could not see how poverty and oppression figured in the alliance that Diana had begun to make. They could not see the phenomenon as 'political' at all: as Linda Grant puts it, in a terrible simplification of issues of thought and emotion:

> The problem, as much for Diana and the 'ordinary people' who shed tears over her death as for the feminists cited above, is that feelings are not politics.
>
> (Grant in Merck 1998: 190)

Such a statement can make sense only if we cling possessively to our own (intellectual's) definitions of politics: politics as highly articulated, coherent, thought-through, pure. The politics around Diana and much of her way of life was by contrast embedded, implicit and under-articulated, contradictory because engaging with a contradictory world.

The 'Dianaized' nation seems to have excluded much (but not all) critical intellectual opinion. I guess that this excluded group included large sections of the educated or college-going middle class, especially perhaps their men. There was little for them to identify with in Diana's life or death. There was plenty to despise in her very un-academic, un-high-cultural persona. The other identifiable source of opposition came from right-wing royalists and conservative liberal Charles-ites who saw Diana as a competitive spoiler of royal dignities and princely projects. From these sources the attempt to curtail mourning ('enough is enough' said on behalf of her boys) and really to bury the Princess and her promise continues.

Most strikingly, in Diana's Britain, previously central categories were thrust to the margins: especially the 'old' royals with their huge privileges and awkward condescensions. The fleeting hegemony of the Diana moment was popular or populist in two senses. It was 'anti-intellectual' in an important sense, but also as Beth Edginton argues, 'the anti-thesis of the Nation-as-Establishment' (*Screen* 1998: 79). The people made their demands as 'citizens' not 'subjects', with the Queen as subject to Her, and the whole royal crew awaiting the dead Princess at the Palace gates.

The dynamics of representation, recognition, identification and transference which focused on Diana shifted the pattern in other ways. It made marginalized categories integral to an exemplary relationship. In terms of sexual categories it was not the Thatcherite 'family' (or even its Blairite version) which was exemplary, but the independent woman seeking to represent herself and have her own project. This independent heterosexual woman made a close alliance with gay and lesbian styles and politics. Gay identities were not simply 'tolerated' but affirmed. Other social identities, usually more marginal still, like the ill and the dying, the mutilated and the disabled, the war victims, the anorexic and the bulimic, were included in Diana's world, and through her in the nation. Many commentators have noted the interracial multicultural composition of the mourning crowds, and in Birmingham and other cities Diana was commemorated in inter-faith religious services.[7] Her relationship with Dodi Al Fayed gave points of identification for Islamic communities within and beyond the British-based diasporas. Again, a category often treated as Other in contemporary nationalist and occidentalist polemics was brought within the nation and the wider 'Us' by Diana's politicization of intimacies.

All this is consistent with our analysis of psychic dynamics. Traditional nationalist paranoias are historically associated with racism and xenophobia. The view of the nation through other eyes is much closer to the positions adopted by those who have the experience of being members of an 'ethnic minority' and who may also be particularly conscious of the mirroring of their place of settlement by public media in other countries. Most important, perhaps, was Diana's style of relationship to the Other, and to the rest in relation to the Other. This was a way of relating that embodied and internalized the Other as a 'good object' and invited others to do the same. It is difficult to say how Diana's 'humanitarian' politics would have developed and how its limits would have been revealed in situations, especially, of marked social antagonism. Yet once the reality of the lives of oppressed groups are really listened to, once 'difference' is really grasped, it is hard for the dominant social categories to remain the same. Of some of this Diana seems to have been aware, within the limits of her politics of 'comfort': 'You can't comfort the afflicted without discomforting the comfortable' were words written on a piece of paper a friend found on her desk beside momentoes of her visits to the Pope and Mother Teresa (Rosa Monckton in MacArthur 1997: 62).

Diana was mourned so intensely because she was widely available – famous and vulnerable – for others to invest in as a source of pleasure, identity and recognition. She combined a powerful redefinition of a traditional (royal) representative function with the ability to acknowledge something of the reality of other people's lives, especially of those suffering from major oppressions and ill-fortune. This endeared her to large numbers of people, especially those who had endured formative experiences of grief and subordination in their own lives. The widespread identifications, face-to-face or through media which always sought to possess even her private selves, set the terms of a passionate, political mourning. Even in her death, Diana bequeathed to others the opportunity to grieve for ungrieved bereavements of their own. Misrecognized by critics as manufactured or sentimental, this mourning was a typical expression of public grief and personal loss, magnified as much by the intimacy and extent of Diana's social connections (face-to-face and mediated) as by modern global media themselves. Above all, perhaps, we grieved, for what we had lost so suddenly and recognized too late. We mourned her lost promises: for some a reformed and more democratic monarchy; for others the non-royal forms of an equalizing public recognition immanent in her 'testing' of monarchy; for all a social order based on care; and a relation to a wider world founded on the respect of ordinary citizens abroad, not on xenophobia, colonial attitudes and militarized missions. Whatever our subsequent histories, the extent and intensity of the mourning for Diana remains as a testimony to the appeal of this version of the future.

Notes

1 I am grateful, however, to many others with whom I have discussed *Mourning Diana*, especially to Mariette Clare, Ali Mohammadi, Barbara Henkes and members of my Research Practice Group and the MA in Heritage Studies at Nottingham Trent University. Special thanks to Deborah Steinberg, who, as a critical reader and editor of this volume, encouraged me to develop further several of the themes in this essay. I haven't always been able to do this within the limited time available.

2 This is a leading theme of several of the essays in Merck 1998, a collection the subtitle of which, *Irreverent Elegies*, signals a certain intention to debunk.

3 It is common in Britain today to see little piles of flowers and messages at the roadside where an accident happened. Commentators have suggested a connection with the major disaster at the Hillsborough football stadium in 1989 where many people were killed – and a major spontaneous commemoration was held (e.g. Matthew Engel in MacArthur 1997: 27).

4 The paragraph that follows is based on a reading of key texts in contemporary identity theory. Particularly formative for my own approach have been Said 1978, Stallybrass and White 1986, Zizek 1991, Benjamin 1990, Dollimore 1991, Bhabha 1994, Sedgwick 1994, Hall 1997.

5 Versions of this process differ according to the type of psychoanalytic theory underpinning the account. The contemporary revival of psychoanalytic thinking in cultural studies is a major presence in theories of Self and Other. In Kleinian theory, for example, introjection is based on an initial projection into the other – so-called 'projective introjection' (e.g. Mitchell 1986: 185). This is critical for processes of identification.

6 I am grateful to Barbara Henkes for drawing my attention to Dianarama, for discussions on Diana, and for sending me clippings.

7 I am grateful to Deborah Steinberg for discussions and information on these themes.

References

Anderson, Benedict (1983) *Imagined Communities: Reflections on the Origins and Spread of Nationalism*, London and New York: Verso.

Benjamin, Jessica (1990) *The Bonds of Love: Psychoanalysis, Feminism and the Problem of Domination*, London: Virago.

Burchill, Julie (1998) *Diana*, London: Weidenfeld and Nicolson.

Bhabha, Homi K. (1994) *The Location of Culture*, London: Routledge.

Campbell, Beatrix (1998) *Diana, Princess of Wales: How Sexual Politics Shook the Monarchy*, London: Women's Press.

Coward, Rosalind (1984) *Female Desire: Women's Sexuality Today*: London: Paladin.

Deutsch, K. W. (1966) *Nationalism and Social Communication*, 2nd edition, Cambridge, Mass., and London: MIT Press.

'Dianarama' (1998) *De Volksrant* (Amsterdam), no. 60, 16 June.

Dollimore, Jonathan (1991) *Sexual Dissidence*, Oxford: Clarendon Press.

Epstein, Debbie and Johnson, Richard (1998) *Schooling Sexualities*, Buckingham: Open University Press.

Flett, Kathryn (1998) 'Hurtling Towards Chaos', *Observer Newspaper Life Magazine*, 23 August.

Gay Times (1997) 'Signs of the Times: The Revolution of the Flowers: Diana, A Tribute' (October), 50–4.

Gellner, Ernest (1983) *Nations and Nationalism*, Oxford: Blackwell.

Hall, Stuart (ed.) (1997) *Cultural Representations and Signifying Practices*, London: Sage.

MacArthur, Brian (ed.) (1997) *Requiem: Diana, Princess of Wales 1961–1997: Memories and Tributes*, London: Pavilion Books.

McGuigan, Jim (1992) *Cultural Populism*, London: Routledge.

Mackenzie, W. J. M. (1978) *Political Identity*, Manchester: Manchester University Press.

Merck, Mandy (ed.) (1998) *After Diana: Irreverent Elegies* London: Verso.

Mitchell, Juliet (ed.) (1986) *The Selected Melanie Klein* Harmondsworth: Penguin.

Morton, Andrew (1997) *Diana: Her True Story – In Her Own Words 1961–1997*, London and New York: Michael O'Mara Books and Simon and Schuster.

Pilger, John (1998) 'The Anniversary of Princess Diana's Death Is a Reminder of the Hijacking of Feminist Journalism by Agony Aunts', *New Statesman*, 26 June 19.

Said, Edward (1978) *Orientalism*, London: Routledge and Kegan Paul.

Screen (1998) 'Special Debate: Flowers and Tears: The Death of Diana Princess of Wales', vol. 39, no. 1 (spring): 67–84.

Sedgwick, Eve K. (1994) *Tendencies*, London: Routledge.

Smith, A. D. (1971) *Theories of Nationalism*, London: Duckworth.

Smith, A. D. (1979) *Nationalism in the Twentieth Century*, Oxford: Oxford University Press.

Stallybrass, Peter and White, Allon (1986) *The Politics and Poetics of Transgression*, London: Methuen.

Steinberg, Deborah, Epstein, Debbie and Johnson, Richard (eds) (1997) *Border Patrols: Policing the Boundaries of Heterosexuality*, London: Cassell.

Wilson, Elizabeth (1997) 'The Unbearable Lightness of Diana', *New Left Review*, no. 226: 136–45.

Zizek, Slavoj (1991) *For They Know Not What They Do: Enjoyment as a Political Factor*, London: Verso.

3

OUR LADY OF FLOWERS

The ambiguous politics of Diana's floral revolution

Susanne Greenhalgh

Take an aerial shot of the Palace with all the bouquets in front of it, draw the line where the bouquets ended, and plant the whole area with flowers that bloom only in August and then disappear for the rest of the year. It would be a nice piece of ephemera that would have a philosophical point.

(Tim Smit in Smith 1998)

Commenting on the power of flowers to symbolize public sorrow for the death of Diana Princess of Wales, Nancy Banks-Smith captured a telling vignette from her viewing of the televised funeral:

Somewhere en route to St. James' one brash, pink, proletarian carnation, thrown at the gun carriage, stuck among the magnificent wreath of lilies. You could almost hear them putting their heads together. 'Who is it? Don't talk to it, Muriel. You don't know where it's been.' Nothing abashed it or shook it off. Pink and perky, it was there as the six-foot guardsmen shouldered the lead coffin. It entered the Abbey without a by-your-leave. It left for Althorp in the hearse. For all I know, it is lying on the grave on the island in the lake. Somebody's thoroughly common or garden carnation.

(Banks-Smith 1997)

Flowers, together with the improvised 'shrines' of which they often formed a part, were indeed the dominant signifiers of the 'people's grief', and the belief that their invasion of the royal strongholds constituted a 'floral revolution' of some kind had great currency at the time. In what follows I ask whether these tokens were indeed politically performative, capable of conveying social protest, or whether they ultimately celebrated continuity rather than change.

Esther Schor has argued for a cultural rather than psychological concept of mourning 'as a process that generates, perpetuates and moralizes social relations among individuals'.

> [M]ourning rarely, if ever, occurs in isolated instances; a single loss may generate multiple instances of mourning, as well as manifold of sympathies that lessen in intensity – but stop where? – as one moves further from the wrought centre of grief.
>
> (Schor 1994: 4)

People all over the world, but especially in Britain, laid claim to grief, and the right to display it, in a way more often regarded as the prerogative of the bereaved family and friends. Crowds queued patiently to sign the books of condolence, to add a message, toy or bunch of flowers to the piles of tributes, to shed tears as though for one of their own, yet acclaim her as a saint or angel – all for a woman whom few had met, but whose image had been part of their lives for the last two decades. Often it was hard to discern where the 'wrought centre of grief' actually was in the mourning for Diana – in the hidden emotions of the bereaved families or on the streets with the 'Princess's people'?

To understand the politics of these tributes it is necessary to recognize the role of flowers in the historical shift from a culture of luxury to a culture of mass consumption, and the fresh light this throws on the continuing commodification of Diana. The more recent phenomenon of improvised shrines at the site of untimely deaths, on the other hand, arguably allowed the expression of both traditional and radical interpretations of the meaning of her life. Above all, as ephemeral objects flowers and shrines not only play an important part in the symbolic discourses of beauty and transience which for Freud were intrinsically linked to 'the great riddle' of mourning (Freud 1957: 303–7) but they may also call in question the durability of any social or political project to which they are appropriated as symbol. As a result of this analysis it is possible, I suggest, to identify at least three political trajectories in the displays of public grief in Britain. The first, which I term the 'policing of mourning', reveals an investment in authoritarian modes of social discourse even as it appears to call for freedom from restraint and tradition, sometimes surfacing in explicitly nationalist or even xenophobic gestures. The second, performed by those Earl Spencer named the 'constituency of the rejected', can be interpreted as a site of emergent political protest, turning the display of sympathy into a call for social and political reformation. Lastly, I point to the ways in which the memorialization processes which followed the funeral helped to recuperate potentially radical aspects of the mourning into a safe traditionalism, especially through the deployment of discourses of religion, commerce, aristocracy and heritage. This interplay between different and even contradictory elements makes the 'floral revolution' itself a complex and ambiguous phenomenon – one which has perhaps still not run its course.

Hearts and flowers: repertoires for mourning a princess

From the first flower outside Buckingham Palace (reportedly laid by a passing taxi-driver a few minutes after the first broadcast reports of the accident) to the 10,000 to 15,000 tons solemnly removed by hand from the various royal sites to mark an end of the public mourning, the flower offerings, more than any other of the 'grave-gifts' of toys, tokens, letters, poems, photographs, votive candles, or even playing cards, became significant properties in the staging of grief. The carpets of flowers outside 'suitable' or 'substitute' sites were scrutinized or celebrated as popular art, as secular worship, or as emblems of a form of 'floral revolution'. Royal attempts at the performance of grief, on the other hand, were all too often seen as demonstrating an inept command of this newly powerful language of flowers, giving impetus to the developing media opposition of heartless formality with heartfelt popular sorrow. It was reported that without Prince Charles's intervention there would have been no royal flowers on the coffin, draped with the heraldic roses and fleur-de-lys of the royal standard, which provided the public with their first visual confirmation of the Princess's death. As public criticism mounted over the absence of the Queen from London, first Princes Andrew and Edward, and later other members of the family, were dispatched on walkabout to view the flowers and messages outside the royal palaces. Charles and his sons made their first photocall at Balmoral on a similar errand, and the gesture of handing flowers to them became the favoured means of conveying sympathy. When, in turn, the princes added these offerings to the piles of tributes they not only deliberately united themselves with the nation's grief (Santino: personal communication), but, in Charles's case, could hint at a public reconciliation, with ex-wife as well as with people, by carrying one white lily away as a token of remembrance (Randall 1997).

Flowers, of course, form the most traditional and conventional feature of funerals and death commemoration in Western culture, dating back to ancient times and early on absorbed into Christian practice, especially rituals directed to tombs of saints (Goody 1993: 123). In Britain, however, flowers largely disappeared from religion after the Reformation, returning only in the mid nineteenth century as part of what has been called the cult of mourning. Always both a part of nature and of society's views about nature, flowers are also a key aspect of culture, that which is brought under human cultivation, and as such, in the form of cut flowers and bouquets, for several hundred years they acted as signs of a European secular 'culture of luxury', which, in the twentieth century, has given place to a 'culture of mass consumption', figured by the cellophane-wrapped blooms that fill the supermarkets and out of which was created what has been termed the floral architecture of Diana's death (Kent 1997: 68). As the anthropologist Jack Goody explains, the culture of flowers 'is always in some sense threatened by its internal contradictions . . . which turn around riches and poverty, excess and restraint' (Goody 1993: 70). Flowers also play a prominent role in the rituals of royal visits, binding royals and people into the reciprocal relationships of gift-giving, gestures of 'respect and affection', which also construct the recipients as 'warm and caring' (Rowbottom 1998: 83).

Whilst flowers might appear to offer a common language, even a medium of symbolic exchange, for royals and people, the 'spontaneous shrines' were intrinsically more complex vehicles for communication. These improvised assemblages of flowers, personal mementoes, photographs, candles and writings at a site associated with sudden death, whether by accident, natural disaster or deliberate human act, are now recognized as a wide spread phenomenon, borrowing their evolving repertoire of properties from many cultures and political or religious events, although the media coverage now regularly given to such activities is perhaps beginning to give them a conventionality that makes the descriptive term 'spontaneous' less appropriate (Santino 1992a, 1992b). AIDS memory quilts, 'walls' of remembrance modelled on the Vietnam War Memorial in Washington, and the personal possessions preserved and displayed in Holocaust museums are all recent influences on such practices, ones which also highlight their potential for political appropriation. George Monger, however, has collected early British instances of roadside shrines to victims of car accidents or violence, some dating back to the turn of the century and apparently associated (at least in the minds of the recorders) with gypsy or tinker practices (Monger 1997: 113). These examples suggest that a perceived sense of cultural difference from the accustomed ways of marking death may be a significant part of the initial power of such assemblages to express private grief in public in a manner which deliberately solicits the attention of passing strangers, even if this becomes conventionalized at a later date (Monger also points out the influence of Mediterranean wayside shrines seen on holidays abroad). Indeed this collaging of elements from different, even potentially antithetical, cultural traditions may be part of the point of the exercise, signalling a desire deliberately to break free of conventional boundaries to the representation of grief or anger at unnecessary death.

In Britain the mourning that followed the Hillsborough football stadium disaster of 1989, in which ninety-five mainly young Liverpool football fans were crushed to death, has been singled out as a key event, both for its creative fusion of rites drawn from sport, Irish Catholicism and youth culture and for the extensive media coverage these received (Walter 1991;

Walter *et al.* 1995; Davie 1993). For two weeks the home ground, Anfield, was turned into a place of pilgrimage for the leaving of flowers, scarves and messages, gestures also spontaneously incorporated into services at the city's two cathedrals (Walter 1991: 611–12). According to Walter this played an important role in drawing attention to, and perhaps disseminating to a wider British audience, the 'expressive' mode of grief later to emerge in reactions to the death of Diana (Walter 1991: 607; Biddle and Walter 1998: 96–9):

> A city retaining an unusual blend of Celtic and old working-class mourning patterns . . . enacted in highly dramatic form . . . was on view to the whole nation. Middle-class people throughout the country saw on Merseyside a model for the handling of grief to which they aspired, yet lacked the communal identity to achieve.
>
> (Walter 1991: 623)

Similar commemorative and initially local responses were made to tragedies such as the terrorist plane explosion over Lockerbie in 1988, and the shooting of a class of primary school children at Dunblane in 1996. In the latter case the focus of commemoration shifted to the cathedral in the heart of the town, and later to the cemeteries, leaving the school itself as first a site of private mourning for the bereaved and later to resume its teaching of the survivors. The signification of grief also became a national action through media coverage of calls for the lighting of window candles and a minute's silence on the Sunday following the deaths, and gave rise to the Snowdrop campaign which lobbied successfully for changes in gun licensing legislation.

The sites of murders and traffic deaths, especially if the victims are young or have children, are now regularly marked for a period of time by flowers, toys and notes, many of them placed there by children, and sometimes these become permanent memorials, both to record private grief and to act as public warnings or condemnation (Monger 1997: 114). Of course the loss of young lives readily becomes a symbol of threat to the future of a society. Although Santino notes the absence of explicit political sloganeering in such memorials in Northern Ireland, which are generally used for expressions of personal and community grief and loss within a rhetoric of prayer or moral questioning (Santino: personal communication), messages at the site of the Omagh bombing, which broke the ceasefire that accompanied the Good Friday agreement in 1998, included explicit pleas for the peace process to continue. A site may also be used for calls for justice as part of a high-profile legal campaign, as in the case of the racist killing of the black schoolboy Stephen Lawrence.[1] In such instances shrines merge with political demonstrations such as candlelit vigils and are clearly intended to be performative as well as expressive, demanding a response from those in authority, most often in the shape of reformation of the institution at fault.

Although shrines have mostly been linked directly with grief, Jay Winter, in his study of first World War sites of memory and mourning, records a 'street shrine' erected in a working-class (and Irish) area of east London to mark voluntary enlistment which was visited by the Queen in 1917 (Winter 1995: 80). This seems more accurately a form of patriotic *display*, reminiscent of those in shop or domestic windows during national events such as coronations, victory celebrations or a world cup contest. It also appears to have a 'finished' quality about it that makes it a 'showing' rather than a continuing performance, demanding that it be admired rather than added to, and curtailing the opportunities for further improvisation. The shop window displays common in the week after Diana's death fall into this category. With the exception of charity shops, which also tended to foreground Diana's good works, especially if directly linked to their own cause, these displays most often referred to the Princess's elegance and fashion sense, often in combination with tasteful flower arrangements (Bowman 1998). They served to merge the established identity and reputation of the company, imaged through the style of its window dressing, with a sense of unity with the community at large, allowing the everyday business of commerce to continue in an aura of muted respect and celebrating social continuity rather than transformation.

Shrines, then, may be erected by those who have suffered personal loss or be gestures of sympathy and community feeling from neighbours or even strangers. In the former case, according to Monger, they can be both an act of loving remembrance and respect and also one of catharsis, thus in keeping with the dominant British view of mourning as a therapeutic process, as the healthy discharge of grief. 'Stranger shrines' on the other hand, he suggests, act as a form of *social* purgation, expressing horror that such things can happen in our society. Equally an act of remembrance, they are also acts of solidarity, community and support for the bereaved (Monger 1997: 114). But in both cases the shrines are closely linked to the scenes of the violent and untimely death. This is also true of the Northern Ireland shrines discussed by Santino. To a greater or lesser extent, for a brief or longer period of time, they make the environment in which they are situated look different to those who pass through, framing a location into a site of memory as well as mourning by making one violent incident the key to its meanings.

Diana fitted the requirements for memorial by spontaneous shrine as the mother of still young children and through her own relative youth, her association with charities on a global scale, and above all her untimely death. However the site of her fatal crash, in a busy urban underpass, made it difficult if not dangerous to reach, and certainly to contemplate or augment.[2] Unsurprisingly the Liberty torch nearly above the accident site became, and remains, a convenient substitute for Parisians and tourists, dedicated in large part to Dodi and Di as a couple and a celebration of their love affair, and rapidly on offer as one of the tour sights of the city. The dominant motif of star-crossed lovers and the stress on their interracial and religious relationship fitted both the stereotypical image of Paris in world culture and the realities of the racial tensions evident in some of its suburbs. For those without the means or the wish to make such a pilgrimage, however, Diana's death abroad posed problems in siting their mourning offerings. It soon became clear that there would be no lying in state, and that the grave would be on private property at Althorp rather than in the family vault in the local church. Although the royal palaces were quickly identified as substitute sites, they had assumed a baleful quality in Diana's version of her unhappy life story. Even to address notes, as it were, to Diana at the royal residences, was to make claims about her status and to offer a rebuke to those who had sought to deny she was a 'real' princess. It was inevitable therefore that there would be condemnation as well as consolation in the messages at the royal gates.

Show us you care: class, nation and the policing of mourning

As Robert Hertz asserted long ago, 'the emotion raised by death varies extremely in intensity according to the social status of the deceased' (Hertz 1960[1907]: 76). Huntington and Metcalfe give a chapter of their book on celebrations of death to 'the dead king', claiming such an event readily becomes 'a symbolic paradigm of our own deaths and the meaning of death itself . . . the royal funeral, effigy and corpse become a highly condensed set of symbols directly representing everyone of the deaths of all the people of the realm' (Huntington and Metcalfe 1979: 182–3). The mourning of Diana has already been analysed as an event the power of which was dependent on acknowledgement of her royal status – a requirement made difficult at first not only by her 'semi-detached' relationship to the royal family at the time of her death but by the extensive media coverage of her 'romance' with Dodi Al Fayed (see Watson 1997). Certainly the public mourning of Diana cannot be understood without reference to the constant comparisons that were made with the style of royal mourning. There has been a growing tendency for the British press to privilege certain kinds of mourning behaviour over others, but this was the first occasion that a royal funeral had been the target for such analysis (see Walter 1994; Walter et al. 1995; Biddle and Walter 1998). Although a royal death, especially of a popular figure, might seem in any case to license a degree of excess in the performance of grief, what was novel, even unique, about responses to the funeral arrangements for Diana was the extent to which both the royal family and less ardent mourners were policed into 'appropriate' shows of grief by sections of the media and the public.

The royal family's mourning, especially for members other than the monarch, has historically shown a progression from marked public ritual to an essentially private style, in accord, until recently, with the majority of its middle- and upper-class subjects and its declining political role (Fritz 1981: 73). However, this 'old sombre stiff-upper-lip' culture of grief, which aimed to keep emotion hidden and thus invisible, came to be widely viewed as yet another symptom of the ways in which the royals were out of touch with many of their subjects, whose 'expressive grief' demanded signs, however small, of feeling as well as fortitude (Biddle and Walter 1998: 96–9). It was a constant media theme in the week before the funeral not only that the sincerity of their grief for Diana was in question but that the royal family's way of death had been tested and found wanting. Behaviour once thought entirely appropriate for a Christian family at the constitutional heart of the established Church was criticized as contravening more central, emotional needs, as when the young princes attended church on the morning after their mother's death, in accord with royal routine and – apparently – their own wishes (see Rowe 1997; Morton 1997: 276).

Much attention was paid to other aspects of royal protocol and formal gestures of mourning, especially as arrangements for the funeral began to emerge (for example the media campaign for Elton John to sing, the increasing of the length of the funeral procession, questions of who would walk behind the cortège, and above all reactions to the absence of a flag at half-mast over Buckingham Palace). The family's return to London, the well-drilled precision of what was, in all but name, a state funeral, given 'a mixed Windsor, Spencer, Metropolitan Police and new Labour choreography' (Pimlott 1998), silenced most criticism but some voices remained raised in protest against the style of mourning employed. A newspaper report told of angry crowd reactions when the cortège first appeared, unaccompanied by any family mourners:

> As news filtered through that the royals would join the cortège later, it was treated with contempt. Rita Myers, 60, of Romford, was full of feeling. 'When you have a funeral, your family follows from your home,' she said. 'It's as simple as that. Kensington Palace was her home. They should have been behind Diana all the way.' Steve Gutteridge, 43, of Bishop's Stortford, said: 'She was all alone when she left her home, and that's disgusting. I don't care what the protocol was.'
>
> (Rayment 1997)

This strand of class-consciousness surfaced also in the examination of the floral tributes and messages (itself once an important part of the mourning ritual of working-class communities). At the funeral itself the much-reproduced image of Prince Harry's small wreath of white roses, with its envelope addressed to 'Mummy', seemed momentarily to reconcile the demands of emotion and restraint, public and private grief, intimacy and decorum that were played out in the press and on the air, and perhaps in the streets. The shower of flowers and applause which followed the hearse on its journey to Althorp, on the other hand, raised both the emotional and religious stakes to an almost theatrical intensity, suggestive of a star taking her final curtain, but also of a procession to display holy remains: policemen handed back flowers to the throwers after the hearse had passed, as though they were relics, hallowed by brief contact with Diana (*The Princess's People*, BBC2, 6 September 1998). The 'people's earl' Spencer manipulated the familiar connotations of flowers as a medium of sympathetic communication and exchange with the public when he released photographs of himself kneeling among the thousands of flowers which had been rowed over to the burial island, an action which led to yet more bouquets at the gates of Althorp and eventual appeals for no more offerings to be left. When the time came to remove the flowers in London the nation was comforted by the sight of guides and scouts reverently sorting fresh flowers to be taken to old peoples' homes from dead ones to be composted for use in the royal parks, whilst the messages and memorabilia were preserved for the Spencer family.[3]

However, the flowers and shrines were also the occasion for xenophobic violence. Two Slovak tourists and a Sardinian youth accused, in separate incidents, of pilfering teddy bears and flowers from the piles of tributes were the targets of angry abuse and even blows from members of the public, and accusations of grave robbing, and stiff sentences from the judiciary. Despite a defence, in the case of the Slovak women, that they had merely taken memorial tokens in accordance with the funeral customs of their own culture, there was an evident assumption that these foreigners were profiteering from, rather than participating in, the national grief for 'England's rose'. Elsbeth Court's study of the child art first produced for the London tributes also identifies a strong sense of nationalism at work in the display of grief:

> Diana was mostly represented by hearts and flowers, by crowns, angels and fairy-tale princesses, with emphasis put on the blonde-ness of her hair. Sometimes a Union Jack was included, sometimes the flag of St George. Not only the imagery but the very careful drawing per se made the English-ness of it all unmistakable. What other culture in the world would have produced a cult along these lines?
>
> (Court in Norrie 1998)

Although Spencer was careful to call his sister a 'very British' girl, an undercurrent of English nationalism was cannily echoed by Bernie Taupin's rewriting of his elegy to the American icon Marilyn Monroe, which turned the lines 'England's green and pleasant land' from William Blake's 'Jerusalem' into 'your footsteps will always fall here, along England's greenest hills', a version which rapidly became almost a new national anthem.

The trend towards the public 'policing' of grief and inappropriate behaviour towards the dead and their mourning continues. On 8 December 1998 two florists were found guilty at Durham Crown Court of stealing floral tributes from a garden of remembrance in North Shields. Although it was said in mitigation that the couple had been forced to sell their business and move house because of the abuse they had received, they were judged 'grave robbers who committed a very shabby, heartless piece of stealing' and sentenced to fines and suspended prison terms (*The Times*, 9 December 1998). But whilst the North Shields florists were indeed found guilty of stealing flowers from a cemetery, the tourists took them from sites where no grave existed to rob, where the body was elsewhere. It was almost as if Diana's grave, for a time at least, was potentially anywhere and everywhere where flowers were laid, and any act of cupidity, carelessness or disrespect towards its floral memorialization became one of desecration. If Diana had, in some intangible way, come to stand for the nation itself, a 'New' Britain with hearts and flowers its symbols, many came to feel that they were strangers in their own land, a covert resistance to a tyranny of tears.

Outside the gates: the rational protest of the rejected

It was this public policing of grief, as well as its excess, which caused right-wing critics to condemn the mourning for Diana as a form of 'sentimental fascism' as well as 'mob grief', its addiction to 'feminine', 'infantile' gesture politics representing the triumph of sentimentalism over the values of Enlightenment rationalism and political order (Steyn 1998: 175; Anderson and Mullen 1998: 18). Schor, however, argues that, far from denying sentiment, the 'achievement of Enlightenment morals was to conjure a phantom public in the private realm; its legacy was to bring to light in the public sphere the ghostly shapes of the heart' (Schor 1994: 9). If mourning can act as 'a force that constitutes communities and makes it possible to conceptualize history' (Schor 1994: 4), the hearts on display during the week of mourning often conveyed both a new sense of community and a desire not simply to share in a moment of history but also to shape its future direction.

It was notable that many of the visitations to tribute sites took the form of family outings (including many couples) and that many of the messages and interviews made deliberate connections with their own family deaths. A number of the notes (along with the e-mails addressed to the on-line shrines) were sent to the young princes, or even to Charles and the Queen, some offering conventionalized expressions of sympathy, others impassioned and highly personal accounts of their writers' own history and feelings. Many of the writings belonged to a genre familiar from sympathy cards and *In Memoriam* notices in local newspapers, which according to Jon Davies provide 'a kind of populist, market-provided mass media chantry' (J. Davies 1996: 53) in which the use of the present tense assumes both the presence of and active living by the dead: 'the living are talking to the dead in the face of the living. They seem to want everyone to know they are in direct connection with their dead' (J. Davies 1996: 54). However far from the 'wrought centre of grief', feelings were often expressed in the same terms that would have been used for a family bereavement. Equally, the offerings varied from images torn from newspapers accompanied by denunciatory slogans or headlines, to private photographs of a meeting with Diana, and placed treasured personal items alongside objects, like candles or ribbons obviously specially bought or assembled with the kind of dedication evident in the home-made birthday cards featured daily on children's television. At times the mood seemed almost one of keeping company with the dead, reminiscent of a funeral wake.

If, as Baudrillard asserts, all political power is finally based on the manipulation and administration of death (Baudrillard 1993: 130), the public's treatment of Diana as one of the family – a sense of relationship driven in large part by the media revelations of her private involvement with individuals in need – must be read politically as well as psychologically. In this discourse of grieving the traditional Western concept of family as both image and manifestation of the ideal state was no longer embodied in the dysfunctional royal family but in the self-image of the crowds themselves, who frequently offered themselves as surrogate 'carers' to a figure popularly perceived, despite her status, wealth and glamour, as victimized, vulnerable and dispossessed. 'Feel the love' exhorted the banner stretched out in front of Kensington Palace. Ross McKibbin concludes that, though this was indeed a heart-felt impulse, it was also represented an 'incomplete and immature' democracy: 'Love, care, goodness are no less valued, indeed are perhaps even more valued, but they are not thought to be found in the social sphere. The remedy for social exclusion or distress is individual action and individual virtue' (McKibbin 1998: 25). (See Monger and Chandler 1998 for further observations on the Kensington Palace shrines.)

But the mourning was not simply a private family affair. Rather it often voiced an inarticulate anger: 'time after time, the scribbler sided with Diana (and Dodi) against 'Them' – ill-defined authority, an uppercrust Establishment that supposedly included the older royals' (Pimlott 1998). Jewish, Muslim, Hindu and Sikh communities all mourned with their own ceremonies and the gay and lesbian community of Manchester laid flowers in the Princess's honour (Wainwright, Bunting and Gibbs 1997). This multiculturalism of both crowds and rituals revealed not a utopian 'rainbow coalition' but the pain of life in a Britain not yet sufficiently free of its colonial past. Gates, fences, walls and boundaries played an important role in the demarcation of mourning (Evans 1998) and many of the mourners found in Diana an image of their own sense of exclusion, their sense of being kept outside the gates of the society to which they belonged.

> Three young black men were clutching each other and rocking gently. One of them, a man with a hard haircut, repeatedly moaned: 'It's all finished, man.' . . . Under one tree (every tree had been made into a different shrine by believers) there was a group of Asian people, being led in soft prayer by an elderly woman with a tasbi (prayer beads). A teenage girl interrupted her, asking her in Urdu not to pray aloud because it would offend other people.
>
> Such terrible apprehension still – about our very presence in this country. On the Thursday night, the whole of London's Southall Park was lit up by candles and chanting prayers by Sikhs, Hindus and Muslims – all of whom felt perhaps that here they could be free to own their bit of the princess and what she meant to them. To us.
>
> (Alibhai-Brown 1997)

The dead princess, especially in the light of her newly publicized charity work for the homeless, victims of AIDS and landmines, became a figure who, it was felt, could 'unite ordinary people, the poor, those who feel oppressed, those who feel marginalised and those of Middle England into one movement' (Bragg 1997). The loss of such an icon of reconciliation exposed a vital absence at the heart of a culture often seen as socially, racially and nationally divided. Diana's death, and the shrines and messages it evoked, made many look at their society differently. And, like her, they wanted the institutions, not just the gestures, to change. In this sense the mourning for Diana resembled Hillsborough, which brought many who were not fans to oppose police abuse as well as football violence, and Dunblane which led to an anti-gun campaign that revealed some of the class basis to gun support (with the Queen's husband on the side of the pro-gun lobby).[4] It expressed horror and grief not just for an individual death but for the wider circles of social distress with which her life had intersected. And it demanded – often explicitly – a better future.

Museums and mementoes: the memorialization of grief

As the first anniversary of Diana's death came and went, the mourning still seemed extraordinary, not least in the way so much of its impact seemed to have vanished away like 'a shadow and a dream'.[5] Newspaper polls found little evidence of mass plans to mark the day, the families' own commemoration was deliberately low-key, and the young princes' call to allow their mother to rest in peace sought to draw a final veil over public grief. Although this was often explained away as 'Diana fatigue', an inevitable mo[u]rning-after an emotional binge, it also revealed the extent to which the events had been successfully reinscribed in tradition. Despite the sense of novelty at the time in retrospect, it is clear that traditional sites, and mainly traditional modes of mourning predominated. Churches and town halls, many of which opened books of condolence, received their share of offerings, as did war memorials, which remain powerful and prominent reminders of mourning in many communities (see J. Davies 1993; Winter 1995). Many commentators contrasted the values associated with Diana with those accentuated by the militarized state funerals of war heroes such as Churchill and Mountbatten, and McKibbin even suggests that the 'feminization' of mourning behaviour among young men is partially explained by their lack of experience of the armed forces (McKibbin 1998: 20). However, British war memorials have always tended to stress both the pity and the inevitability of war, and although feminine images are infrequently part of their iconography, when present they generally signify peace and care towards the dead and wounded (J. Davies 1993: 120–1), allowing them, despite some reservations from the British Legion, to provide a context for acknowledgement of Diana's charitable work, especially her campaign against landmines. Even when 'secular' sites such as shops, shopping malls, motorway flyovers were made part of the collage of mourning simply by the positioning of a candle or a bunch of flowers, and the witnessing of the sight/site by a passer-by, these shrines signalled continuity rather than change, investing the everyday networks of a late-capitalist economy with a temporary aura of community, reminiscent of the ways in which some supermarkets have experimented with hosting services on religious holidays.

Those who wished to underplay the power of the mourning as a political force indeed often explained it away as a religious impulse. Paul Johnson, writing in the *Daily Mail*, had no doubt that the mourning for Diana constituted a 'spontaneous, collective religious act of the nation in honour of a new saint' (Johnson in Ferguson 1998). In the updated version of his biography of the princess Andrew Morton endorsed the orthodoxy that candlelit Kensington Palace Gardens had been transformed into 'a place of dignified pilgrimage that Chaucer would have recognized' and concluded that Diana's story was 'part of a religious cycle of sin and redemption, a genuinely good and Christian woman who was martyred for our sins' (Morton 1997: 278). Roland Boer argues that such examples can be regarded as 'the first properly global manifestation of civil religion', containing the necessary ingredients of 'a public event, the invocation of religious discourse, and the preservation of ruling class hegemony' (Boer

1997: 86, 85). Transference of the established associations with sanctity of Mother Teresa, who died days after Diana, media emphasis on her charitable work, together with the power of the mythic narrative structures circulating around the idea of the fairytale princess, made her a suitable candidate for the status of civil religious saint (85–6), complete with her own shrines. The most explicit manifestation of this civil beatification came when the Chancellor of the Exchequer, Gordon Brown, against a soundtrack of violin music, paid effusive tribute to Diana on the popular religious programme *Songs of Praise* (BBC1, 30 August 1998), proclaiming her a new Florence Nightingale:

> I think we were all surprised by the numbers who appeared to give flowers, and that outpouring of very personal emotion. But I don't think, in retrospect, any of us should be surprised that she meant a lot. Because she shone a torch into areas of life that a lot of people had been happy to forget.
>
> (Brown in Prescott 1998)

Even when the shrines had been dismantled and the bouquets cleared away, flowers continued to figure prominently in the memorialization that took over from mourning, often foregrounding similar issues of class, nation and the policing of mourning.[6] The Diana, Princess of Wales Memorial Committee set up in December 1997 to advise the government on suitable forms of commemoration, included a memorial garden in Kensington Gardens in its final four proposals 'subject to public consultation'. In fact this was to become a highly contentious project (still unresolved at the time of writing) which aroused strong opposition from residents of this prosperous borough appalled by any prospect of a return of the mourning masses. Disquiet at the prospect of some kind of 'Dianaland' theme park in the heart of the capital as well as at Althorp, already foreshadowed in the commercial tours and charity 'Diana trails' along the funeral route, echoed the class-based distaste expressed by James Stevens Curl towards the 'mass-produced excrescences' to be found in contemporary cemeteries:

> The symbolic, and the eternal version of an ancient Classical tradition that was related to designs for death going back thousands of years were suddenly and violently abandoned. They were replaced by marble hearts, by plastic ash-containers, and by the well-tended and excessively coloured rose-garden.
>
> (Curl 1993: 366)

A similar concern with 'good taste' is evident in the controversy over the decision by the Memorial Fund Committee (responsible for overseeing the charitable use of money from public donations and the sales of 'Candle in the Wind') to grant the American soft toy company Ty permission to bring out a purple 'Princess' Beany Bear, complete with white embroidered rose on its chest and a poem in the religious style of so many of the mourning verses on its ear tag:

Princess

Like an angel, she came
from heaven above

She showed her
compassion, her pain,
her love

She only stayed with us
long enough to teach

The world to share, to
give, to reach
(*Guardian* 26 April 1998: 16)

For many this fusion of commerce and commemoration, like the use of Diana's name on a margarine tub, was hard to justify despite large donations to the Princess's charities. If it had been felt unwise to label the people's offerings 'cheap' or 'tacky', many of the souvenir products on the market, from T-shirts to collector dolls, could be safely condemned, by the Prime Minister as well as the press, as an affront to the memory of 'our nations's golden child'.

It is scarcely surprising, therefore, that at Althorp the remembrance was kept far away from 'tabloid mourning' (Morris 1997), in the best of taste and carefully neoclassical in style to blend with the eighteenth-century architecture and landscaping of an aristocratic stately home. The central memorial tablet of the three created for the lakeside 'temple' (a folly salvaged from the demolished Admiralty building by a former Earl) surrounded the Princess's silhouette with carved garlands of roses and forget-me-nots, in recognition that flowers were 'the most potent symbol of the nation's grief' (Althorp Official Web Site 1998), and the theme was continued in more romantic fashion by the planting of a hundred white rambling roses to veil the monumental urn and plinth on the island and the floating of white water lilies on the lake alongside the four black swans already resident (Pearson 1998), all in addition to trees planted by royal guests on previous occasions. When the museum dedicated to the princess opened in July 1998, visitors walked on a floor sprayed with rose petals through the 'people's tribute' room, to the accompaniment of classical music and a video of BBC coverage of the week's events, though the ornamental bench presented to the Earl by estate workers in memory of his sister was rapidly lost from view beneath the familiar piles of flowers from well-wishers. After a respectful interval for contemplation souvenirs could be selected from a range packaged discreetly in the purple of royalty and half-mourning.

As Zygmunt Bauman has argued, the art collections, architecture and memorials of the aristocracy are such successful testimonies to the power of the 'precious ore of time-defying ancestry' to ensure immortality, that its 'charms and mascots . . . minted, fit for marketing and available for private acquisition' remain objects of desire and key ingredients of the heritage industry (Bauman 1992: 56). Despite the republican sympathies popularly read into Earl Spencer's funeral oration (which actually contained an explicit pledge of allegiance to the Crown), the shrine he created for his dead sister replaced her safely in an aristocratic pantheon, literally out of reach of her public. By putting not simply Diana but her mourning into a museum, the whole extraordinary phenomenon could take its place where all the other stories of royal wives and rebels belong; in the colourful pages of a picture-book version of England's enduring heritage.

Conclusion: where have all the flowers gone?

'Saying it with flowers' was regarded as the most simple and direct way in which to speak about the meaning of Diana's death, but in reality the appropriateness of this discourse lay precisely in its ambiguities. Far from providing a universal 'classless' language it highlighted social divisions and national insecurities. The excesses of the flower mountains drew attention, especially in the context of Diana's much-publicized charity work, to the need for restraint, voiced by those who called for mourners to give charitable donations rather than bouquets. The more 'natural' royal style that Diana was claimed to possess might seem suitably represented by equally 'natural' flowers, but as increasingly hybridized products of a global market (many of the flowers in the tributes came from South America or Africa via the brokers of the Netherlands) their artifice and packaging (it was a subject of frequent comment that the flowers were presented in their wrappings) also spoke to the way in which in life and death alike she remained a commodity for others' use, always in danger of becoming a transient rather than durable object of meaning (see Bauman 1992: 10).

The transience of the floral tributes, their ambiguous and shifting play of meanings, and the intrinsic placelessness of the shrines seem to speak of temporary remembrance, rather than enduring monuments, even if some of them have themselves been memorialized and preserved in museums and exhibitions. The 'ghostly shapes of the heart', figured in the sentimental rhetoric of the flowers, poems and drawings of the crowds, are, finally, not easy to decipher. Free of an intimate connection with an actual site of death, whether grave or killing-ground, these material manifestations of a diffused circle of grief and sympathy often resembled the idiosyncratic memory-boxes gaining popularity among proponents of 'natural death' ceremonies, suggesting that whatever meaning there was private rather than communal and lay in the parts rather than any whole. At times indeed they seemed a rehearsal of all the many forms that mourning can take in a multicultural, multidenominational society. Where difference was everywhere it became a kind of conformity, or a cancellation out of meaning, resisting integration into a coherent political or social reading.

Although it is true that the cult of mourning for Diana, like the culture of flowers, was threatened by its own internal contradictions, it also provided a language in which to articulate not only grief but the desire for fundamental social change. Its shrines and messages provided rich repertoires in which to speak of liberation as well as of authoritarianism, of hope and resolve as well as alienation. By collaging the mourning gestures of many traditions, and inventing new ones, it took on the kind of energy, which, Maurice Bloch suggests, can be a form of violence, opening the way to needed social change (Bloch 1992; D. Davies 1997: 19). Aspects of this mourning did indeed provide the form of catharsis that Augusto Boal ascribes to Athenian tragedy, which sustains an existing hegemony (Boal 1979: 36–46) but it also paradoxically provided a framework for the clarification, rather than purgation, of social dissent. In this sense it was a process that indeed generated, perpetuated and moralized social relations (Schor 1994: 4), a site of memory as well as of mourning. After it, Britain would never look quite the same.

Acknowledgements

I am grateful to Jennifer Chandler, Sandra Kemp and Jack Santino for generously sharing their ideas and research with me.
This essay is dedicated to the memory of Rossy Pitt-Brooke (1954–96), who would have had a lot to say on the subject.

Notes

1 The black teenager Stephen Lawrence was stabbed to death in London in 1993. Police failed to follow up evidence that a number of white youths were implicated in his murder, and the only charges brought were in an unsuccessful private prosecution by his parents in 1996. After a formal complaint to the Police Complaints Commission, a Home Office inquiry was established, chaired by Sir William Macpherson, into the circumstances surrounding the murder and, more generally, the investigation and prosecution of racially motivated crime. Its report, made public in February 1999, was highly critical of the Metropolitan Police's handling of the case. In December 1998 Channel 4 screened a message by the Lawrence parents as an alternative to the Queen's traditional Christmas Day broadcast, and a dramatization of the tribunal, *The Colour of Justice*, was performed at the Tricycle Theatre, Kilburn, in January–

February 1999 and broadcast on BBC2, 21 February 1999. The day after the Macpherson Report appeared, the memorial plaque at the site of Stephen's death was daubed with white paint.

2 The BBC reporter Kate Adie later claimed that it was because this setting was so 'banal' that the television coverage shifted to the laying of flowers outside Kensington Palace, helping to turn news into a human interest story and publicizing the evolving gestures of mourning (Gibson 1998: 6).

3 Undertakings were made to treat flowers left to commemorate the first anniversary of the death with equal respect, though these were left in place for only two or three days.

4 The Dunblane parents were also criticized by a right-wing Conservative MP for being too 'emotional and hysterical' in their campaign against handguns.

5 This phrase, derived from the Russian Orthodox Liturgy, was set to music as part of the anthem 'Song for Athene' by John Tavener which concluded the funeral service.

6 The mourning was also 'immortalized' in live performance at the Edinburgh Festival: for example David Benson's re-enactment of the funeral, *Nothing But Pleasure*, and *Flowers in the Park*, 'a thought-provoking experience offering moments of light relief to the grief' which portrayed 'ordinary folk' paying floral tribute (Glaister 1998: 13).

References

Alibhai-Brown, Yasmin (1997) 'An Asian, a Socialist and a Tear for Diana', *The Times*, 12 September.

Althorp Official Web Site (1998) 'Urn and Temple – Edward Bulmer', http://www.althorp-house.co.uk

Anderson, Digby and Mullen, Peter (eds) (1998) *Faking It: The Sentimentalisation of Modern Society*, London: Social Affairs Unit.

Banks-Smith, Nancy (1997) 'Trail of Tears', *Guardian*, 8 September.

Baudrillard, Jean (1993) *Symbolic Exchange and Death*, trans. Ian Hamilton Grant, London: Sage.

Bauman, Zygmunt (1992) *Mortality, Immortality and Other Life Struggles*, Cambridge and Oxford: Polity Press.

Bickford, Anne and Lavelle, Siobhan (1997) 'Places to Mourn Diana' in Re: Public (Ien Ang, Ruth Barcan *et al.*) (eds) *Planet Diana: Cultural Studies and Global Mourning*, Kingswood, New South Wales: Research Centre in Intercommunal Studies, University of Western Sydney, Nepean: 61–6.

Biddle, Lucy and Walter, Tony (1998) 'The Emotional English and their Queen of Hearts', *Folklore*, vol. 109: 96–9.

Bloch, Maurice (1992) *Prey into Hunter: The Politics of Religious Experience*, Cambridge: Cambridge University Press.

Boal, Augusto (1979) *The Theater of the Oppressed*, trans. Charles A. and Maria-Odilia Leal McBride, London: Pluto Press.

Boer, Roland (1997) 'Iconic Death and the Question of Civic Religion', in Re: Public (Ien Ang, Ruth Barcan *et al.*) (eds) *Planet Diana: Cultural Studies and Global Mourning*, Kingswood, New South Wales: Research Centre in Intercommunal Studies, University of Western Sydney, Nepean: 81–6.

Bowman, Marion (1998) 'Research Notes: After Diana', *Folklore*, vol. 109: 99–101.

Bragg, Melvyn (1997) 'The Fate that Will Launch a Thousand Books', *The Times*, 8 September.

Curl, James Stevens (1993) *A Celebration of Death*, rev. ed., London: B. T. Batsford.

Davie, G. (1993) 'The Anfield Pilgrimage', in Ian Reader and Tony Walter (eds) *Pilgrimage in Popular Culture*, Basingstoke: Macmillan: 201–19.

Davies, Douglas J. (1997) *Death, Ritual and Belief: The Rhetoric of Funerary Rites*, London and Washington: Cassell.

Davies, Jon (1993) 'War Memorials', in David Clark (ed.) *The Sociology of Death: Theory, Culture, Practice*, Oxford: Blackwell: 112–28.

Davies, Jon (1996) 'Vile Bodies and Mass Media Chantries', in Glennys Howarth and Peter C. Jupp (eds) *Contemporary Issues in the Sociology of Death, Dying and Disposal*, Basingstoke: Macmillan: 47–59.

Evans, Margaret (1998) 'The Diana Phenomenon: Research in the East Midland', *Folklore*, 109: 101–3.

Ferguson, Euan (1998) 'Once More-With Feeling', review section, *Observer*, 30 August: 1–3.

Freud, Sigmund (1957) 'On Transience' in *The Standard Edition of the Complete Psychological Works of Sigmund Freud, Volume XIV (1914–16): On the History of the Psycho-Analytic Movement, Papers on Metapsychology, and Other Works*, trans. J. Strachey, London: The Hogarth Press and The Institute of Psycho-Analysis: 303–07.

Fritz, Paul S. (1981) 'From "Public" to "Private": The Royal Funerals in England, 1500–1830', in Joachim Whaley (ed.) *Mirrors of Mortality: Studies in the Social History of Death*, London: Europa Publications: 61–79.

Gibson, Janine (1998) 'TV News "Has Heart" Since Diana's Death', *Guardian*, 31 August.

Glaister, Dan (1998) 'Diana: The Revolution', *Guardian*, 12 August: 13.

Goody, Jack (1993) *The Culture of Flowers*, Cambridge: Cambridge University Press.

Hertz, Robert (1960[1907]) 'Contribution to a Study of the Collective Representation of Death', in Rodney and Claudia Needham (eds) *Death and the Right Hand*, Aberdeen: Cohen & West.

Huntington, Richard and Metcalfe, Peter (1979) *Celebrations of Death: The Anthropology of Mortuary Ritual*, Cambridge and New York: Cambridge University Press.

Kent, Phillip (1997) 'The Building of Death', in Re: Public (Ien Ang, Ruth Barcan *et al.*) (eds) *Planet Diana: Cultural Studies and Global Mourning*, Kingswood, New South Wales: Research Centre in Intercommunal Studies, University of Western Sydney, Nepean: 67–70.

McKibbin, Ross (1998) 'Mass Observation on the Mall', in Mandy Merck (ed.) *After Diana: Irreverent Elegies*, London: Verso: 15–24.

Monger, George (1997) 'Modern Wayside Shrines,' *Folklore*, vol. 108: 113–14.

Monger, George and Chandler Jennifer, (1998) 'Pilgrimage to Kensington Garden', *Folklore*, vol. 109: 104–08.

Morris, Jan (1997) 'The Naughty Girl Next Door', *Time* vol. 150, no. 11, 15 September.

Morton, Andrew (1997) *Diana: Her True Story – In Her Own Words 1961–1997*, London and New York: Michael O'Mara Books and Simon Schuster.

Norrie, Jane (1998) 'Drawn to Diana', *London Evening Standard*, 2 January.

Pearson, Dan (1998) 'In Diana's Footsteps', *Sunday Times*, 2 August.

Pimlott, Ben (1998) 'After Diana', *Sunday Times Review*, 30 August.

Prescott, Michael (1998) 'Ministers Furious as Brown Says He Is "Continuing Diana's Work"' *Sunday Times*, 30 August.

Randall, Colin (1997) 'Young Princes Take Heart from Compassion of Public Mourners', *Daily Telegraph*, 6 September.

Rayment, Tim (1997) 'The Public Cry Out for their Lost Princess', *Sunday Times*, 7 September.

Rowbottom, Anne (1998) '"The Real Royalists": Folk Performance and Civil Religion at Royal Visits', *Folklore*, vol. 109: 77–88.

Rowe, Dorothy (1997) 'Being Good isn't Good for the Family', *Guardian*, 2 September.

Santino, Jack (1992a) '"Not an Unimportant Failure": Rituals of Death and Politics in Northern Ireland', in Michael McCaughan (ed.) *Displayed in Mortal Light*, Antrim: Antrim Arts Council.

Santino, Jack (1992b) 'Yellow Ribbons and Seasonal Flags: The Folk Assemblage of War', *Journal of American Folklore*, vol. 105: 19–33.

Schor, Esther (1994) *Bearing the Dead: The British Culture of Mourning from the Enlightenment to Victoria*, Princeton: Princeton University Press.

Smith, Geraint (1998) 'Diana's Gardens "Would Be a Poisoned Chalice"', *This is London*, 16 July, http://www.thisislondon.co.uk

Steyn, Mark (1998) 'All Venusians Now: Sentimentality in the Media' in Digby Anderson and Peter Mullen (eds) *Faking It: The Sentimentalisation of Modern Society*, London: Social Affairs Unit: 163–79.

Wainwright, Martin, Bunting, Madeleine and Gibbs, Geoffrey (1997) 'Nation Pauses in Silent Tribute', *Guardian*, 6 September.

Walter, Tony (1991) 'The Mourning after Hillsborough', *Sociological Review*, vol. 39, no. 3: 599–625.

Walter, Tony (1994) *The Revival of Death*, London: Routledge.

Walter, Tony, Littlewood Jane and Pickering Michael (1995) 'Death in the News: The Public Invigilation of Private Emotion', *Sociology* vol. 29, no. 4: 579–96.

Watson, C. W. (1997) '"Born a Lady, Became a Princess, Died a Saint": The Reaction to the Death of Diana, Princess of Wales', *Anthropology Today*, vol. 13, no. 6: 3–7.

Winter, Jay (1995) *Sites of Memory, Sites of Mourning: The Great War in European Cultural History*, Cambridge: Cambridge University Press.

4

BE(LONG)ING

New Labour, New Britain and the 'Dianaization' of politics

Valerie Hey

Introduction

When Tony Blair was elected on 1 May 1997 with a landslide, I experienced the electoral annihilation of the radical right as a visceral, almost orgasmic pleasure. I also knew that this euphoria was bound to be short-lived. Best just enjoy the momentary lightness of being – of deliverance to Planet New-Labour/New-Britain.[1] Jonathan Freedland suggests that there was a shift in the zeitgeist that promised a 'more open and tolerant, less macho, less miserable society' (*Guardian*, 3 September 1997): in short, a 'feminization' of politics.

This chapter is concerned with exploring how the dialectic of positive change – 'things can only get better' – configured public responses to the death of Princess Diana. Her particular popularity and the subsequent intense reactions at her death occurred in part because 'Diana' was caught up in and positioned by some New-Labour/New-Britain political themes but also because she, literally and in fantasy, personified certain 'outlawed' emotions – of expressivity, compassion and caring. John Vidal captures the force of the exceptional identification shown by people the night before the funeral:

> Almost to a person they say they feel that Diana spoke to them personally, and gave them hope, when they were at the bottom. Ex-prisoners, single mothers, the deaf, the lame, the crippled, lie down together. She cared, they say. *Others who should have known better did not.*
>
> (*Guardian*, 6 September 1997, emphasis added)

The construction of this unlikely community of feeling suggests the capacity of the 'irrational' to dismantle even the most apparently invincible of political projects. As Martin Engel argued at the time:

This week has provided the final proof that Margaret Thatcher was wrong, there is such a thing as society. And it sometimes asserts itself in ways that no-one can predict and most struggle to comprehend.

(*Guardian*, 6 September 1997)

Mapping the 'unpredictable' and 'irrational' requires that we consider how subjective investments are secured. A post-structuralist interest in desire and emotion(s) allow us to think about how differently located people come to 'want what they want' (Walkerdine 1990: 89). This chapter has two interrelated currents. First, it is an attempt to place my own 'surprising' reactions to Diana's death by reading these through the lens of feminist post-structuralism. Second, it considers how, particularly after her death, New Labour span (and more importantly was able to spin) a particular political iconography of the life/death of the Princess into its hegemonic re/New/al project. In short, my argument is that the Princess's role as 'outcast' (however implausible in 'real' terms) created space for some complex co-identifications by 'other' outcasts – the socially marginalized, including political 'exiles' from within socialism and feminism (Epstein and Steinberg 1996).

It seems to me that, whilst the political and personal investments held within these disenfranchised positions (as well as their underlining fantasies or desires) were already in play before the Princess's death, these were intensified after her death and projected into the prevailing equations that made up the New Labour mantras: of social inclusion, community and a revivified sense of socially responsible compassion.[2]

Left behind? the complex responses of the left

When Princess Diana died on 31 August, I heard the news on the radio in complete disbelief. After all, Diana's image had been ubiquitous. I was transfixed by the media coverage throughout that Sunday. I also felt queasy about my own 'politically incorrect' level of interest in the extravagant coverage. Apparently, I was not alone amongst members of the academic left. For example, a recent report of a seminar about Diana, takes an almost apologetic tone:

Why has Princess Diana become a topic for academic seminars? Consideration of the reaction of the mass media, institutions, but mostly of ordinary people after her death offers enough material for a broader discussion about deeper transformations which are occurring to British society . . . Many academics were also surprised by their own feelings and reactions to Diana's death.

(*LSE News and Views*, vol. 14 [11], 1998)

Here, the shared captivation by emotional public spectacle appears troubled by a recognition that this may not *quite* constitute a legitimate object of critique, the contradiction being carried by the elitist opposition between 'ordinary people' and 'academics'. This defensive concern about legitimacy effects much of what the academic left mis/understands in the Diana phenomenon.

Predictably, responses in the left split over interpretations about her 'political quotient'. Was she 'progressive'? or 'reactionary'? This is what I have called elsewhere the 'dipstick' approach. The metaphor implies a practice in which a critical commentator (usually a left male), inserts his probe into a phenomena, in order to test its revolutionary or reactionary class meanings. Some were in no doubt. John Lloyd was outspoken in his critique of the 'new establishment' of 'supersonic wealth' and condemned Diana's personal style as 'let it all emote art' and 'touchy feelie populism' (*New Statesman*, 3 October 1997). Many commentators pointed to the immense contradictions between Diana's wealth and what they called her 'claims on' victimhood. 'Diana lit the world and obscured it' (Lloyd, *New Statesman*, 3 October 1997). Another lambasted: 'There is a nasty whiff of the masochistic in the new "iconic" populism. Diana fought tigerishly to keep hereditary royal titles and fortunes for herself and annex them for their children' (Christopher Hitchens, *Nation*, 29 September 1997). Katha Pollitt in the same publication compared reactionary Mother Teresa with Princess Diana's mythic status, noting the strange paradox that 'that the two women most adored (in the late twentieth century) are medieval figures of the princess and a nun'. Hitchens accused Princess Diana, like Mother Teresa, of using 'the poor and the sick as "accessories"'.

This savaging left little ground for acknowledging ambivalences in reactions, much less scope for understanding Diana's evident appeal, *despite* the gulf between 'ordinary' people and her inordinate personal wealth. In contrast, Joan Smith, along with other feminist and pro-feminist voices, used a different, more engaged tone:

> . . . from the beginning [Princess Diana] had a special meaning for women which meant she was 'not some distant glamourous figure but someone with whom they felt an *intimate connection*.
> (*Guardian*, 2 September 1997, emphasis added)

Other writers perceived different equivocations, especially Diana's uncanny capacity to make her access to the monarchy work as a critique. Julie Burchill, for example, casts Diana as the 'People's Destroyer':

> She showed up the House of Windsor's total lack of rapport with, or affection for, its people with cruel clarity.
> (*Guardian*, 2 September 1997)

The main faultline in the critique cut across class and gender lines. Diana's life and the public's reactions to her death were, as a consequence, read through competing frames. One position construed class at the expense of *any* gender analysis, effectively pursuing a sub-variant of the 'rich bitch' line. She was dismissed as an overrated, reactionary idol. Her iconic appeal was construed teleologically as a testimony of her regressive impact. From an opposing more feminist-influenced position, she was seen as bringing a different sort of political language to the previous merely ceremonial function of monarchy. Her post-divorce profile was seen to have consolidated broader and more engaged political themes which had disturbed both tradition and traditional categories of analysis.

Some writers simply refused *any* serious critical engagement, berating 'us' from their lofty perch on the moral high ground. Lloyd's call for an end to 'the intrusion into us of the manipulation of our emotions by the production of an icon' could not help, given its pre-emptive (possibly hysterical?) refusal to think emotional 'collusion' outside of pejoratives. Many commentators considered that the mere open display of feelings were suspect at best, and at worst, fascist – lurid and frankly rather absurd comparisons with the 'mindlessness' of 1930s Germany were invoked (Chris Dunkley, *Financial Times*, 9 September 1887 cited in Kirby 1998: 31). There is another chapter to be written about the 'emotionophobia' shown in such aggressive reactions to popular responses. How often, for example, were popular responses constructed as abnormal?[3] It occurs to me that for people to construct standing quietly in queues (to sign the books of condolences) and the floral revolution as pathological and dangerous 'excess' tells us far more about fears amongst the elite of the 'Other', whether this is the 'masses' or their messy displays of 'modest' public grief.

Neither right-wing misogyny nor cynical socialist dis/enchantment assist us here: though the latter may look cool, it does so only because it works by positioning engaged work as recuperated collusion. Taking up a feminist post-structuralist analysis is riskier but likely to prove far more generative. As an approach committed to exploring the micro-relations of self/subjectivity and social relations, it is extremely useful in understanding the making of personal affiliations. However, this level of analysis *alone* cannot show us how individuals' desires come to be articulated together into a *cultural* performance of *collective* behaviour, nor can it say much about the economic, social and communicative practices and conditions within which such 'fixings' between people and between people and their shared 'objects of desire' occur.

In order to understand these relations between the 'production', 'consumption' and 'mourning' of Diana, we need to take back the classic left notion of the market but then specify the particular cultural configuration of markets abiding in late modernity. Jane Kenway's notion of the 'postmodern market',[4] drawing as it does on Valerie Walkerdine's (1990; 1997) work on identification, desire and consumption, offers a useful starting point for such a reworking.

Supply and demand: the paradox of postmodern markets and 'community'

According to Kenway's model, postmodern markets can be distinguished by several interactant features. They are predominantly constituted through globalized technological modes of communication with a reliance on associated forms of scientific rational knowledges. Postmodern market forces have the ability to disorganize the traditional solidarities of class, transcend the boundaries of state and nation and reconfigure gender, ethnic, class, age, region and international relations (Kenway 1998). Such shifts are accomplished by the intensification of commodification as 'capital is increasingly able to stake a claim to more and more so called "private" space' (Hey 1996: 355). It is the crucial additional emphasis on consumption in the depiction of postmodern markets (Kenway 1998) that can help us specify the unique features that structured people's reaction to the death of Diana. In this model there is a central move to read consumption as cathexis – as about *desire*. Kenway draws on Rosalind Coward's powerful insight that in the intensification of commodification 'dissatisfaction is constantly recast as desire' (Coward 1984). Kenway notes also that should desire collide with 'the constraints of possibility' (Kenway 1995: 17) it is more likely that the recasting implicates the more troubling emotions of anxiety and frustration. Theoretical recognitions of the material *and* psychic features of postmodern markets ground the following analysis of reactions to Diana's death.

It is, by now, axiomatic to note that the powerful destabilizing consequences of economic restructuring are most keenly felt by the already disadvantaged. This is especially the case where the response of the radical right has been to withdraw from welfare provision (Epstein and Kenway 1996). The state is an evaluative rather than a welfare one (Neave 1988). Moreover, these social, political and material changes have been felt by groups outside of the predictable categories of social and economic marginalization. The dispossessed now potentially includes the old middle class (Epstein *et al.* 1998). It is clearly not possible to argue through all these features of postmodern markets, but three main factors are pertinent in reading the Diana phenomenon. First, is the (pedagogic) role of the West's enormous media capacity. Second, is the demoralized and fragmented nature of the British, especially English, polity and civil society under the legacies of the radical right. And third, is the role of desire in impelling new forms of (emotional) resistance to the seemingly implacable hegemony of the market. By noting points of articulation amongst these factors – it is plausible to locate aspects of Diana's appeal here – in people's desire to

recast or manage the multiple anxieties of 'an age of manufactured uncertainties' by seeking and securing a place as one of 'the people'. This
(be)longing represented a popular accumulated sentiment which attached
subjects to both the Princess and to the New Labour state since each
promised (in different though overlapping ways) routes back to 'society'.

The role of the media: intertextual resources

The globalized techno-capitalism of the West has an unparalleled capacity
to transmit events supra-nationally and simultaneously. We now count
audiences for spectacular events in billions. Since this highly responsive
techno-ability is under the commercial control of the producers of CNN and
News International, it could be argued that the growing personalization of
news (of which the Diana phenomenon was a most potent example) arises
because human interest stories (along with sport and music) share core
features of (emotional) 'connexity' (Mulgan 1997) which render them one
of the few grammars capable of securing a global reach. However, the public
reactions to Diana's death went well beyond the personal or emotional and
showed a political edge that actually baffled most commentators. This is not
to deny the role of the media but rather to suggest that in certain distinct
and unprecedented ways it did not *lead* public opinion so much as *follow* it.

In claiming public space to celebrate Diana's life and death, people
extemporized a repertoire, including ritual practices borrowed from sources
beyond their own immediate experience. Here the media *were* important in
offering visual evidence of comparable events – the national mourning for
Dunblane was frequently cited. Both episodes provoked a spectacle of grief
(candles, flowers and vigils). Yet the Greenham Common 'embrace the base'
event provides a stronger, more politically charged reference point. The
Greenham action was one of the few times that a mass feminist action was
prominently and sympathetically displayed in the tabloid press. It was
'photogenic' in a way that other 'actions' were not. This was because it
offered both the potent image of a communal 'long shot' (an aerial view of
thousands of women and girls embracing the base) and also 'close-ups' of
personal memorabilia, allowing scope for individual identification.
Unknowingly perhaps, the currency of protest at Greenham exactly suited
a popular (if problematic) format.

The global media did not *cause* people's reactions to Diana's death. Nor,
more significantly did they provide the inflexion of political resistance in
people's affirmation of their attachment to Diana and *what she stood for*.
'Candle in the Wind', light and flowers may now seem a cliché but what
these symbolized was an oppositional agenda – a commitment to care,
compassion, empathy which defined itself both against the radical right's
legacy including the uncaring impacts of globalized economic and social
uncertainties. In this light, fixing a self into a civic space through an

identification with Diana meant effectively standing *against* the indifference of the market and the indifference of 'people who should have known better'. What occurred on the streets of London and across Britain out-manoeuvred even the fast forces of postmodern technologies to capture it. We need to look more centrally at the mobilization of feelings stimulated by Diana.

'The People's Princess': emotional fixtures and imagined communities

It is painfully significant that Diana lived her brief public life under the radical Right and that her life ended in the honeymoon period of the New Labour landslide. The triumph of New Labour was accompanied by a rhetoric of community, interdependency and inclusion. It was perhaps this mood of suppressed 'collectivism' that demonstrated people's desires for an alternative to individualism and which Diana's activist persona – her visits to the homeless; participation in AIDS charities; the landmine campaigns and fund-raising for women's refuges – seemed to embody. In the context of nearly twenty years of anti-collectivist free market forces, Diana stood out as an oppositional figure. So we need to look at the specific social, psychic and political dynamics that compelled this recognition as popular constituencies came to identify with Diana and to 'demonstrate' about her death. How was this cathexis put together?

Being

Classic representations of Diana's public persona featured her seemingly boundless capacity to touch 'ordinary people'. After her death 'ordinary' people she had 'touched' offered their personal videos of her, perhaps to display her 'off-camera' authenticity. Certainly many felt as if they 'knew her' in validating her purported fine-tuned interpersonal skills. It was certainly true that her image as a flawed (but warm) human being was sufficiently robust to rescue her from the frozen protocol and formality of the royal family. She was unique amongst the royal household in seeming to possess a genuine modern empathy. We have also to recall that the 'other' woman with a contemporaneous high profile at the time was Margaret Thatcher. Their reigns were almost coterminous. The public investment in Diana can be seen as overdetermined by this coincidence. Whilst Diana became synonymous with compassion, Mrs Thatcher relished her reputation for ferocity as the 'Iron Lady'. Psychoanalytic concepts of projection, intro-jection and splitting have plenty of purchase and productive scope within the Diana/Mrs Thatcher binary narrative.

Diana's earliest pronouncements about the redemptive power of 'love' and 'hugs' could not have been in starker contrast to Mrs Thatcher's pronouncements about success, hard work and discipline. If one erred in the 'Thatcher family' one was at risk of a severe 'handbagging',[5] whilst any fall from grace in the Diana household was imagined more as an opportunity for redemptive understanding. Diana was identified with a language of connectedness and 'emotional literacy' drawing on the (so easily parodied) stock phrases of self-help manuals. Margaret Thatcher, in contrast, constructed success as a privatized accomplishment in a can-do culture of self-seeking competitive individualism – the Spice Girl as opposed to the self-help paradigm. Failure under the Right was stigmatized as a moral lapse and the state was not looking to pick up, much less reconnect, the pieces.

Under the radical Right some of us might have preferred psychologically to invest in the 'good mother' Diana (altruism, self-sacrifice, self-less, connection) rather than the punitive 'bad mother' Margaret (self, separation, selfish). After the death of Diana and the 'death' of the Right, there was plenty of 'scope' for desire and remorse amongst those of us who felt guilty that they had been (un)avoidably implicated in a political project that put self-'interests' first. This is true of those who resisted the drift to authoritarian populism (Hall 1988). In this context, the rescuing of rapport by Diana carried people's repressed longings, for a polity beyond the mere appeasement of the sovereign self, 'She cared, they say. *Others who should have known better did not*'. It was as if Diana had carried the psychic cost of our collective refusal or inability under Thatcherism/Majorism of identifying with the 'other' in an 'us'. Maybe the repressed that powerfully returned was a compound desire for inclusion not only in a more humane polity but in one that could only be made possible through a communal striving for a new 'better (less self-interested) me'.

Be(long)ing

If part of the new polity was inflected by an optimistic desire for self-improvement, in which 'Things can only get better', this surely resonated with Diana's apparent boundless capacity for self-invention and 'fresh starts' (selling her dresses, divorcing Charles, overcoming bulimia). Her capture of the popular imagination also lay in a powerful reassertion of popular desires to 'belong'. These politics of connection represented a civic bid to make an 'emotional community' which involved the literal and metaphorical taking back of space appropriated (and then closed down) by the anti-state and anti-civic practices of the previous Conservative administrations. Princess Diana as 'the People's Princess' had become a resource (however unlikely) of hope. Her modelling of the politics of be(long)ing spoke back to people's desire to belong and was sufficiently potent to hold within its appeal a range of complex and contradictory positions.

As I have suggested, understanding people's rekindled commitment to the social requires an acknowledgment of the collective psychic costs of living in a pessimistic 'moral economy' mandated by nearly two decades of radical right market ideology. Having made the 'commitment' in the election, to a new polity, people felt bereft because the 'uncrowned princess of hope' had been killed, at the precise moment when she should have been installed in the new royal family of New Labour. It was precisely because so many of these longings were unspoken and unconscious that they emerged paradoxically at the point of rupture at her death. At that moment it seemed that what had formerly been private acts of identification surfaced into the open (conscious) in a 'unity of affect' capable of carrying multiple recognitions constructed across class, 'race', ethnicity, sexuality, region, religion, age, gender and lifestyle difference. At this point it was possible for the various fragments to 'come out together' to produce a distinct form of solidarity – one premised on imagined socio-politico-emotional bonds. These feelings of wishing for positive cultural change – 'Things can only get better' – New Labour had sensed, stimulated and responded to.

As I have noted, commentators put the events of Diana's death and the New Labour ascendancy together since both signalled aspirations for unity. However, analysts privileged the 'media' in their explanation at the expense of understanding what it was about *Diana* that had galvanized popular sentiment. It became evident that a central aspect of the public construal of Diana was her widespread appeal from amongst multiple constituencies. This popularity framed the 'people's funeral' in significant ways to set up the emotional, political and social grammars available for the media event. Writers, however, tended to overlook the work of counter-hegemony that had gone on *before* Diana's death. They sought instead to ground the public's reactions in the retraditionalizing narrative rendered in the media:

> Defining Diana's death as a media event is a useful way of understanding the public's response. The response is both common to media events and specific to the content of the particular event. The generic response is one of unity and shared experience. In an age of audience fragmentation via multiple channels, of political apathy and individualistic values, a media event offers a moment of collective ritual participation exaggerated by its very rarity. It reconnects us through traditional formats still retained by the now beleaguered public service broadcasters to those traditional emotions of pride, unity and belongingness central to British nationhood and History.
>
> (*Psychologist*, November 1997)

We need to problematize the cosy notion of Britishness, since it has historically been constituted out of old and neo-conservative themes of *exclusions* (Gilroy 1987; Arnot 1992). Yet, it is equally wrong to ignore the unity that *was* put in place, however precariously, in the aftermath of Diana's death. As I have argued, this took the form of an ethical search for 'an imagined (better) community' (Anderson 1991).[6] One aspect of this 'unity of affect' reflected widespread longings for human contact, a longing that implied a recognition of responsibility for others. The other element related to more intimate themes which resonated with women's demands for male emotional literacy.

Princess Diana's refusal of sexual shame, demonstrated, as I argue below, in her *Panorama* interview, offered scope for a gender and indeed a feminist identification through her insistence on 'outing' the sexual politics of private life. It was Diana's unique role as the relay of the public, private, personal and political agendas of popular dissent that established the conditions for her iconic status in life and in her death.

The feminist princess

Like other feminists in the 1980s, I followed the story of Diana, through the prescient but politically ineffective 'Don't Do it Di' campaign – the actual wedding ceremony, the kiss, the babies, the clothes, the transformations, the eventual disintegration of the marriage, the bulimia, the recovery, the flirtation with feminist therapy and the rebirth into political 'activism'. But the defining moment for me in the (quasi-feminist?) fairytale was her ruthless but elegantly understated expose of the sexual politics of elites in the infamous *Panorama* interview. Here was the number one sexual icon dramatizing dissatisfactions that millions of 'ordinary' women shared. Her critique implied the emotional bankruptcy not only of Charles but of patriarchal marriage itself, and it was compelling. She placed the 'private' on the political agenda in a pointed way and drew explicitly (if eclectically) on feminist themes. She spoke about her search for an independent identity and her refusals to be sidelined – of her struggles against the repressiveness of her husband's household. Her stated public refusal to put up with the royal *ménage à trois* or to 'go quietly' accounts for her place in popular consciousness as the premier member of the 'first wives club'.[7] This is another reason why her death was felt so deeply – here was a dissenting if fractured (feminist?) voice right at the heart of the British establishment. Yet of course, it was a highly privileged voice – the voice of private education, of finishing schools and blood sports, of servants and conspicuous consumption. But for many people (including me) these divisions were dissolved and the usual distance between 'them and us' imploded in those defining moments of her main (indeed all) public appearances, the *Panorama* interview, her landmine campaigning, her funeral.

New Labour: new subjectivity?

Decca Aitkenhead got it right when she remarked that 'here *at last* is a chance for us to demonstrate both to each other and to ourselves that we are not selfish individuals leading nuclear lives, and that we still *yearn* to do something good and right' (*Guardian*, 5 September 1997, emphasis added). Aitkenhead identified one unlikely figure among the crowds – a 'punk with a wreath', a sight which apparently elicited 'inordinate public pleasure', seeming to confirm that 'even social deviants care! Maybe 'we're okay after all.' The verb 'yearn' is significant, because 'at last' these public (re)actions affirmed a newly fashionable belief that longing for the 'other' was permissible. What we saw was the emergent pleasure in accepting the existence of human needs. By showing up as a contributor to the 'floral revolution', people effectively demonstrated that the private pursuit of individual greed was not all there was to life.

How then can we locate the role of the death of Princess Diana within the ongoing New Labour project? A necessary part of establishing consent for this new hegemony[8] had entailed the hailing of 'us' into new Labour subjectivities. Instead of 'shareholder' we have had a shift to 'stakeholder' with its softer, non-market-oriented notions of regained 'community'. New Labour pre- and post-election discourse talked and continues to talk of 'social exclusion' and the need to substitute 'network riches' (Perri 6 1997) for 'network poverty'. Before the election, the discourse of community was put in the service of a claim for notions of 'society' and 'social responsibility' against which the 'sleaze' and 'fat cat' excesses of monopoly capitalism were viewed contemptuously as 'Other'. A critique of greed was central in New Labour's successful dislodging of the old moral economy. Diana's rededicated public life appeared to enact similar sentiments, her death consolidated this shift in popular consciousness.

The public responses to her death – namely its occupation of civic society – the Kensington Gardens flower ground (compared to the 'private' tributes in shops) and the funeral crowds themselves, embodied a different form of legitimacy for a new modern polity – one that, however flawed simultaneously broke with tradition (the demonstration of emotion in contrast to the stereotypical Anglo reserve), and yet these forces simultaneously harked back to times of imagined greater social solidarities. This was achieved by re-presenting a notion of mutual interdependency that derided the illusion of autonomy carried in the wilder excesses of neo-liberal ideologies (Johnson 1991). Bernstein is instructive in pointing out the provenance of this New Labour house style:

> We can consider Blair's New Labour entry into the official pedagogic arena as launching a new prospective identity. An identity drawing on resources of a different past. An amalgam of notions of community (really communities) and *local responsibilities to motivate and restore belonging in the cultural sphere*, and a new participatory responsibility in the economic sphere. Thus the underlying collective of New Labour appears to be a recontextualising of

the concept of the organic society, the retrospective identity would be projected by 'Old Labour'.

(Bernstein 1997: 168, emphasis added)

In the context of the New Labour project, it was not at all surprising that Tony Blair took charge in framing how we were to react to the death of Princess Diana. Blair's apparently 'personal' tribute to her captures the New Age political wisdom:

The people everywhere, not just here in Britain, but everywhere kept faith with Princess Diana. They liked her; they loved her; they regarded her as one of the people. She was the People's Princess.

(BBC 1 news coverage, 1 September 1997)

It is the 'kept faith' that is, as Rosalind Coward argues, 'just right' not only because it registers a gendered identification of 'a woman struggling to transcend her personal difficulties and make her life . . . useful', it also carries (at least for this interpreter) another layering of half-conscious projected meanings that capture another 'keeping faith' – a longed-for return of a different equally troubled and struggling heroic form (popular oppositional socialism?).

Yet it is hard to fathom quite what long-term gains flow from this unlikely 'unity'. Some commentators spoke of a republican surge that found expression in displays of popular resentment about the royal family's own (inept) public response. People were not impressed by the 'stiff upper lip' and 'business as usual'. Civic society demanded a dialogue – a formal or informal recognition that something had happened that needed to be taken account of. Tony Blair's interventions undoubtedly rescued the royals from their incompetence. We were then offered a more 'informal' Queen in her necessary pro-Diana broadcast, the lowering of the flag on Buckingham Palace against the great God protocol which as one pundit noted is the 'cousin of deference' and then the 'People's funeral'. As one Conservative columnist wrote, citing a vox pop, 'They used to tell us what to do. Now we tell them' (Ross Benson, *Daily Express*).[9] But was this shift of greater significance beyond the consolidation sought by New Labour? What of the potentialities for a more radical change of heart? What of the role of the academic left in reading the events and its aftermath?

Conclusions: a change of heart?

Princess Diana became a 'screen goddess' in the Thatcherite era in no small part because she solicited an identification with 'us' against 'them' – just as some of 'us' bought into our desires for her as solace – resources for optimism – as a buttress against the 'accumulated popular injuries' accrued under conditions of free-market individualism (Johnson 1991) and the disappointments of failures of alternative political projects of socialism or feminism. She had accommodated, amongst other fantasies, a belief that at least one powerful someone was actually personally concerned about 'her' people.

In her actions and their representation we/she redrew the border between herself and Prince Charles, the traditional monarchy as well as Mrs Thatcher's manic hyper-rationality. She and 'us' constructed an 'accomplice' counter-hegemony that built upon numerous symbolic and psychic resources: firstly a desire to redeem ourselves as social beings and in the process recognize the other as a fellow traveller. We conferred a pedagogic role on her through our longings. It was a role that traversed the personal, private, political and public. It was in some ways an exemplary modern identity in that it displayed the costs of seeking out equal relations with men in the late twentieth century, as well as the possibilities of reclaiming the self, when men refused the challenge. It was also a role showing what it might be like to stop aspects of the arms trade or refuse the fears and taboos associated with the stigmatized condition of AIDS or speak out about domestic violence. In part, this was a powerful intervention because Diana became (and at times sought to be) public copy. As Rosalind Coward perceptively noted, women's concern for Diana entailed moments of 'recognition' about 'how her life would turn out [which] was often a concern for themselves'. Her transformation from an initially gauche, then elegant 'exhibit' and latterly as engaged in a redemptive project of compassionate political activism or symbolism captivated the popular imaginary as a story of a symbolic survivor.

While she was clearly massively privileged, Diana had sought to reposition herself. She had shown herself capable of pulling herself out of the Sloane set, She had left school with no more certification than a prize for the 'best kept hamster'. She had taken the only career opportunity allowed the 'idle rich' and transmuted this by adopting herself to a world of political, controversial 'causes'. She had demonstrated a different style – a more open, informal 'democracy' of 'rapport' that managed, as Rosalind Coward argues, to *transcend a range of 'differences'*: hence her iconization. By the time of her death, she had reinvented herself. Compassion was to become her signature. These shifts in her own positioning were sustained by our co-investments in this alternative humanist project. Her 'people' became greedy consumers of 'transgressive' cultural messages that were worked back into civic society. Unwittingly or at least, unconsciously, Diana and 'us'[10] were co-conspirators. And the fact that she, or rather our projected fantasies of her,[11] became the political unconscious of all the radical right despised, namely the 'unsuccessful' – the poor, sick, lonely and outcast – is remarkable. It took Tony Blair's political acumen to recognize the depth of personal connection felt by 'the people' for 'their' princess and to give 'permission' for these private feelings to convert into potent spectacle – a paradoxical celebratory/mourning/grieving emblem of a 'more compassionate'[12] sharing, caring Britain. But what will be the longer-term effects of the Diana summer? What does the repositioning of the royal family imply? What will be the new gender, ethnic and class meanings constructed in the relegitimation of public or community selves? What are the prevailing emotional registers of New Britain? Is it true that the new 'confessional culture' indicates the feminization of Britain? My own analysis of aspects of New Labour's communitarianism suggests that it has as many *re*-traditionalizing themes as modernizing ones.[13]

Acknowledgements

I should like to thank Alison Kirton for her initial encouragement and her subsequent invaluable help in collecting relevant press coverage of reactions to the death of Princess Diana. I would also like to express my appreciation to the editors for their sensitive and insightful commentary on an early draft which enabled me to put my ideas into sharper focus. Any flaws that remain are mine.

Notes

1 The New Labour leader Tony Blair enunciated the mantra at the 1994 Labour Party Conference 'Our party – New Labour – Our mission – New Britain' (quoted in Jonathan Freedland, *Guardian*, 18 September 1997).
2 Some of these feelings and aspirations have found another home within the newly branded caring, sharing Conservatives.
3 I have found Cynthia Cockburn's initial exploration of the 'Macho Men of the Left' productive when I first read it ten years ago. It still points to important and as yet unresolved issues in the left's political project about creating an inclusive socialist politics and polity (Cynthia Cockburn, *Marxism Today*, April 1988: 18–23).
4 I have found Jane Kenway's work immensely productive in trying to think through the relations of class, consumption, gender and desire. See Kenway 1995, 1998.
5 Handbagging was what Mrs Thatcher was said to do to errant ministers who caused her displeasure. The expression captured (amongst other things) Mrs Thatcher's personal authoritarian no-nonsense power.
6 In terms of my own rethinking on subjectivity, identifications, identity and social class, I am struck by how often in Richard Hoggart's autobiography about his growing years as a working-class Northern boy and young man (Hoggart 1991) the themes of community and solidarity stand out as critically important unsentimental and necessary modes in conditions of poverty and deprivation. It is these (residualized?) memories of solidarity and community that I think lie in popular consciousness as traces capable of being reinscribed. They appear to me to be felt as charitable impulses wider than the defensive solidarities of a narrowly conceived industrially based class struggle.
7 The name of a popular Hollywood film about the solidarity between a group of women who have all been divorced as their husbands' first wives.

8 See Hey (forthcoming).

9 The point is not that the New Labour administration 'saved' the monarchy but it is of course significant that already prior to her death Tony Blair had apparently summoned Diana to discuss her future 'ambassadorial' role. Quite clearly New Labour is not republican though it has taken the opportunity to enact its 'modernization' project in terms of 'downsizing' the royal circle and other revisions to its prestige. Most importantly it seems that the Queen has had a 'wake up' call about the distinction between deference and democracy and now has to consider much more carefully the modes in which the 'people's consent' might have to be secured.

10 This 'us' is necessarily imprecisely specified.

11 According to David Cannadine (*Guardian*, 6 September 1997), she was 'a screen on which to project a multiple set of postmodern identities; part Eva Peron, part Mother Teresa, part Marilyn Monroe'. It is a neat irony that Elton John's lyric 'Candle in the Wind', taken up by people spontaneously and used as a mourning (performative) tribute to Diana, more than held its original meanings despite being overwritten by Bernie Taupin. See Christopher Hitchens' witty and irreverent piece in *The Nation* 'Four Poems and a Funeral' (29 September 1997) on other subliminal resonances.

12 Tony Blair on *Breakfast with Frost 1*, September 1997.

13 Hey forthcoming; Hey 1998.

References

Aitkenhead, Decca (1997) *Guardian*, 5 September.

Anderson, Benedict (1991) *Imagined Communities: Reflections on the Origin and Spread of Nationalism*, 2nd edition, revised and extended, London and New York: Verso.

Arnot, Madeline (1992) 'Feminism, Education and the New Right', in M. Arnot and L. Barton (eds) *Voicing Concerns: Sociological Perspectives on Contemporary Education Reforms*, Wallingford: Triangle.

Bernstein, Basil (1997) 'Official Knowledge and Pedagogic Identities: The Politics of Recontextualisation', in I. Nilsson *et al.* (eds) *Teachers, Curriculum and Policy: Critical Perspectives in Educational Research*, Umea, Sweden: Department of Education, Umea University.

Blair, Tony (1997) *Breakfast with Frost*, BBC, 1 September.

Burchill, Julie (1997) 'The People's Destroyer', *Guardian*, 2 September.

Cannadine, David (1997) *Guardian*, 6 September.

Cockburn, Cynthia (1988) 'Macho Men of the Left', *Marxism Today*, 18–23 April.

Coward, Rosalind (1984) *Female Desire*, London: Paladin.

Coward, Rosalind (1997) *Guardian*, 2 September.

Demos Collection (1997) Issue 12: 'The Wealth and Poverty of Networks: Tackling Social Exclusion', London: Demos.

Engel, Matthew (1997) *Guardian*, September.

Epstein, Debbie, Elwood, Jannette, Hey, Valerie and Maw, Janet (eds) (1998) 'Introduction', in *Failing Boys? Issues in Gender and Achievement*, Buckingham: Open University Press.

Epstein, Debbie and Kenway, Jane (1996) 'Feminist Perspectives on the Marketisation of Education', *Discourse*, Special Issue, vol. 17, no. 3 (December).

Epstein, Debbie and Steinberg, Deborah Lynn (1996) 'No Fixed Abode?: Feminism in the 1990's', *Parallax*, vol. 3: 1–6.

Freedland, Jonathan (1997) *Guardian* 18 September.

Gilroy, Paul (1987) *There Ain't No Black in the Union Jack: The Cultural Politics of Race and Nation*, London: Routledge.

Hall, Stuart (1988) 'The Toad in the Garden: Thatcherism among the Theorists', in C. Nelson and L. Grossberg (eds) *Marxism and the Interpretation of Culture*, London: Macmillan.

Hey, Valerie (1996) 'A Game of Two Halves: A Critique of Some Complicities Between Hegemonic and Counter Hegemonic Discourses Concerning Marketisation and Education' *Discourse*, Special Issue, vol. 17, no. 3: 351–62.

Hey, Valerie (1998) 'The Demos Girls: New Labour, New Feminine Subjectivities? Some Questions of Gender, Generation and Education', paper presented at the CCS Conference 'Education in Late Modernity: Beyond Narrowing Agendas', 10–12 June, Institute of Education, London.

Hey, Valerie (forthcoming) 'Reading the Community: A Critique of Some Post/modern Narratives about Citizenship and Civil Society', in P. Bagguley and J. Hearn (eds) *Transforming Politics: Power and Resistance*, London: Macmillan.

Hitchens, Christopher (1997a) 'Throne and Altar', *The Nation*, 29 September: 7.

Hitchens, Christopher (1997b) 'Four Poems and a Funeral', *The Nation*, 29 September: 9.

Hoggart, Richard (1991) *A Local Habitation: Life and Times Vol. 1 1918–40*, London: Chatto and Windus.

Johnson, Richard (1991) 'My New Right Education', in R. Johnson (ed.) *Education Limited: Schooling, Training and the New Right Since 1979*, London: Unwin Hyman.

Kenway, Jane (1995) 'The Marketisation of Education: Mapping the Contours of a Feminist Perspective', paper presented at the ECER Conference, Bath, UK, September.

Kenway, Jane (1998) 'Local/Global Labour Markets and the Restructuring of Gender, Schooling and Work', paper presented at the American Association for Research in Education conference, San Diego, April, International Symposium on Gender, Education and Globalization.

Kenway, Jane and Epstein, Debbie (1996) 'Introduction: The Marketisation of School Education, Feminist Studies and Perspectives', *Discourse*, Special Issue, vol. 17, no. 3: 301–14.

Kirby, Mark (1998) 'Behind the News 4: Death of a Princess', *Capital and Class*, no. 64: 30–41.

Lloyd, John (1997) 'Life Without Diana', *New Statesman*, 3 October: 26–7.

Mulgan, Geoff (1997) *Connexity: How to Live in a Connected World*, London: Chatto and Windus.

Neave, Guy (1988) 'On the Cultivation of Quality, Efficiency and Enterprise: An Overview of Recent Trends in Higher Education in Western Europe 1968–1988', *European Journal of Education*, vol. 23 (1/2): 7–23.

Perri, 6 (1997) 'Social Exclusion: Time to be Optimistic', Introduction to Demos Collection, Issue 12: 'The Wealth and Poverty of Networks: Tackling Social Exclusion', London: Demos.

Pollitt, Katha (1997) 'Thoroughly Modern Di', *The Nation*, 29 September: 9.

Smith, Joan (1997) 'You, Me, Her, Us' *Guardian* 2 September: 6.

Vidal, John (1997) *The Guardian*, 6 September.

Walkerdine, Valerie (1990) *Schoolgirl Fictions*, London: Verso.

Walkerdine, Valerie (1997) *Daddy's Girl: Young Girls and Popular Culture*, London: Macmillan.

5

RHETORIC, NATION, AND
THE PEOPLE'S PROPERTY

Joe Kelleher

Ambivalent mediators

In this chapter I intend to consider the 'Diana events' in relation to a nexus of theoretical issues that are to be gathered here under the rubric of 'rhetoric'. Or, it might be fairer to state, I intend to 'cite' the Diana events, already subsuming the empirical–historical into the realm of the rhetorical, as an exemplary occasion of rhetoric's reappearance in late twentieth-century public life as a particular ground for considering both the ethics and the ambivalence of political communion. That phrase 'Diana events' will be used throughout as a shorthand to suggest how an occasion, along with a collection of incidents, performances and discursive practices may themselves be gathered up in a discursive network through which the *meaning* and *import* of events is *contested* in the manner of a competition over rights and privileges: in short, rights of property, and the privileges of the upper hand.

'Rhetoric' (the word and the practices it refers to will be further elaborated below), in this context, is to serve – so to speak – as a two-handed technology. On the one hand it comprehends how empirical events may be constituted and exchanged among participants (performers, witnesses), through and *as* discursive practices. On the other, it serves as a mode of metacritical practice, a methodology of analysing and bringing to light interests, power-plays, and ideological sleights of hand that may function as the 'ends' of rhetorical 'means'. As such, in serving to bring together the parties to an agreement, while at the same time functioning as the analytic light by which disputed and contradictory interests may be brought to view, rhetoric engages in both a binding and a rupturing. Rhetoric, that is to say, is an ambivalent mediator. This is an ambivalence, I would suggest, that we would always feel ourselves to be familiar with – whatever our unfamiliarity with a more 'academic,' or 'historical' understanding of the codifications of the *ars oratoria*, the art of persuasive speaking, since the classical eras. Rhetoric was a discursive technology, certainly, that would function to mediate between the specifically situated parties to a dispute. It was the means by which an orator at a public tribunal – a representative speaker in the arena *of* the 'public' would seek to bind an audience of listeners, to persuade them to the rights and wrongs of a claim, or a point of view, or a course of action. Surely, though, we must also think of rhetoric as a mediator that marks and at the same time binds the apparent ruptures between metadiscourses, such as the historical and the contemporary, the academic and the everyday, the theoretical and the empirical, the other and the us. That ambivalent rupture appears particularly when the 'rhetorical' is identified in the terms of the pejorative – an identification that dismisses the discourse of the other 'as' rhetoric but thereby seeks to bind present listeners to a (rhetoricalized) conviction at the site of the here and now.

The occasion for such processes to operate at large tends to be a moment of political transition, crisis or uncertainty. Such occasions and processes are exposed with as much analytic clarity as we could wish for in Shakespeare's *Julius Caesar*, where the 'plain blunt man' Mark Antony (or so he presents himself: 'here I am to speak what I do know') incites the populace to war on the occasion of a funeral oration, setting his own speech in opposition to the more apparently practised rhetoric of his opponent Brutus. Antony appears to offer the people a claim to their proper inheritance through a discursive exchange over a desecrated corpse that only the people, through violent action (in this case) in the corpse's name, can return to proper sanctity (III.ii.74–273). The result, of course, is civil war – a rupturing of the commonalty – the first incident of which is the arbitrary murder of a man for the mere crime of sharing a name with one of the conspirators. It is Mark Antony's speech, not Brutus's, that fully achieves the three functions (incitement to action, forensic demonstration and *epideictic* – effective, appropriate – oratorical display) codified in classical rhetoric.

However, we do not need to look only to literature for our examples. As I have been writing this chapter the world media have been relaying the competing rhetorics that have constituted the public-relations offensive over the American–British bombing of Iraq during the so-called Operation Desert Fox. In a televised press conference immediately after the cessation of the bombings, the Iraqi deputy prime minister Tariq Aziz responded to the reported statement of the British prime minister Tony Blair that the raids had put Saddam Hussein 'back in his cage' with the claim that 'This is the old rhetoric of a liar'. The rhetoric of the anti-rhetorical bluff, at the same time, was backed up with an index of the empricism of the corpse, renewing again the ambivalent rupturing alliance between rhetoric and empiricism, as Aziz gave his government's official count of the numbers of Iraqi military dead: '62 martyrs'. The numbers of civilian dead, at present, remain unquantified.

The Diana events, considered in these contexts, may seem hardly to compete at the level of critical significance. However, it is my contention that there is critical mileage in considering these events as – let us say – a paradigm instance (although of course with their own historic and cultural specificity), an exemplary occasion within the frame of modern rhetorical–cultural operations at large. The very extent to which the events were rhetorically constituted; the extent also of their occupation of our contemporary rhetorical technology of the mass media; not least the ways in which those media – for all their techno-modernity – seem to offer occasions for almost Aristotelian exercises in oratorical–political address: all these qualify the Diana events as a *rhetorical* event *par exellence*. So, for instance, for many people in Britain their first encounter with the news was through replays of Tony Blair's performance to camera on the Sunday morning after the car crash in Paris. Blair's speech was the statesman's threnody, fully appropriate both in its occasion and in its performance. There was more to the speech, however, than the dignified respect paid to the passing of a public figure. This was a recently elected Labour prime minister, whose party had at last (overwhelmingly) overcome nearly two decades of Conservative Party government – a period of right-wing political hegemony that had seemed at times interminable, as if electoral democracy were only a rhetorical screen for an unimpeachable supra-democratic political agenda governed exclusively by the interests of international capitalism. The Labour Party's overcoming of their (and our) opponents was, however – perhaps inevitably – wrapped up in the rhetoric of a 'new' governance that was to return the political agenda somehow to 'us', to the interests of the 'people', and in such a way that our interests would be recuperated over and against the divisive ideologies of *self*-interest that had characterized the time of the previous administration. Certainly the election victory was celebrated in such terms. Now, barely four months after that victory, the new prime minister was, it appeared, coming into his inheritance and ours, speaking on this Sunday morning on behalf of the people, speaking of 'the People's Princess', performing a rhetorical gesture of popular gathering over the symbolic capital of a significant dead body.

I am not necessarily identifying (or performing) a cynicism here, but only for the moment marking out what appeared – even then – the first move in a series of rhetorical appropriations of Diana's death and person that, as the series escalated, became more manifest in their rhetoricality. So, subsequently, the people too got in on the act, and no longer were performances played out exclusively within the frame of mass media technology. The laying of flowers against the royal residences, the vigils and occupation of public spaces (particularly in London), the demand filtered through the broadcast media for Elton John and Bernie Taupin to renew their working relationship: these were the gestures of a relatively unmediated popular rhetoric (or the rhetoric of a popular demand) that was for a moment fully tuned in to the specific demands of place and occasion. Might this even be something approaching popular activism? We had, after all, experienced the events of 1989 in eastern Europe as part of the Christmas television schedules, so we were familiar with the genre. More recently in Britain, during the winter of 1994–5, we had even gone into the streets ourselves (or at least the A-roads of Kent) to prevent the transport of baby cows to France (see Bhattacharyya 1998: 283–5). We were developing a taste for such behaviour, and maybe we did not require governments or media to do our talking for us. More accurately, however, during September 1997 there was something of a guarded *ambivalent* alliance in Britain between the media and the people: the people, on the one hand, threatening to hold the news media to ransom for what was perceived in many quarters as their hounding of Diana – even to her death – while at the same time feeding on the stories and the 'tribute' photo-spreads, licensing the media to operate as *rhetors* on our behalf, to name, appropriate and internalize us *as* 'the people', as long as all our interests appeared to be in common.

As for the mass media themselves, they seemed at times to be running to catch up, mediating their rhetorics to the *moment* of the popular mood, the mood of a demand. I was struck, watching the funeral on television, by one instance where the voice-over commentator – all deep-toned deferential solemnity and soft-polished phrases – was suddenly and unceremoniously replaced (it seemed) by written subtitles. I did not even have to reach for the volume control. It was like a blip-second fantasy made real of truly inter-active television. Nor was the ceremonial programme immune, as the funeral oration by the Princess's brother – who seemed to be putting in his own bid for what in future would be right and proper, articulating the hint of an agenda of constitutional change – was succeeded by acknowl-edgment from a crowd who were claiming the perogative, even if they were not in the Abbey where the oration was given, of being the proper (properly mediated) inheritors of the import of Earl Spencer's address.

However, as the rhetoricality escalated so too, I would argue, did the ambivalence of its affect. Rhetoric seems to operate according to the logic of a rechargeable half-life, ever insidious, but a half-life nevertheless. As the people's rhetoric repeats its claim to speak in the people's proper name, one begins to ask – as one, among others, *of* the people – what (and whom) is really being mediated here? That is to say, as one identifies the rhetoric 'of the people', identifies it *as* 'rhetoric', one may experience not so much the privilege of an inheritance so much as the distance of a disenfranchisement. As some of the graffiti daubed on the London Cenotaph during the recent bombings of Iraq put it, 'Not in my name.' But to speak, then, of and to rhetorical events (and the raids, for those of us who did not experience actual bombs falling on our homes, were given as *rhetorical* events, as means towards a discursive persuasion) is to be entangled in a subjection to a real ambivalence. As with that anti-war graffito, one's refusal of a certain rhetorical dispensation may be framed in terms of the particular variant of a syllogism, the *enthymeme*, that Aristotle throughout his treatise on the oratorical arts identified as the foremost trope of rhetorical persuasion. This figure was the appeal to probability whereby one or more premises of the syllogism are left unexpressed as their truth is given to be self-evident. That is to say, one argues from within the space of one's own subjection, taking that as the 'given,' staking one's right to make a refusal on the very basis of the rhetorical incorporation that is the object of the refusal itself. It is I, as one of you, who insists upon my right not to identify myself as one of the 'us'. And what is more, there are many others I am sure of my kind. In such a space the critical analysis of rhetorical manoeuvres becomes tricky. It is tricky, for instance, to turn from rhetoric to empiricism if the ground – the motive – for such a turn is the fact of one's already being a fully paid up member of the rhetoricalized contest. So, one continued to watch the events unfold on television with as much fascination as displeasure, storing up instances to be employed someday maybe in an academic critique and did this rather than turning off and forgetting about the whole business. Because that will not do either. I am implicated here. If I seek some way out of this impasse, or more likely some way of considering it better (or more usefully) I should turn not away from rhetoric but in the direction of an understanding of rhetoric's larger scene. This may not amount to a history of rhetoric, but it may begin with some thoughts about rhetoric *as* history.

Rhetoric the revenant

Audits of the two thousand year or so decline of what Roland Barthes called 'the old rhetoric' (Barthes 1988), the classical orator's art of expressive and impressive (persuasive) speech, have guarded against recognizing that decline as a death. A brief sketch of rhetoric's fall into 'intellectual discredit' (Barthes 1988: 43), its history as 'an ironic tale of diminishing returns', might run along the lines of an account of the epistemic decolonization of what Ricoeur refers to as 'the vast empire of rhetoric' (Ricoeur 1978: 9, 10). Philosophy in this story seeks self-determination, and independence from disciplinary restrictions of the art of persuasion to theories of style and classifications of parts of speech. The chapters of this account could begin with Socrates' arguments with the Sophists, they might work through the sometime parodic re-appearance of rhetoric as a desiccated scholasticism in the later Middle Ages and the Renaissance, and would have to take in Enlightenment and Romantic denunciations of oratorical manipulation in the name of unrelativized free inquiry and the apparent self-sufficiency of evidence – the evidence, as Barthes narrates it, of the personal, the rational, and the sensory.[1] Or, as we might recognize such things today – a princess's (and her people's) deployment of the language of feeling; the bill-toting politician's appeal to 'reasonable' common opinion; and the function of an image in persuading us to buy a commodity, an idea or an allegiance, as if purchase were inheritance all along. (One might think of the oratorical demagogue in Shakespeare's play showing at last the 'poor dumb mouths' of 'sweet Caesar's wounds' and letting them speak for him, but as suggested already there are enough more contemporary examples, and with mechanical and electronic reproduction more pervasive ones too.)[2] As we find ourselves implicated in these evidences we may feel bound to recognize that rhetoric, to borrow some recent theoretical parlance, is a *revenant*: a ghost that returns.[3] One might go so far as to suggest that it returns *as* 'theory'. That is not to offer a reduction of the diversity and critical value of theories to an all-inclusive rhetoricality, although a neo-Nietzschean account of the rootlessness of modern being, or a Foucauldian focus on power–knowledge constructions of history as 'discourse' could take us some distance down this path.[4] Rather, the suggestion is offered simply to observe how courses specifically devoted to critical and literary theory in higher education programmes, and the function of the theorists' passages and proper names as *loci classici* in much of the academic writing that claims good grades and professional advancement, bears a resemblance to the educational function and 'place' of rhetoric in the early humanist *trivium*.[5] Of course, though, rhetoric – or 'rhetoricality' – to the extent that it might function as *the* ambivalent figuration of our transdisciplinary, heterogeneous modernity, does not only appear as critical theory. It operates now in our understandings of philosophy, social science, the paradigm shifts of scientific 'progress', aesthetic history, mass media technologies and popular culture, and the 'dense tangle of our triviality' in the '*pragmata* of everydayness'. '*Modernism is an age not of rhetoric, but of rhetoricality*, the age, that is, of a generalized rhetoric that penetrates to the deepest levels of human experience' (Bender and Wellbery 1990: 34, 25)[6] Whatever our competences and literacies with regard to the specific oratorical arts of 'rhetoric' as such, an occasion such as the Diana events makes apparent the extent to which a generalized rhetoricality pervades the constitution of public life, as well as informing the critical purchase we might make upon that constitution.

Whether we theorize or not, and whether we do or do not believe ourselves to be believers in ghosts, rhetorics of one sort or another may continue to spook us, by challenging our convictions with regard to what we are, what we know, and what would or would not be good for us to do. We may consider that our political life is not really any more governed by the persuasiveness of what is said or not said in our public forums; we may consider many of our contemporary representatives to be not up to the job even if that were so; we may anyway refuse to defer to the presumptuousness of one who would speak on our behalf, or who would aim to sway our convictions with fine words; and we may say *we* use writings these days, not speeches. We may believe – like some late modern echo of Plato's and

Socrates' challenges to the Sophists, and in spite of what we have absorbed either deliberately or otherwise of postmodern scepticism with regard to the eternal verities of truth, love and beauty – that there are unbridgeable distances between the realities of our lived experiences and any definitive purchase that 'mere rhetoric' (to revive the cliché) might make on those realities. We may even – most obviously perhaps, especially if we know just a little about it – insist that the *ars oratoria* as such, with its formalized structural divisions into *inventio* (coming up with something to say), *dispositio* (arrangement of what is arrived at), *elocutio* (style and ornament), *memoria* (committing to memory), and *actio* (gestures and diction, the actorly performance), its overnice specification of the juridical, deliberative, and epideictic functions, or its arcane deployment of tropes and *topoi* and suchlike, is itself an arcane and irrelevant specialist interest, not part of our cultural map, neither proper nor pertinent.[7]

With regard to those structural divisions of rhetoric's parts, let alone the philosophical or 'everyday' objections to the rhetorical *techne*, there was a whittling down at work from the earliest days. 'The last two (*Actio* and *Memoria*) were rapidly sacrificed, as soon as rhetoric no longer concerned the spoken (declaimed) discourses of lawyers or statesmen, or of "lecturers" (epideictic genre), but also, and then almost exclusively, (written) "works"' (Barthes 1988: 51). This exclusion was at work already in Aristotle's text. However, there may be more at stake here than the history of a merely *disciplinary* division between what George Kennedy has characterized as the differences between 'Primary' (primarily an oral act of persuasive enunciation relating to the specificity of an occasion) and 'Secondary' rhetorics (in the latter 'the speech act is not of central importance; that role is taken over by the text', and its aim may be to gain credit in the eyes of an audience for an 'author') (1980: 4–5). What may be at stake, rather, is an issue of ethics, which for StephenTyler is *the* issue in the apparent decline, through 'the separation of reason and passion' and the driving of discourse 'from the world of deeds into the world of words', of rhetorical discourse's 'original ethical system' (1978: 167). The ethical issues in the separation of reason and passion are made pertinent by Eagleton when he suggests that one might be persuaded of an argument without feeling called upon to act, that a Marxist even may also have to be something of a Platonist, which is to say that passion and reason, 'rhetoric and dialectic, agitation and propaganda', would have to come together in a concern for 'justice, a moral concept itself only calculable on the basis of social knowledge, as opposed to *doxa* or ideological opinion' (1981: 112–13). We are in the realm here not of a rejection of rhetoric but a sublation of its moralizing discourses into morality proper. The Diana events, we may remember, were pervaded by moralizing discourses, discourses directed against the behaviour of *others*, from outraged condemnations of the paparazzi, through to implications levelled against the Windsors' treatment of the errant princess.

The Platonic position is given in the *Phaedrus*, which has confused some readers who would take it as a disjointed dialogue on love and *also* rhetoric. We might offer instead the suggestion along with Barthes who writes of the Platonic psychagogy as an 'eroticized rhetoric', or Ernesto Grassi who insists on 'the "moving" function' of Plato's true rhetoric, the leading of souls through the connection of knowledge with *eros* and thereby *pathos* (1980: 32, 25) that the rhetoric offered by Plato in the *Phaedrus* to save our souls would have to be 'a dialogue of love' (Barthes 1988: 19).

I would argue that the silencing of *actio* and *memoria* in the rhetorical schema is contributory to the ways in which we might forget the gestic appearance of rhetoric's ethical potential. It seems interesting (although maybe it also seems obvious) that recent work in theatre and performance studies that has addressed itself to ethical social and cultural relations (in intra- and intercultural contexts) has focused its analyses – sometimes to the exclusion of textual (written) objects – on the rhetorical arts of gesture and memory.[8] Theatre aside (and ethics aside also perhaps), *actio* and *memoria* have become indispensable determinants of the rhetorical performances – borrowing, even if at a remove, the Aristotelian definition of rhetoric as the 'ability, in each case, to see the available means of persuasion . . . to be able to observe the persuasive about "the given," so to speak' (Aristotle 1991a: 36–7)[9] – offered in the arenas of the contemporary mass media. In this light we might consider, with a view to our focus here on the Diana events, the responses that follow on a mediatized (and ever after 'live') oratory, such as the British Prime Minister Tony Blair's accomplished performance to camera on the morning of the Princess's death mentioned above. There *actio* (or the to-be-perceived absence of it) and *memoria* (ditto) – through the potential eliding in the convictions of witnesses of 'from the heart' with that which may or may not have been committed 'to heart' – becomes a vital technology in the rhetorical domain of a tele*visual* scrutiny.[10] At stake in such performances (*if*, that is, we are justified in reading them as aiming at a persuasion of others' convictions – the true politician would presumably deny such opportunism) is the achievement of a negative rhetoric (like the techniques of post-Stanislavskian realist acting) that aims to convince with a reality effect, over and against a public's refusal to purchase a too explicit mimesis. This may be as much as to say, along with Eagleton, the refusal to purchase an ideology, a refusal to be included in the ideological designs a performance might have on us, even as it draws us along, infecting our memory, determining the significance of our acts and gestures – subjecting us, even in spite of ourselves, to the very rhetorics by which we constitute ourselves as loyal (or not so loyal) 'subjects'.[11]

As I wish to argue here, with particular focus on rhetorical performances in Britain attendant upon the death and commemoration of the Princess of Wales, rhetoricality haunts us, and it does so right at the spot where we would articulate that first person plural, that 'we', that 'us', in the name of which we would have done with rhetorical pretensions. Our rhetoric (our true rhetoric) after all, if there were to be such a thing, is not *that* rhetoric, not *those* orations and ceremonies and gestures; not that funereal music, thank you; not that voice-over, please; not that way of judgmentally observing, appropriating, – or even addressing – a dead person. Especially not a dead person that we claim as our own, in thousands upon thousands of bouqueted petitionary devotions, laid up very impressively against the royal properties like a piece of mass installation art, a slap-in-the-face outdoing (or belated acknowledgement) of all those conceptual artists who pursued the avant-garde's rhetorical sublation of art and life while leaving us the people, and what we can access (and it is us after all who live the life), supposedly out of the equation. (See Bürger 1984.)

Further if it is, as it was for Socrates, at the death that we will be judged, when the orator's arts alone will serve as no sort of a defence (Plato, *Gorgias*, 527a), there is, among other things, a *last* judgement at stake, where 'the truth will out' but according to a logic of an historical problematic. The rhetoric of others is old already, old, unjust, and misleading. Our proper rhetoric, on the other hand, and its disclosure of truth, is something to come. And there are, as there always were and will be, rhetorics to come. We might, while still mindful of the particular 'restricted rhetoric'[12] of the classical orator, recall Socrates' argument in the *Phaedrus* as an anticipation of a rhetoric to come, a rhetoric that would lead other souls (i.e. a psychagogy) through a combination of dialectic skill, analytic care for the nature and passions of addressees, and a primary philosophical concern that 'would be moved chiefly by love of the beautiful' (Nichols 1998: 21; *Phaedrus*, 273d–e). As for *existing* rhetoric, this is attacked by Socrates (particularly in the *Gorgias*, where the focus is mainly on the political governance of public and private life) to the extent that it divides pleasure from justice, pursuing immoderate desires through pandering flattery. The 'true rhetoric, or a true political art, that would strive to make citizens more just and better', remains for Socrates a 'possibility' (Nichols 1998: 20), a consummation devoutly to be wished perhaps, but maybe more imminent (impending as a temporal event) than immanent (inherent in the present state of affairs).[13]

All of this may point us in the direction of a suggestion that, while rhetorics of one sort or another may abound, not only mouldering away somewhere in outmoded conventions, or niggling in the seminar rooms and overlooked pages of academia, but re-appearing to irritate us otherwise in the shiny new rhetorical technologies of the mass media (who *know* what is 'in the public interest') and the brand-hawking of 'new' party politics, a displeasure or mistrust of those that do so may itself be an expression of a rhetorical desire, a desire *of* rhetoric, the rhetoric of the other. Our framing then, even in spite of ourselves, of Rhetoric as the big Other wherein our desires, particularly our political desires, are articulated somehow otherwise to how we would or should hear them, may find echo in the peculiarly ambivalent identifications, during the Diana events, of a 'democratic' (and sovereign) people with the peculiarly symbolic (or 'royal') operations of governance, power and privilege: the nexus of the people, the powers that be, and the dead Princess, each of which appears to engage in a mutual metaphorization. The people, after all, in spite of what we effected with our voice at the recent general election, may suspect again we are not as sovereign as we feel we have a right to be. The Princess too, we remember, had her royalty only for a term, a term bounded by marriage and divorce. As for the powers that be, whoever they be they are not, surely, not really, the family Windsor, but at least we know where *they* live, and they do hang a flag outside to show that they are at home. So, although there may have been a more prevalent awareness at large than was allowed in the British news media at the time that none of this actually *mattered* that much, still much public space and time was given to negotiations over whether, for instance, Buckingham Palace should or should not, would or would not, fly the Union Flag at half-mast for the People's Princess.

Identification in this instance is made at the site of a death, and a royal death at that. One might, then, elaborate on the proliferation of 'royalty' tropes in arguments over the death and revenance of rhetoric, as in Genette's critique of the 'centrocentism' of the generalized restriction of rhetoric in theories of figural discourse that tend to set up 'at the very heart of rhetoric or what is left of it – not the polar opposition of metaphor and metonymy, which still left room for a little air to circulate and to blow here and there a few "débris d'un grand jeu," but metaphor alone, frozen in its useless royalty' (Genette 1982: 114–15). At least, we would remember that rhetorical speech 'marks, and is marked by, social hierarchy. Rhetorical speech adheres to power and property' (Bender and Wellbery 1990: 7). As Eagleton puts it, even as classical rhetoric served as a sort of politicized literary criticism, its 'intention' being 'systematically to theorise the articulations of discourse and power, and to do so in the name of political practice: to enrich the political effectivity of signification', it was at the same time a textual training of the ruling class in techniques of political hegemony (1981: 101).

At the death, we hope, rhetoric will have its true face on, although like Socrates we may not put too much faith in others' ability to recognize it. It may still be – as with King Hamlet's ghost with his visor down – hard to effect or incorporate a definitive identification, and hard to know or say how to make the shift from rhetoric to just acts, what with the times being out of joint, and the battlements recently – and at this late hour of the day – echoing to reports of indulgences in the court (a court sustained by a tenuous legitimacy at that), reports that might be better honoured in the breach than in the observance. As the Prince himself elaborates, this sort of thing might give us a bad name amongst the other nations. And as has already been cautiously observed by sources close to the business, all this bodes some eruption to the state. It may provoke conspiracy theories. Or, at the very least (or the very most) a ripple of improper applause interrupting the ceremonies at Westminster Abbey – in response, thoughbeit, to the oratory of an hereditary aristocrat. All of which, of course, is not to suggest that power is 'merely' symbolic; but rather to worry at the justice of some of the symbolizations on offer: to wonder, for instance, what is 'the people' claimed – and claiming – in the circulation of a phrase, 'the People's Princess'. How did we get to be *there*? Who let *us* in? And what did we think we were on?

Rhetoric, witness and testimony

Rhetorical demonstration, etymologically speaking – especially if we hold on to the significance of *actio* and *memoria* – is a bringing to sight, 'a "showing" . . . and thus in the original sense "theoretical" (*theorein* – i.e., to see)' (Grassi 1980: 20).[14] Attendant upon any persuasive showing is the act of witness of those who would be persuaded, and the establishment thereby of what I wish to characterize here as a *constituency* of conviction – which, as I shall attempt to show, may be just as much to say a fractured constituency determined after all by ambivalence. The Diana events were characterized by calls for a showing and a seeing. The powers that be, for instance, should show a proper response, and that response had better be cognizant of the constituencies on whose behalf it was articulated, never mind conventions of etiquette. So the Conservative Party leader William Hague, recently instituted in that job since the electoral defeat of John Major, was criticized for speaking on the Sunday morning on behalf of his local parliamentary constituents, not at all what was called for, rather than (as Blair did) on behalf of all the people. Just so, although the niceties of custom might preclude the gesture, it was demanded (as mentioned above) that the official royal residence in London should fly the Union Flag at half-mast in acknowledgement of one who was – as far as the people were concerned – to all intents and purposes (divorce notwithstanding) still a princess. The organs of these demands – who would also of course, in the public interest, serve as the media of record and witness – were the newspapers, although mediated witness would be supplemented by any means possible. With regard to this last, friends of mine who joined the crowds in central London reported that the universal gesture, as the cortège passed, was the lifting overheard of pocket cameras optimistically pointed in the direction of an event that was otherwise, for most people, invisible. Rhetoric, in this light, might be that which serves as a persuasive technology mediating between the co-ordinates of *testimony* (authentic and proper performance) and *witness*, articulating that which is offered in return to the people's demand for authority to show a certain face, and thereby – through one or another mode of dissemination – mapping the imaginary site of a peopled space, an 'imagined community', a constituency of concerns and interests.[15]

However, if this were so, then it must also be allowed that all rhetorical technologies of showing and witness at this time – particularly (with the initial blaming of news photographers as the cause of the fatal crash) the technologies and rhetorics of the mass media – were crossed over with ambivalence.[16] It is an ambivalence, caught between insistent demand and endemic mistrust of the pursuit of political self-interest, that characterizes certain rhetorical performances in late twentieth-century public life. These range from the ridiculous to the critical, from the public scrutiny of intention-to-truth-telling in a US president's videoed (and then rebroadcast) testimony to a grand jury over the exchange of lovers' gifts and sophistic definitions of sexual intercourse,[17] through the rash of apologies on offer (or not) these days by representative figures for one or another historical abuse of peoples, to the institution of a truth commission in South Africa, or a post-Agreement public inquiry in Northern Ireland into the policies and actions of the Royal Ulster Constabulary. In occasions such as these, the return of rhetoricality – although of course now it would not suffice for us to give credence merely on the basis of oratorical accomplishment – recovers some of its genealogical origin from fifth-century BC Sicily where, after the overthrow of tyrants, the art was instituted as a means to recuperate property rights, through public inquiry, at a moment of significant political transition.

As has been argued by Samuel Ijsseling, among others, rhetoric 'nearly always has something to do with property, with acquired or supposed rights, and with prestige and privileges' (Ijsseling 1976: 11). As such, one face of the rhetorical ambivalence is that it may articulate a subversive challenge to the status quo while at the same time attempting to effect a conservative recuperation of an ante quo. This seems to be echoed in the ambivalence around the Diana events between simultaneous deference towards and transgressive challenge to the prestige and privileges of royal authority. Perhaps the property at stake there was the Princess herself, through the demand that somehow the 'Queen of Hearts' might be ceremonially returned, by a royal family who had seemingly had done with her anyway, to the hearts of the people who had become (and were all along) the rightful possessors and possessees of her person. This in itself would then be a persuaded response to a particular rhetorical performance (disseminated again by the mass media), Diana's prospective crowning herself as constitutional monarch of the people's emotions in the interview she gave to the *Panorama* television programme. Contestations of property and privilege, thereby, are dispersed – with a significant touch of theatrical semiotics (not least Diana's impressive somatic performance in that interview, but I am also now thinking again of the theatricalized function of various *places* over the course of the events, the site of the crash, the gates and railings of the royal residences, the Abbey and the funeral route, the wooded isle of the princess's interment on the Spencer family property, for which nevertheless tickets would soon be available) into the symbolics of performative language. Here, to the extent that 'possession only exists by virtue of the word' (Ijsseling 1976: 11), the *discursive* ambivalence of rhetoric makes its appearance, which is perhaps how we best recognize it. The return of rhetoric, that is to say, activates ambivalence through instituting property disputes *as* discursiveness. And, in so doing, it opens up the fractures within which community, the constituency of the 'us', is somehow experienced as disenfranchisement.

It seems fair to suggest – and certainly as much has been said in commentaries since the event – that the seemingly universal valorization of languages of 'feeling' at that time gave rise, at the same time, to feelings here and there of profound disquiet. It was as if, in the discursive appeal to passion and the demand for passion to be brought to light and shown – and be seen to be shown – here now and in England, through identification with a certain figure of celebrity, that some 'other' constituency was being constituted, over one's head as it were. Who *are* these coming to the sacrifice? we might have been inclined to demand of ourselves in a sort of Keatsian awe, to the extent that any one of us – watching the events unroll from home through the television where there was only one show to be seen, or taking another sort of tube ride over to gaze upon Kensington Palace and all her flanks with garlands drest – might have felt themself at the same time fascinated with the scene but somehow disenfranchised by it, somehow missing the plot. The silence (or screening out) then of dissenting voices had something of the mythological about it, as if Actaeon might be punished again for stumbling upon the scene of the celebration of Diana's mysteries, a mystery that amounts to an enigma, the enigma of truth and beauty some might have had us believe, but more like 'the renewed enigma of rhetoric': 'the affective social tie – that is, the whole domain of suggestion, mimetico-affective contagion, the magical power of words, and so on', reposing perhaps 'on the equally hypnotic tie with the *Führer*–Ego–Ideal', but after all

> hid[ing] nothing, dissimulat[ing] nothing or only the nothing, the absence of any ground, of every *subjectum* and every subject. It is the irrevealable enigma of a *mimesis* that is all the more effective and 'technical' because it has nothing of its own, and because it creates from nothing.
>
> (Borch-Jacobsen 1992: 73)

How is one to speak to such an enigma? For Mikkel Borch-Jacobsen 'there is absolutely nothing to say about it unless it be to repeat, following Freud and so many others, that this enigma is not that of truth'. However, this 'does not render it any less powerful, as those who have tried to silence rhetoric have always recognized'.

Among those latter are philosophers of the European Enlightenment, who expressed disquiet with the rhetorical affect, particularly with regard to its interventions into the social–political praxes of science, education, religion, law and civic dispute. In the work of John Locke and, later, Immanuel Kant there is not so much a silencing of rhetoric as attempts to delimit its domain, to figure it as an elsewhere, or banish it even to one or another supplementary arena. Locke dismisses rhetoric as an abuse of language in a world where 'Wit and Fancy finds easier entertainment . . . than dry Truth and real Knowledge' (Locke 1979: 508; book III, chap. 10, sec. 34). Ornaments of speech, 'all the artificial and figurative application of Words Eloquence hath invented, are for nothing else but to insinuate wrong *Ideas*, move the Passions, and thereby mislead the Judgment; and so indeed are perfect cheat'. Rhetoric, therefore, 'that powerful instrument of Error and Deceit', according to the Lockian empiricist ethics that worries over the divorce between terms and ideas, between the common meanings of words and the false ideas that moralistic language-use might lead us into, is suitable for neither information nor instruction. However, Locke does allow – and it is integral to his argument – both the pleasure and efficacy of rhetorical manipulation. Indeed, in this passage, rhetorical arts function as the enjoyable (though not enjoyed by Locke, we presume) supplement to 'dry' empiricism. They serve 'rather Pleasure and Delight, than Information and Improvement' and their prevalence (too 'various' and 'superfluous here to take notice') abounds: in 'Harangues and popular Addresses', in handbooks of rhetoric, in the establishment and 'great Reputation' of professors of the art, and in the pleasure people still take at large in being deceived. Kant's argument also is involved in marking the ethical limits of enjoyment. And for Kant, even more so perhaps than for Locke, rhetoric returns – even as it is dismissed – as a sort of irreducible surplus or supplement, the supplement we might say of *jouissance*.[18] For Kant the arts associated with rhetoric belong properly to poetry.

> I must confess that a beautiful poem has always given me pure delight [*vergnügen*], whereas reading the best speech of a Roman public orator, or of a contemporary parliamentary speaker or preacher, has always been mingled with the disagreeable feeling of disapproval of an insidious art, an art that knows how, in important matters, to move people like machines to a judgment that must lose all its weight with them when they meditate about it calmly
>
> (Kant 1987: 1978; part I, sec. 53)

Rhetoric, when improperly applied outside the arena of aesthetics to 'civil laws or the rights of individual persons', is both dangerous and demeaning, 'unworthy of any *respect* whatsoever'. The 'machinery of persuasion' serves self-advantage, it pre-empts and imprisons free judgement, it is mechanistic, and nor is it sufficient for rhetorical persuasion to be used for laudable ends 'for it is not enough that we do what is right, but we must also perform it solely on the ground that it is right'. Moreover – unlike poetry which is always preceded by the calling-card of aesthetic intentions – rhetoric is shameless in its deployment of the illegitimate technologies of theatricalized display, seeking 'to sneak up on the understanding and ensnare it by a sensible exhibition'.

However, even the anti-rhetorical polemic itself is delimited, both in the *Essay Concerning Human Understanding* (1689) and the *Critique of Judgment* (1790), to a paragraph-length effusion, as if – even as one attempts to put oneself (or one's text) at a disrespectful distance from the 'machinery of persuasion' – one is obliged, if only as briefly as possible, to get one's hands oily tugging its levers. That is, one is implicated in the constituency of conviction even as one seeks, rather like the unconvinced citizen bearing unwilling witness to the national rhetoric of conviction performed over the passing of a celebrity royal, to stand by one's disenfranchisement. Therein lies the determination of ambivalence. The predicament seems akin to what Slavoj Zizek identifies as that of the liberal intellectual today in the face of the apparently irrational rhetoric of resurgent late twentieth-century European nationalism, who will 'refuse it, mock it, laugh at it, yet at the same time stare at it with powerless fascination' (1993: 212). Zizek accounts for the passionate rhetoric of nationalist identifications in psychoanalytic (specifically Lacanian) terms, and like Borch-Jacobsen above he characterizes the process as an 'enigma', which is to say here the enigma that sustains racist fantasies, 'the enigma, impenetrability, of the Other's desire' (236). It is an enigma that finds congruence with Kant's ambivalence towards the alien locutionary *place* (rather than the process itself) of aesthetic enjoyment when occupied by the rhetorical machine; and it is worth noting here that the Kantian dismissal – 'Moreover, both in Athens and Rome, [rhetoric] came to its peak only at a time when the state was hastening to its ruin, and any true patriotic way of thinking was extinct' (Kant 1987: 198) – concludes with the historicization of something like a *nationalist* problematic. Congruities between ambivalence, rhetoric and the imagined identifications of political subjecthood are common enough. Nietzsche opens his lecture series of the early 1870s with the observation that rhetoric 'is an essentially republican art' and then immediately plays the quizzical note. 'It is [in the classical eras] the highest spiritual activity of the well-educated political man – an odd notion for us!' (Nietzsche 1989: 3). Freud, in a classic essay on the ambivalences of psychic identification, penned during the First World War and the violent self-conflagration there of national–imperial machineries, equates the structure of mourning with 'the reaction to the loss of a loved person, or to the loss of some abstraction which has taken the place of one, such as one's country, liberty, an ideal, and so on' (Freud 1991: 252).

What is interesting for me here is that Zizek's account of the disastrous performativity of nationalist discourse, the instituting of its reimagined communities and the production of racist hatred (and by extension, self-hatred), is based upon an analysis of (rhetorical) property disputes over the substance of *jouissance*, or enjoyment. For Zizek, the revenance of racist nationalisms since the disintegration of Communism in eastern Europe might be theoretically accounted for in terms of narratives of the 'Theft of Enjoyment'. What is at stake is not simply symbolic identifications made manifest in ceremonies and 'so-called' value systems, but the enigma of the irreducible 'Nation–Thing' that can only after all be accounted for in tautological terms ('"the real Thing," "what it really is about," etc.', 202). This serves as the concealed structuring principle of our fantasized identification of the threatening other's improper, 'excess[ive]' enjoyment;[19] and serves at the same time – as the stakes in the 'imaginary castration' (205) we enact upon ourselves as we partake in nationalist–racist fantasies – to structure our concealment from ourselves that all along *we never possessed what was allegedly stolen from us* (203).

The recuperation of a spurious enjoyment as property, by means of the empty speech of sophist tautologies that persuade groups of people to recognize themselves as the legitimate inheritors of discursive power over others, was of course the rhetorical problematic as far back as the texts of Plato. If there is a solution to the problem, it may at the very least have to take a rhetorical form. This is Zizek's suggested solution, which is to 'sap' somehow the 'unconscious belief in the "big Other" of power . . . exposing the power's ultimate impotence', which may in the first instance need amount to no more than the performance of a rhetorical double-bluff. 'Sometimes . . . the only truly subversive thing to do when confronted with a power discourse is simply to *take it at its word*' (237). And, perhaps, this is not so far after all from Socrates' solution, which was to take the Sophist at his word, to scrutinize his word through the method of the dialectical face to face, depending in the last instance not on what might accrue from the tribunal of the Other towards one's own store of pleasure and advantage but on one's own ethical relation to what one knows oneself of truth, love and beauty.

It may seem that to address the Diana events, to return to these at last, in the context of the violent historical disasters that Zizek speaks to, is to fall foul of the classic rhetorical failing identified by Socrates two and half millennia ago, a blowing out of proportion, making small things seem great. I allowed as much earlier in this chapter, and would not be unsympathetic to such an objection. Perhaps as much might be said of the exponential rhetoric surrounding the Diana events themselves, and Nietzsche's diagnosis of the rhetorical imagination as arising 'among a people who still live in mythic images and who have not yet experienced the unqualified need of historical accuracy' (Nietzsche 1989: 3) would not be impertinent here. I would suggest also, however, in a return to what was mentioned of Socrates and Plato above as imagining the true rhetoric of a last judgement, a rhetoric to come, as a recuperation – in spite of history – of what is truly *proper*, that we might also recall, along with such objections, Walter Benjamin's ambiguous insistence that 'the chronicler who recites events without distinguishing between major and minor ones acts in accordance with the following truth: nothing that has ever happened should be regarded as lost for history'. For Benjamin the proper historical imagination engages – as did rhetoric from the beginning – in a 'redemption', a recuperation from and on behalf of the past (which is to say from and on behalf of the dead) of all the past's citable moments, for the sake of an historically rupturing justice, a 'Judgment Day' in effect (Benjamin 1977: 256). It is not enough, however, as far as the historical materialist is concerned, to recognize the past '"the way it really was." . . . It means to seize hold of a memory as it flashes up at a moment of danger . . . The danger affects both the content of the tradition and its receivers. The same threat hangs over both: that of becoming a tool of the ruling classes' (257). This surely, among other things, is the danger Socrates, unambivalently, set his dialectic against: the danger of rhetoric. It is the danger, also, that Zizek suggests we might outface by outfacing the big Other and 'tarrying with the negative'. Perhaps also although much more ambivalently it was the danger made manifest, recognized and articulated in the complex rhetorics that competed over the property of the People's Princess. Like Aristotle's rhetorician, sometimes we have to take what is '"given," so to speak'.

Notes

1 As well as Barthes and Ricoeur I recommend the following accounts of the decline and (as we shall see) modernist return of rhetoric: Eagleton 1981; Tyler 1978; Genette 1982; Borch-Jacobsen 1992; Bender and Wellbery 1990.
2 For a structuralist analysis of 'The Rhetoric of the Image', particularly interesting in the present context for its account of the naturalization of vague connotated notions of 'nation*icity*', see Barthes 1984.
3 For a book-length analysis of the revenance of a certain rhetorical injunction, eliding King Hamlet's ghost with the still-pertinent texts of Marx and thereby problematizing any dismissal of such injunctions as 'merely' historical, see Derrida 1994.
4 See Foucault 1987. The key Nietzsche text would be Nietzsche 1976. On the modernist convergence of rhetoric and philosophy in 'discourse' see Angus and Langsdorf 1993. For a querying of the neo-Nietzschean analyses as providing a rhetoric that 'was to end up as that vigorous demystifier of all ideology that itself provided the final ideological rationale for political inertia', see Eagleton 1981: 108.
5 For Barthes the agenda of the old rhetorical pedagogy was no way 'neutral' nor immune to concerns of power. 'We can see how far such pedagogy forces

speech: speech is beset on all sides, expelled from the student's body, as if there were a native inhibition to speak and it required a whole technique, a whole education to draw it out of silence, and as if this speech, learned at last, conquered at last, represented a good "object relation" with the world, a real mastery of the world of men' (Barthes 1988: 26).

6 I am also indebted to Bender and Wellbery for the previous list. For a not dissimilar audit see Fish 1989: 471ff.

7 For a clear mapping of rhetoric's parts and functions see Barthes 1988; Kennedy 1998; or of course Aristotle. The most easily available text is Aristotle 1991b. For a more exhaustively scholarly edition see Aristotle 1991a.

8 A brief reading list might run as follows: Roach 1993; Read 1993; Roach 1996; Phelan 1997; and Diamond 1997. For a work on ethical relations between gestic performance and storytelling as a technology of remembering, and thereby the rhetorical mapping of cultural identities, see Bhattacharyya 1998. For a fascinating overview of visualized memory theatres and the *techne* of the rhetorical *memoria* see Yates 1984.

9 See also here Barthes's notion that 'there is a kind of stubborn agreement between Aristotle . . . and our mass culture, as if Aristotelianism . . . survived in a corrupt, diffused, inarticulate state in the cultural practices of Western societies – a practice based, through democracy, on an ideology of the "greatest number," of the majority-as-norm, of current opinion' (1988: 92).

10 As suggested already, Blair's performance throughout the events was brilliant. The disciplined brilliance of a specifically *rhetorical* performance was perhaps definitively cemented in the words of the reading he gave from 1 Corinthians 13 at the funeral. 'Though I speak with the tongues of men and angels, and have not charity, I am become as sounding brass, or a tinkling cymbal . . . When I was a child, I spake as a child, I understood as a child, I thought as a child: but when I became a man, I put away childish things.'

11 A key text here, focusing on the necessary ambivalence of a range of theories of rhetorical subjection (and the enabling production of various subject positions), through Althusser, Foucault, and Freud is Butler 1997.

12 'The history of rhetoric has been that of a *generalized restriction*' (Genette 1982: 104).

13 For Socrates' ideal vision of philosophical–rhetorical psychagogic husbandry to come see *Phaedrus*, 276e–277a. From Nichols's translation: 'But much more beautiful, I think, is the seriousness that comes into being about these things, when someone using the dialectical art, taking hold of a fitting soul, plants [*phuteuo*, also "begets"] and sows with knowledge speeches that are competent to assist themselves and him who planted and are not barren but have seed, whence other speeches, naturally growing in other characters, are competent to pass this on, ever deathless, and make him who has it experience as much happiness as is possible for a human being' (Plato 1998: 88).

14 See also Fish 1989: 471, who speaks of rhetoric as a 'seeming', a rising to sight in advance of speech.

15 The phrase of course is Benedict Anderson's, in relation to the nation, that 'imagined political community – and imagined as both inherently limited and sovereign'. The structures by which Anderson elaborated his definition of the nation have a touch of the rhetorical about them, as each of the self-imagined community live in 'the *image* of their communion', communities distinguished 'not by their falsity/genuineness, but by the *style* in which they are imagined', a mode of imagining the genealogy of which Anderson locates

in the age of Enlightenment and Revolution (that is, from the late eighteenth century) challenges to the '*legitimacy* of the divinely-ordained, hierarchical dynastic realms'. Imagined relations, impressive and incorporative style, and contests over legitimacy, these are the terms of the rhetoricality of nation-ness (Anderson 1991: 6–7).

16 The ambivalence was nicely brought out in the cover joke of the banned issue of the magazine *Private Eye* at the time, which played upon hypocritical prurience over the rumour that there were photographs to be had somewhere of the crash and its victims.

17 Of course the Clinton issue was also critical. As mentioned above, at the time of writing impeachment proceedings had only been delayed by a timely bombing raid on Iraq, itself in part the result of an escalation of face-saving national rhetorics. Clinton's performance to camera may have seemed comic, or pathetic, even tragic, but there is little to laugh about in the American right's attempted mobilization of rhetorical materials to short-circuit democratic processes.

18 We should be careful here. As Zizek points out in an argument that I shall pick up shortly, 'enjoyment (*jouissance, Genuss*) is not to be equated with pleasure (Lust): enjoyment is precisely "Lust im Unlust"; it designates the paradoxical satisfaction procured by a painful encounter with a Thing that perturbs the equilibrium of the "pleasure principle." In other words, enjoyment is located "beyond the pleasure principle"' (Zizek 1993: 280).

19 For a book-length study of the figuration of libidinal excess in modernist literary and philosophical rhetorics see Weiss 1989.

References

Anderson, Benedict (1991) *Imagined Communities: Reflections on the Origin and Spread of Nationalism*, London and New York: Verso.

Angus, Ian and Langsdorf, Lenore (1993) 'Unsettled Borders: Envisioning Critique at the Postmodern Site', in I. Angus and L. Langsdorf (eds) *The Critical Turn: Rhetoric and Philosophy in Postmodern Discourse*, Carbondale and Edwardsville: Southern Illinois University Press: 1–19.

Aristotle (1991a) *On Rhetoric: A Theory of Civic Discourse*, trans. G. A. Kennedy, New York and Oxford: Oxford University Press.

Aristotle (1991b) *The Art of Rhetoric*, trans. H. C. Lawson-Tranced, London: Penguin.

Barthes, Roland (1984) 'The Rhetoric of the Image', in *Image-Music-Text*, ed. and trans. S. Heath, London: Fontana: 32–51.

Barthes, Roland (1988) 'The Old Rhetoric: An Aide-mémoire', in *The Semiotic Challenge*, trans. R. Howard, Oxford: Blackwell: 11–94.

Bender, John and Wellbery, David E. (1990) 'Rhetoricality: On the Modernist Return of Rhetoric', in J. Bender and D. E. Wellbery (eds) *The Ends of Rhetoric: History, Theory, Practice*, Stanford: Stanford University Press: 3–39.

Benjamin, Walter (1977) 'Theses on the Philosophy of History', in *Illuminations*, ed. Hannah Arendt, London: Fontana/Collins: 255–66.

Bhattacharyya, Gargi (1998) *Tales of Dark-Skinned Women: Race, Gender and Global Culture*, London: UCL Press.

Borch-Jacobsen, Mikkel (1992) 'Analytic Speech: From Restricted to General

Rhetoric', trans. D. Brick, in *The Emotional Tie: Psychoanalysis, Mimesis, and Affect*, Stanford: Stanford University Press: 62–74.

Bürger, Peter (1984) *Theory of the Avant-Garde*, trans. M. Shaw, Minneapolis and Manchester: University of Minnesota Press and Manchester University Press.

Butler, Judith (1997) *The Psychic Life of Power: Theories in Subjection*, Stanford: Stanford University Press.

Derrida, Jacques (1994) *Specters of Marx: The State of the Debt, the Work of Mourning, and the New International*, trans. P. Kamuf, New York and London: Routledge.

Diamond, Elin (1997) *Unmaking Mimesis: Essays on Feminism and Theater*, London and New York: Routledge.

Eagleton, Terry (1981) 'A Small History of Rhetoric', in *Walter Benjamin, or Towards a Revolutionary Criticism*: London: Verso/New Left Books: 101–13.

Fish, Stanley (1989) *Doing What Comes Naturally: Change, Rhetoric, and the Practice of Theory in Literary and Legal Studies*, Oxford: Oxford University Press.

Foucault, Michel (1987) 'Nietzsche, Genealogy, History', in P. Rabinow (ed.) *The Foucault Reader*, Harmondsworth: Penguin: 76–100.

Freud, Sigmund (1991) 'Mourning and Melancholia', in A. Richards (ed.) *On Metapsychology: The Theory of Psychoanalysis*, The Penguin Freud Library, vol. 11, London: Penguin 251–68.

Genette, Gérard (1982) 'Rhetoric Restrained', in *Figures of Literary Discourse*, trans. Alan Sheridan, Oxford: Blackwell: 103–26.

Grassi, Ernesto (1980) *Rhetoric as Philosophy: The Humanist Tradition*, trans. J. M. Krois and A. Azodi, University Park: Pennsylvania State University Press.

Hill, Geoffrey (1985) *Collected Poems*, Harmondsworth: Penguin.

Ijsseling, Samuel (1976) *Rhetoric and Philosophy in Conflict: An Historical Survey*, trans. P. Dunphy, The Hague: Martinus Nijhoff.

Kant, Immanuel (1987) *Critique of Judgment*, trans. W. S. Pluhar, Indianapolis: Hackett.

Kennedy, George A. (1980) *Classical Rhetoric and Its Christian and Secular Tradition from Ancient to Modern Times*, London: Croom Helm.

Kennedy, George A. (1998) *Comparative Rhetoric: An Historical and Cross-cultural Introduction*, New York and Oxford: Oxford University Press.

Locke, John (1979) *An Essay Concerning Human Understanding*, ed. P. H. Nidditch, Oxford: Oxford University Press.

Nichols, James H. Jr (1998) 'Introduction: Rhetoric, Philosophy, and Politics', to Plato, *Phaedrus*, trans. J. H. Nichols, Ithaca and London: Cornell University Press.

Nietzsche, Friedrich (1976) 'On Truth and Lie in an Extra-Moral Sense', in *The Portable Nietzsche*, ed. and trans. Walter Kaufmann, Harmondsworth: Penguin: 42–7.

Nietzsche, Friedrich (1989) *Friedrich Nietzsche on Rhetoric and Language*, ed. and trans. S. L. Gilman, C. Blair and D. J. Parent, New York: Oxford University Press.

Phelan, Peggy (1997) *Mourning Sex: Performing Public Memories*, London and New York: Routledge.

Plato (1998) *Phaedrus*, trans. J. H. Nichols, Ithaca and London: Cornell University Press.

Read, Alan (1993) *Theatre and Everyday Life: An Ethics of Performance*, London and New York: Routledge.

Ricoeur, Paul (1978) *The Rule of Metaphor: Multi-disciplinary Studies of the Creation of Meaning in Language*, trans. Robert Czerny, Kathleen McLaughlin and John Costello, London and Henley: Routledge and Kegan Paul.

Roach, Joseph R. (1993) *The Player's Passion: Studies in the Science of Acting*, Ann Arbor: University of Michigan Press.

Roach, Joseph R. (1996) *Cities of the Dead: Circum-Atlantic Performance*, New York: Columbia University Press.

Tyler, Stephen A. (1978) 'Meaning', in *The Said and the Unsaid: Mind, Meaning, and Culture*, London and New York: Academic Press: 163–7.

Weiss, Allen S. (1989) *The Aesthetics of Excess*, Albany: SUNY Press.

Yates, Frances (1984) *The Art of Memory*, London: Ark.

Zizek, Slavoj (1993) *Tarrying with the Negative: Kant, Hegel, and the Critique of Ideology*, Durham: Duke University Press.

6

THE CROWD IN THE AGE OF DIANA

Ordinary inventiveness and the popular imagination

Valerie Walkerdine

The public response to the death of Diana is not a fabrication of the media. It is a revelation of the country we have become. The Princess of Wales will be remembered as someone whose circumstances imposed the necessity of self-invention. Her frail and maimed spirit became strong by surviving the breakdown of an archaic marriage. Her death disclosed a country which is already more modern than its politicians have understood.

(*Guardian*, 3 September 1997: 15)

It will be remarked that among the special characteristics of crowds there are several – such as impulsiveness, irritability, incapacity to reason, the absence of judgement and of the critical spirit, the exaggeration of the sentiments, and others besides – which are almost always observed in beings belonging to inferior forms of evolution – women, savages and children, for instance.

(Le Bon 1896: 17)

A mob is by definition fickle. It lacks political nouse or political sophistication and is always dominated and motivated by emotional considerations. That's what distinguishes it from political protest or political expression.

(Susie Orbach, *Guardian*, 12 August 1998: 7)

Hysterical masses and revolutionary crowds

In the week that followed the death of the Princess of Wales, commentators were at first obsessed by the idea of 'mass hysteria'. Few observers, it seemed, could understand just how people in their right minds could grieve so openly and volubly for a woman they had never met. By the end of the week Martin Jacques, former editor of *Marxism Today*, was ushering in the 'Floral Revolution'. People Power was on the agenda. Indeed the tide against mass hysteria began to turn when television commentators spoke to the crowds leaving flowers and queuing to sign the books of condolence to discover that they were not mindless zombies but actually could make coherent, even rational, arguments about the importance of the princess and the importance of their presence and mourning.

But the debate about the minds of the masses, the ordinary people who laid their tributes, is very far from new. Indeed, it ushered in the mass movements and phenomena which accompanied the birth of the twentieth century, and it is symmetrical that they should appear once more at the century's end.

Gustave Le Bon was a French royalist who wrote a treatise on the phenomenon of the crowd roughly one hundred years after the French Revolution. In this book *The Crowd: A Study of the Popular Mind* (1896), he popularized views which were current in Europe and which became central to the inception of social psychology as well as the psychoanalysis of groups. For Le Bon, the crowd, mob or mass had a 'collective mind', and that mind was governed not by rationality but by unconscious instincts, building on earlier notions that the masses are sick, overly sympathetic and sensitive, too close to unreason (Foucault 1979; Blackman 1996). The mass of the people then showed a marked resistance to the acceptance of the government of reason, and their coming together in a crowd signalled the danger of their primitive animality and their potential to destroy the forces of reason and indeed of liberal democracy. Crowds of ordinary people were dangerous because they could display a pathological irrationality which had to be corrected by their separation and inculcation into rational subjects. For Freud, who followed Le Bon's ideas closely (Freud 1957) and adapted them for his own ends, the mass of the people had to be made to renounce the easy pleasures of their 'instinctual impulses' in favour of 'substitutive satisfactions' (Freud 1961: 206). It is easy to see the significance of such views on the masses for the volatile years of the century which followed, and indeed. appreciate the importance of a psychological project and the part it had to play in the attempt to civilize the unruly masses. It is interesting then, that Diana was not only herself understood as an 'overly sympathetic and sensitive' person, but she was also a deeply 'psychological' one, in the sense that she was able to express and discuss her emotions in a way that was to be seen to be completely foreign to an emotionally remote royal family.

In this chapter, therefore, I want to explore the place of Diana in the psychological and political project of civilizing the masses and the role of the latter in understanding her significance to the 'ordinary' people who mourned her.

The other side of the 'mass hysteria' and its evocation of those restless antisocial crowds is the spectre of revolution and people power. I want to argue that they are two sides of the same coin. One exhorts the people to behave like rational subjects, the other demands that they should rebel and invokes a discourse which assumes that they must, at last, have had the ideological shackles removed from their eyes or their consciousness in order to see things as they really are. Usually, in such revolutionary stories, it is the intellectual who leads them on to see the true state of their own misery. In this scenario it is difficult to see who this intellectual could be, unless it is the hapless Martin Bashir, *Panorama* interviewer to the Princess. Indeed, I want to argue that this constant psychological and political belittling of the place of the emotions and the ideas of ordinary people, is at the heart of a political mistake about the nature of what happened. The attempt to understand and control the masses, whether by left, right or centre, has had at its heart a problem with understanding ordinary people as anything other than psychologically lacking, whether it be by virtue of their irrationality or their inappropriate consciousness. The psychological project which was marshalled to make them into appropriate citizens or revolutionary footsoldiers indeed produced the very people who rebelled in such an unexpected way and whose very mourning and protests were still to shake and worry the chattering classes. If the people were doing it all on their own how could it possibly be all right?

This 'revolution' embodied pain, love and loss rather than rage and was not, in the main, perpetrated by angry young men, nor by traditional agents of revolution but by the very people who would usually be regarded as deeply conservative. Add the fact that many of these people included in their mourning the invention of new spiritual rituals garnered from 'New Age' practices and you have all the elements to suggest that 'the people' have cracked. But that is because many commentators had failed to engage with what the lives of ordinary people had been like except to comment on the new media communities of soaps or the absence of sociality.

But, indeed, the problem goes further than this. The form assumed by any revolution or uprising or mass movement from 'below' is always a surprise and cannot be contained within pre-existing discourses. Psychological and sociological discourse, cannot contemplate ordinary people as agents of transformation, except in and through a theory of government and hierarchical leadership that privileges political action and whose inverse is the hysterical mob who do not know what they are doing. In these traditional discourses, social change is always described as political transformation. These theories of the social in which the state has a central place contain an implicit notion of hierarchically ordered sociality, a notion of ordinary people as disempowered and a notion of ordinary behaviour as irrational. Hence crowd emotions, unorthodox spirituality and the spontaneous actions of ordinary people are forever pathologized (Studdert 1999).

The idea that ordinary people could understand something that others had missed through all the hyperbole thrown at them by the media, and could recognize what they wanted to do about it in a practice of profound social and political comment and, indeed, protest, is beyond the comprehension of many of the broadsheet and intellectual commentators. Either they were duped into mass hysteria by the media or they produced a people power which would make sense only when harnessed and guided by the state. This is why sections of the broadsheet press began the week with wild claims about mass hysteria and ended it in serious discussion about the fall of the house of Windsor: only these extremes could be countenanced within the discourses that the press and the 'so-called' experts had set up.

Psychological selfhood and self-invention

If the civilizing project of liberal democracy was to produce a rational subject capable of accepting the moral and political order, a self-governing citizen, then the production of a rational autonomous subject was central to this process (Henriques *et al.* 1998). What has been practised for most of the twentieth century, with increasing urgency and increasing acceptance, is a project through which the animal, instinctual subject (taking the emotions as the object of rational discourse), the subject of the masses, is to be remade as a subject capable of understanding, judging and amending its own psychology and indeed one which can understand self-transformation as a key issue both to self-improvement and to managing the exigencies of daily life. The huge number of self-help volumes and the insistence of television chat-shows (from Oprah to Parkinson to Letterman) tell how we are to present our selfhood to public scrutiny, mirrored by the work equally accomplished in the social work office, school or law court, for example. At the century's end, this is a culmination of what was a scientific project at its beginning. Ordinary people are not made in the image of the autonomous psychological subject: they are to become it. Blackman (1999) argues cogently that Diana stood as an icon for that ordinary transformation, and in doing so placed herself as a subject in need of change, just like the masses and unlike the cold and distant royals.[1] Indeed, Blackman argues that Diana displayed the very features that had been understood by Le Bon and his predecessors as the dangerous characteristics of the masses: sympathy, over sensitivity and a feminine irrational. 'Emotionality, irrationality, fragility, passivity were markers of a femininity that lay outside the rational celebrated in western cultures. However these very characteristics had also become part of a project of self-development where the ability to feel, to nurture, to empathise and confess were valorised and celebrated as part of a new "culture of intimacy"' (1). Blackman argues that it was Diana's appeal to these characteristics and her presentation as someone who was capable of both self-transformation and rising above and beyond her circumstances with courage that appealed to many ordinary women struggling to adapt themselves. Blackman continues:

> Diana's confession of suffering was constituted within a discourse of self-help and coping. In the contemporary cultural sphere transformations in the way psychopathology signifies are occurring. Madness is no longer constituted as irretrievably Other, but an(other) which can be worked upon and transformed (Rose, 1996). From the confessional spaces of chat shows to the pages of women's magazines 'failures' of personal existence are presented as stimuli for change and self-transformation. Failure and psychopathology can be overcome and transformed on a route to self-development. These cultural practices promote a desired image of femininity where women are addressed 'as if' they have the capacity to be autonomous, in control, independent and choosing. Failures in these capacities signify as failures in coping which can be improved on the path to self-betterment and self-empowerment.
>
> (1999: 4)

It was ordinary women who knew more than others about the dreams of self-transformation, who lived in marriages where princes no longer stayed for ever and often left for a younger model, leaving them to bring up children alone, while struggling to earn a living. It is these women, who, throughout the Tory 1980s and 1990s, struggled to hang on to 'love', caring and kindness against a Thatcherite self-promotion. No wonder then that Diana's confessions left them feeling that at last someone had articulated just how bloody hard it was to attempt to become an autonomous woman and just how sick the struggle could make you. Small wonder also that the invectives of the tabloid press[2] produced a massive groundswell of indignation and dissent on the part of those very subjects who had been struggling so hard. It is as though a gigantic wave of identification with that struggle flooded all before it at her death. Nothing was going to be allowed to silence that struggle any more and if she articulated the desperate hurt that people had been feeling then who would not want to mourn the embodiment of all that pain and love? It was that wave which momentarily flooded the country in the aftermath of her death and when the water receded the barrenness of the Conservative era with its greed and selfishness was left for all to see. It is deeply ironic that it turns out that it was Diana not Margaret Thatcher who was the icon of the 1980s. As Blackman points out, it is predominantly women who were the 'ordinary people' who valorized Diana, but, as I want to show in the next section, this was at a moment of profound class and gender transformation within Britain and elsewhere. Becoming a psychological subject is not a simple human accomplishment, but a struggle in which the push to become an autonomous subject is managed and regulated, pathologizing other characteristics through which difficult lives are lived, but which exist in the margins of modern life. That those characteristics mix to produce a rebellion of the damned, is hardly surprising.

Gender, class and labour in New Britain

It was perhaps the hit film *The Full Monty*, released in 1997, which first captured the mood for popular culture of what had been happening for some time in Britain and elsewhere. That is, the manufacturing base of the country had been eroded during the 1980s, leaving the industrial heartland as a wasteland, supplanted by financial industries, which, along with the communications and service sectors, became the mainstay of the British economy. Traditional male working-class occupations dried up and, as the film shows graphically, many working-class men struggled to find new forms of work, having to cope as they did with the rise of women's employment and economic power, though, of course, many women were still employed in low-paid, part-time work. However, another media product, a BBC serial *The Missing Postman*, perhaps illustrates well the gendered reactions to the huge and terrifying changes that were taking place. The missing postman is a man who is made redundant but refuses to give up his work by cycling around the country personally delivering his last sack of letters. He becomes a *cause célèbre* and a fugitive in the process. On his travels he meets many men who have themselves lost their jobs and are now working in service industries. It is they who most count him as their hero, the man who refuses to give up. The desperate losses suffered by these men leave them with no sense of how to cope with their loss and where to move on to. As they struggle to comprehend the savageness of the changes that confront them, many such men are also overwhelmed by wives who cope with this change in different ways and who face the prospect of self-transformation with more accomplishment and positivity than they do. In the serial, the missing postman's wife 'comes to life' after her husband's disappearance, demolishing the interior of her home and remaking it with such panache that the media crews eventually sent to interview him turn instead to her dramatic interiors. She is remade as an interior decorator with a lucrative living at the very moment he is broken by defeat. His only way out it seems is to leave again on an adventure to deliver one more letter to Italy.

At the moment of Diana's self-transformation many women were economically as well as domestically and personally having to remake themselves. This process, sometimes referred to as the 'feminization of the economy', produces not only a huge change in class relations but a huge shift of gender as well. It may be that may of the men who had to face the terrible mourning of their work and manhood began to have to face the emotionality and self-transformation that Diana embodied too. It is at this moment that so many commented on the loss of the British stiff upper lip and dwelt on the image of men too laying flowers and crying in mourning. Indeed one television documentary highlighted a man who said that he had not been able to mourn the death of a parent but was openly and publicly mourning the death of Diana. It was a time at which there was a lot of loss to mourn about, doubtless mixed with the catharsis of the end of the Tory years and the end of the feeling perhaps that the lid still had to be kept on things in order to keep going in the dark days that it seemed would never end. So, for the ordinary people of Britain, so much was changing and those changes were, and are still, painfully difficult. It was the discourse of self-help which gave many the psychological resources to cope and which provided a heroine of self-transformation.

It is significant that 1997 also produced a new tome from the Labour Party think-tank, Demos. Entitled *Tomorrow's Women* (Wilkinson *et al.*), it set out a version of the feminization-of-the-economy thesis, drawing on market research data. Its tone was very celebratory, stating that 'as male jobs disappear, women's importance in society is set to rise, as is their confidence' (8). They divide women into five 'personality' types, which themselves provide an important indication of the type of self-invention favoured in Blair's Britain. These types of women put forward by Demos speak of the necessity of the very self-fashioning in relation to the new labour market discussed above. They are 'Networking Naomi', 'New Age Angela', 'Mannish Mel', 'Back to Basics Barbara' and 'Frustrated Fran'. Of these, it is 'Frustrated Fran' who would be categorized as the most traditionally working-class, though class is never mentioned. 'Fran's are understood as coming from social groups C1, C2 and D and are often single parents in poorly paid often part-time work. It is these women who, claims Demos, are locked out of the brighter future offered to their better-educated and middle-class sisters. The use by Demos of market research categories builds patterns of identity based on models of consumption: these are the new wage-earners, the women, who, like the missing postman's wife, must go and create themselves a work identity, one which accords with the new labour market and the new labour force. Demos talks of 'Fran' becoming 'increasingly marginalized' and 'frustrated at the success of other women, resulting in anger, pessimism, frustration and rage, which could be set to explode'. In September 1997 it didn't so much explode as implode. Indeed it seems as though Demos could understand angry sentiments expressed only as rage not as love, or loss or a desire for kindness or spirituality. It seems as though the same tired old notions of angry working-class masculinity have been dressed up in the service of the new femininity.

Indeed, the four types of femininity discussed by Demos, apart from Fran, suggest the avenues of remaking and self-invention which belay the struggles of the ordinary people with which this chapter has been concerned. For

Demos, these are mere descriptions, not discourses through which new feminine subject positions are produced and regulated. However, there are those in Britain who argue that the feminization thesis presented by Demos and others blurs another change which has happened and continues to happen within Britain. That is that women are being allowed to enter the professional and managerial labour market at precisely the time at which the status of professions in particular is changing. Adonis and Pollard argue that

> the thirty years since the mid-1960s have seen the rise of the Super Class – a new elite of top professionals and managers, at once meritocratic yet exclusive, very highly paid yet powerfully convinced of the justice of its rewards, and increasingly divorced from the rest of society by wealth, education, values, residence and lifestyle. It is a seminal development in modern Britain, as critical as the rise of organized labour a century ago, and rivalled in contemporary significance only by the denigration of the manual working class.
>
> (1997: 67)

They argue that the professions now have far less status and are paid far less than this new elite in the financial and multinational sector. Women are thus being allowed entry into professions at precisely the time when these professions are being devalued and high-flying men are going elsewhere. It is this new, largely male, super-class that eighteen years of Tory rule allowed to flourish and which witnessed the huge changes of gender and class relations that I have mentioned. This period then is one of massive transformation of the social fabric of Britain, but a transformation which leaves patterns of inequality no less stark but differently organized. Thus the terror of those working in the public sector, about the loss of security, status and salary, the loss by most people of any sense of job security, the uncertainties meeting young people with low or no qualifications, which have changed the patterns of gendered employment so dramatically. All this in a context in which Britain is witnessing no absence of wealth, especially in the south-east. Indeed the media are full of stories of executives on million-pound bonuses enjoying spending sprees. In all of this turbulence a longing for love, kindness, caring and stability is hardly surprising.

Such momentous changes have certainly not destroyed inequality but they have changed it, so that the old certainties of community support in traditional working-class areas have been badly dented. In this scenario, constantly remaking oneself is a necessity for all, no matter where their social location. The loss of jobs for life has affected all sectors of the working population. And in the realm of consumption, late capitalism in the West operates saturation marketing techniques, which attempt to create demand for marginal goods and services. These marketing techniques use refined emotionality to feed an ego desperate for self-invention and convinced of the need for personal transformation as a means to keep at bay loss of status and poverty in this changing world.

I am proposing therefore that 'the necessity of self-invention' attributed to Diana in the *Guardian* quotation which opened this chapter is a painful necessity for the ordinary people who mourned her and a way of coping with today's uncertainties where it is no longer possible to know who, what or where you are or are supposed to be. It is also clear that the state and the market encourage these transformations as long as they stay within certain defined boundaries. It is the Diana experience that shows to us where these 'official boundaries' of self-transformation lie. It is revealing that in the weeks following Diana's funeral it emerged that production and attendance at for instance cinemas had been dramatically reduced in the week of her death. This revelation corresponded with apparently officially sanctioned requests from Elton John and Diana's children for mourning to be curtailed, a request that corresponded with the decision to begin the removal of flowers and which was repeated on the anniversary of her death one year later. The limits of allowable personal transformation had been clearly defined. Obviously ordinary people are not only more modern, as the *Guardian* suggests, but also more creative and inventive and more of a danger than they are usually given credit for.

It is this point which brings me back to the issue of the political place of the ordinary people in modernity. That is, that both the psychological and sociological projects depend upon a complex intertwining of subject and state. The people who sat around the trees of Kensington Palace gardens lighting their candles were not waiting to be led – they were leading. They were daring to express those maligned characteristics of emotionality and spirituality and they were making new practices of sociality. They were fashioning them out of the cast-off detritus of rational government. Of course the regulation of them as subjects was formed from the discourses and practices through which their psychological and social reinvention was socially sanctioned to appear, but they made something out of what they had. It is they who showed what can be done without the benefit of any intellectual leadership to show them the way. Perhaps that is why the person they mourned presented herself as an educational failure, but one smart enough to become a major international figure. At the century's end we are witnessing the possibility of a different kind of politics. New ceremonies, new ways to live, new ways of coping all offer testimony to the ways in which ordinary people struggle with the exigencies of self-invention in a rapidly transforming world. In this world self-invention has both to be sanctioned and intensely regulated: Demos women and crying men are okay but extended mourning practices are not. This is not a reading of an autonomous self-reflexivity in a 'third way' but an attempt to understand the complexities of self-production and the ways in which that self-production cannot be contained even by the very forces of government which deemed it necessary. Despite everything, modernity does not have the measure of the subject.[3]

Notes

1 This opposition should be seen as an opposition between two forms of rationality: the expression of emotionality is, after all, championed in Oprah Winfrey etc. as being a rational act, a claim that has done much to undermine older notions of emotional self-control.
2 '[Diana] was pathetic. And anyone who thinks otherwise is as disturbed as she is' (*Daily Express*, 23 November 1995).
3 I am indebted to David Studdert for the political model that implicitly underpins this paper.

References

Adonis, Andrew and Pollard, Stephen (1997) *A Class Act*, London: Hamish Hamilton.

Blackman, Lisa (1996) 'The Dangerous Classes Reading the Psychiatric Story', *Feminism and Psychology*, special issue on Class.

Blackman, Lisa (1999) 'An *Extra*ordinary Life: The Legacy of Ambivalence', forthcoming in *New Formations*.

Foucault, Michel (1979) *Discipline and Punish: The Birth of the Prison*, Harmondsworth: Penguin.

Freud, Sigmund (1957) *Group Psychology and the Analysis of the Ego* in *The Standard Edition of the Complete Psychological Works of Sigmund Freud, Volume XVIII (1920–22): Beyond the Pleasure Principle, Group Psychology and Other Works*, ed. and trans. J. Strachey, London: The Hogarth Press and the Institute of Psycho-Analysis: 69–143.

Freud, Sigmund (1961) *A Short Account of Psychoanalysis* in *The Standard Edition of the Complete Psychological Works of Sigmund Freud, Volume XIX (1923–25): The Ego and the Id and Other Works*, ed. and trans. J. Strachey, London: The Hogarth Press and the Institute of Psycho-Analysis: 191–209.

Henriques, Julian, Holloway, Wendy *et al.* (1998) *Changing the Subject: Psychology, Social Regulation and Subjectivity*, London: Routledge.

Le Bon, Gustave (1896) *The Crowd: A Study of the Popular Mind*, London: Fisher Unwin.

Rose, Nikolas (1996) *Governing the Soul*, London: Routledge.

Studdert, David (1999) 'The State and Sociality: Some Preliminary Thoughts', University of Western Sydney.

Wilkinson, Helen, Howard, Melanie *et al.* (1997) *Tomorrow's Women*, London: Demos.

7

DIANA AND RACE

Romance and the reconfiguration of the nation

Mica Nava

Every now and again there are cultural events which freeze-frame the transformed and transformative elements of a historical period. Princess Diana's death and the week which followed exposed to the world the lineaments of a new British nation which bore no resemblance to the conventional heritage images disseminated around the globe in travel posters, films and BBC dramas over the last decades since the Second World War and the decline of empire. The lead role, it is true, still belonged to a princess, but the supporting cast – the metropolitan populace – was composed to a remarkable extent of the visibly different dark-skinned children and grandchildren of Britain's former colonies, bolstered by a cosmopolitan ragbag of migrant physiognomies from around the world. And more striking still: in this new scenario the lover of the golden-haired princess was dark-skinned and from somewhere else as well. The public face of Britain was no longer white. This new picture of the nation, captured and played back on the endless hours of television footage, was transmitted not only to the world outside. It registered and was constitutive of a transformation in the domestic consciousness as well.

Something analogous happened in France in the summer of 1998. Again a single much-publicized event – the victory in the World Cup of France's multiracial football team – momentarily re-imaged and reconfigured for the global eye as well as for the French themselves the meaning of Frenchness. Like the death of Diana, the incident served to reveal and consolidate – albeit more contentiously than in the case of Britain, given the strength of the racist right in France – a new set of national identifications. In common, both events represent the largely unanticipated consequences of the dissolution and diaspora of former imperial populations. They are in this sense specific to the late twentieth century. Though inevitably rooted in Europe's colonial past, they constitute a historical break, a new beginning.

But these major shifts in national identifications require a catalyst, and in Britain it was the death of Diana that served to define the new mood. The media accounts of her public recognition of racial others in her renowned charity work and her public romance with Dodi Al Fayed captured the imagination of a modernizing culture, still basking in the climate of optimism and anti-traditionalism generated by the Labour victory earlier in the year, and projected on to the screens and consciousness of the world during the course of that one intense week a new British rainbow nation. Although a sexual relationship between an aristocratic cosmopolitan English woman and a racially other man has not been without historical precedent in this century,[1] and thus is not specific to the post-colonial period, what was remarkable and new in this instance was the exposure of the affair in the public domain and, particularly in the weeks after the couple died, its favourable popular reception. This can be attributed partly to the decline in deference towards royalty among the media in the period since the war, leading to the mass circulation of information about hitherto unpublicized events, and partly – and importantly – to transformations in sexual politics with the associated increase in personal freedom for women which have meant that Diana was less constrained by the need to protect her sexual 'reputation'.[2] In a context in which revelations about the private lives of celebrities have become routine and confessional practices are increasingly commonplace, one of the features which in the end seems to have contradictorily defined Diana and Dodi's modern interracial romance was its place in the gallery of everyday mass culture and hence, despite its high profile and the feverish fascination that it elicited worldwide, its surprising ordinariness.

Within hours of Diana's death on 31 August 1997, British television and press coverage of her life and the mode of her dying was intercut with accounts and images of public mourning. The widespread and uninhibited demonstrations of grief following the news of the fatal accident were initially as much of a surprise as the death itself, but, before the day was out, these emotional displays had been established as a key feature of the Diana phenomenon. So the sense of national and then international loss, the style of mourning and the mourners themselves, all became objects of media interest. The focus of attention was widened to include not only Diana and the circumstances of her death but also the response of the people. And from the start, as was noted by journalists, camera operators and spectators alike, the many thousands of mourners included a remarkably large number of black, brown and non-Anglo-Celtic faces. Among those captured on our screens leaving tributes at the different shrines and waiting in line for many hours to sign condolence books, or just hanging out, racial and cultural diversity was far more visible than is usually the case in British media representations of public events.[3]

As the bouquets of flowers accumulated there emerged a growing sense of surprised pride in this new inclusive nationhood, even among the conservative press. There was also a recognition that the new multicultural Britain may have contributed to the new symbols and style of mourning. Emotional display, flowers, candles and incense at public shrines are not part of the history of British funeral practice. Initially there seemed to be some trepidation about speaking of racial difference. On the evening of the death, BBC reporter Margaret Gilmore at Kensington Palace referred several times to the astonishing response of the public and the fact that, as she put it, 'people from all sorts of walks of life, of all ages, from all over the country, even from abroad – so many ordinary people' were there, yet, although the camera lingered on black faces she could not quite bring herself to single out racial difference. However within a day or two, most of the newspapers were commenting openly on the 'multi-ethnic' mourning:

> Young, old, black and white, they came to pay their respects . . . Prince Naseem Hamed[4] was among the earliest . . . Mourners of all creeds prayed according to their faith . . . Catholics, Moslems and Sikhs . . . A Nigerian woman read a poem of lament for 'My Beautiful Diana, My Sister'.
>
> (Pukas and Gallagher 1997)[5]

Some of the papers confidently celebrated this new nationhood and unity: 'In our grief for Diana, there is none of that old British reserve. We are united as never before . . . It is the new British spirit, the spirit of Diana, proclaimed proudly throughout the land' claimed the *Mirror* (4 September 97) in an editorial illustrated by a cartoon entitled 'United Kingdom' which depicted mourners of different race, class, religion and age – a rainbow coalition[6] – linking hands in front of a flag at half-mast and binding together the landscape of the nation.

The unity of emotion and sense of collective loss represented by the press was sufficiently flexible to permit the coexistence of a range of identifications, and in London differences of allegiance solidified over the week of mourning so that by the funeral itself the principal shrines had developed their own distinct symbolic associations: Buckingham Palace was for middle-Englanders and the tourists; Kensington Palace, the most densely packed with flowers and other offerings, provided, as Diana's home, the gravitational pull for her supporters and the critics of the royal family; and the department store Harrods was for those who celebrated the coupledom of Diana and Dodi and wanted to commiserate with the Al Fayed family (or perhaps were just in need of refreshment: Harrods had a stall which served free food and drinks to those waiting to sign their books of condolence).[7] Of course not everyone was aware of these distinctions. Some people were indifferent or hostile and kept well away.[8] Others stayed at home and watched the whole thing on the television, and many of those who trekked into town admitted only to curiosity and the need to witness for themselves the seismic transformation in British culture, so visited all three sites. But informal canvassing as well as the early allusions of reporters suggest that blacks, Asians, gays, single mothers and others who located themselves outside mainstream British culture and identified in some way with the oppressed and vulnerable, were more likely to visit Kensington Palace and Harrods than Buckingham Palace, and some of the written tributes left with the flowers confirm this.[9] For instance among the many thousands at Kensington Palace were the following two richly evocative and moving messages:

> Queen of the Coloured Hearts
> Queen of the Devastated
> Queen of the Unloved Ones
> Queen of the Unknown
> Love from the Unknown
> > (*Daily Mail*, 4 September 1997)

and:

> Dear Diana
> Thank you for treating us like human beings not criminals
> From the lads at HM Prison Dartmoor
> > (*Daily Mail*, 4 September 1997)

So what was rendered visible in the days following the fatal accident in Paris and Diana's death was evidence of her astonishingly wide appeal and her ability to unify people from across the social spectrum. Most striking of all was her ability to speak to and recruit into her orbit those groups who considered themselves marginalized from the more orthodox political processes. Even the Labour Party in its most euphoric and victorious moment, after its May 1997 victory, could boast relatively little support from the young, the unemployed and ethnic minorities. In the days following the 1997 election landslide, the Labour Party's publicists issued press releases and photos celebrating its one hundred women MPs, but there was no similar promotion for the handful of non-white and ethnic minority MPs. Many on the left were struck by Blair's failure in this respect and were disappointed that the Labour Party was not making a greater effort – or was too afraid of middle-England – to win the confidence of blacks and Asians and recruit them as supporters and participants in the new political project.

In contrast, Diana effortlessly captured the support and the imagination of those groups without losing the constituencies of the centre.[10] In this sense she became, as Martin Jacques has put it, 'a new kind of public person, a new kind of leader'. She was a unique 'representative of cultural modernity' who exposed

the chasm between the traditional institutions of governance –
Westminster and Buckingham Palace – and the culture and concerns of the people . . . Tradition, deference, protocol, hypocrisy,
men in suits . . . were progressively besieged by authenticity,
emotion, informality, the female . . . Diana's appeal was quintessentially of our time

(Jacques 1997: 6–7)

Diana's style of being in the public world – her spontaneity, warmth and
vulnerability, her *in-touchness* – showed up the limitations not only of formal
political processes – even of the left – but also of the old-fashioned,
emotionally constrained and out-of-touch royal family. Her treatment at
their hands, her visible disappointment with her life and her sensate longing for something better is partly what mobilized the extraordinary process
of mutual recognition and identification between herself and the people.
Her friend Rosa Monckton offered an insight into the texture of this
process:

Diana had a huge capacity for unhappiness, which is why she
responded so well to the suffering of humanity. She felt real pain
. . . she had a unique ability to spot the broken hearted and could
zero in on them. She was relentless in her ability to give.

(Monckton 1997)

Diana's life experience, her own traumas and humiliations, led her to
identify with the marginalized and needy. And they in turn identified
with her.

Among those with whom she identified at this intuitive level were people
with AIDS, the young urban homeless, the victims of landmines, the
socially marginalized and excluded. Her passionate determination to
make a difference led her to radical political positions not easily tolerated
by governments and what she called 'the establishment'. Thus for instance,
she believed in a transfer of resources from rich countries to poor (Hencke
1997);[11] she intervened with considerable effect in global politics on the
question of landmines (despite being accused of being 'a loose cannon' by
leading Tories) and had meetings planned with Labour Party women MPs.
So her charitable impulse went beyond the conventional parameters of
Victorian philanthropy. She was prepared to engage politically (although
she insisted that what she was doing was not political) and endured criticism and even ridicule in order to change things. Unlike most other
members of her class involved in charitable work, her practice was fuelled
by more than just a sense of duty and some compassion.

Her psychic formation, rooted partly in the experiences of her childhood
and her powerful identification with outsiders, extended beyond charity to

her friendships and the people she dealt with in her professional life, and of course finally also to her lovers.[12] Although this is surprisingly overlooked – or at least uncommented upon – in the endless media portrayals of her, after her separation from the royal family she made a series of both formal and personal contacts with foreigners and racially 'other' first-generation British. At one level these relationships confirm the analysis of her as an icon of the modern more open and more fluid Britain. Paradoxically it is the very lack of attention to racial and cultural difference in these interpersonal exchanges that signals cultural modernity. The taken-for-grantedness of the trans-racial, transcultural social encounters suggests a kind of *post*-anti-racism, and marks a significant – if uneven – British cultural transformation that was reflected in the composition of her mourners after her death. Yet, at the same time, these relationships with outsiders also signalled her awareness of the history of social exclusion in Britain and can as well be read in part both as a marker of her own sense of not belonging and a challenge to the traditionalists – whether in Buckingham Palace or the Clapham omnibus.

There were a number of such encounters or friendships, some of them more publicized and notable than others. Her firm of solicitors was Jewish, as was her psychotherapist, and one of her closest women friends was Brazilian. For the first high-profile media event instigated and controlled entirely by her, the *Panorama* interview, considered by the BBC its coup of the year, she selected (or accepted) as her interviewer not a Dimbleby or any of the other established mandarins of the BBC but a relatively unknown journalist, Martin Bashir, of Indian Muslim origin.[13] About the same time she seems to have been introduced to the Egyptian heart surgeon Magdi Yacoub at a charitable event organized by Mohamed Al Fayed (Fayed had been a friend and associate of her father's for ten years and she maintained contact after her father's death). Through Yacoub, Diana met Hasnat Khan, a heart surgeon of Pakistani origin, described as 'dashing' by the *Mail*, with whom she seems to have had an affair (or was 'romantically linked' as the newspapers put it coyly). During this same period she made several private visits and at least one on behalf of charity to her friends Jemima and Imran Khan in Pakistan. Whether she met up with Hasnat Khan in Pakistan was not reported in the press. However, Imran Khan is reputed to have said that 'there was hardly any non-Muslim who worked in a Muslim country with as much devotion and dedication as Diana demonstrated for the sick and poor in Pakistan' (Streeter 1997). The claim was grandiose; notwithstanding, the photos of her cradling a dying child in Imran Khan's cancer hospital in Lahore received worldwide coverage and enhanced her compassionate reputation.[14] At the same time she took advantage of her convenient geographical location and 'slipped her bodyguards' to pay a social visit to Hasnat Khan's family (*Daily Mail*, 1 September 1997). All this certainly made an impact on the Islamic world. Diana's multifaceted and respectful relationship with Muslims was noted by the countries of the Middle East and Asia (as well as Britain) and raised again in the conspiracy allegations which circulated after her death.

The British press was low-key about Diana's romance with Hasnat, perhaps because she made little of it herself. And besides he wasn't famous. Dodi Al Fayed was a different matter. The relationship was considered serious almost immediately because so little effort was made to hide it. It was public from the start, and newspapers and apparently her friends spoke of love, passion and happiness. Yet Dodi was an unexpected and transgressive choice. This was mainly because his father, Mohamed Al Fayed, was loathed by the Tory Party and considered rather disreputable by most sectors of the British public, even those who were Harrods customers. As an Egyptian in pursuit of British citizenship (which was twice refused), he had offered cash to Conservative MPs to ask questions in Parliament and then exposed their corruption, so, although his actions had contributed to the May 1997 Labour victory, his complicity meant that he had few public defenders.[15] Dodi, his oldest son, was, like his father, an Egyptian, a Muslim and a multimillionaire, and in addition had a reputation as a playboy.[16] Moreover the family wealth was no more than a generation old, made in trade rather than inherited. So for Diana to have a highly visible affair with Dodi was certainly a rebellious act. She was challenging the conventional loyalties and snobbery of significant sections of her own class and also of a good part of the traditional body politic of the nation. In taking up with a Muslim, she was also embracing (in the view of most white British) the least favoured exogenous cultural and religious group.[17] Yet despite all this the press were remarkably kind to Dodi and the Al Fayed family, particularly in the days immediately following the accident.

During that first week many of the papers compared the Al Fayeds with the royal family, and the Fayeds emerged in the kinder light. They were represented as warm, welcoming, authentic, informal, generous and cosmopolitan (breakfast consisted of coffee and croissants) – all qualities considered absent in the royal family. 'They made Diana feel wanted and loved' (*Express*, 1 September 1997). Although references were made to Dodi's previous love affairs with glamorous women, he was depicted as caring and sensitive: 'Women liked, trusted and confided in him' (Cunningham 1997). His ex-lovers remained his friends, and one of them is quoted as saying, 'He was the kindest, gentlest man who took infinite care about his friendships' (Roberts 1997). Unlike Charles, Dodi was described as 'having nothing remotely pompous about him'.[18] Like Diana, he had had a difficult childhood with separated and warring parents. Additionally he seems to have had a special and populist touch with Diana's sons: he hired a private disco for them and his young half-siblings during their holiday in Saint-Tropez (Hall 1997). His partial residence outside Britain, in Paris and California – his cosmopolitanism – must also have been attractive for Diana. But perhaps finally, as the *Express* succinctly put it, 'Dodi's role as an outsider to the establishment which Diana felt had so badly let her down during her 15-year marriage, may have been just what attracted the princess to him' (Crosbie 1997). There was something modern, different and satisfy-ingly *political* about her choice of Dodi. Although he was extremely wealthy, his social marginality made her relationship with him an act of protest against the rigid protocols and emotional constraint – the traditionalism – of the monarchy.[19] Like the *Panorama* interview, the affair with Dodi was a public retaliation against her former husband and his relatives. It was a defiant Romeo-and-Juliet romance and was recognized as such by the hundreds of thousands who left messages of support and remembrance to them both together – to Di *and* Dodi – and who projected on to her their own fantasies of insurrection against parental prohibition and their desire for something emotionally fulfilling and *different*. The mood was even reflected in the BBC, which, as part of its rescheduling after the couple's death, screened the 1960 American film *Guess Who's Coming to Dinner* about a love affair between a black man and a white woman.

The fantasy, the desire for something different, seems to have been so powerful that in the end even Diana's critics and opponents in the press seem to have been won over and expressed support for her relationship with Dodi.[20] Although this might have been no more than courteous and contingent, given that the two were now dead, it could also be interpreted as an attempt to reflect public sentiment, to stay in the mainstream. It is also likely to have been an act of reparation for the notorious press harass-ment and damaging stories of the past which were so strikingly disavowed in the days after the crash. Finally the turnaround might also in part have been a challenge to the Queen, a response to her refusal to participate publicly in the mourning. What is clear is that, during the period imme-diately following Diana's death, the British nation was reconfigured and a different mood prevailed. There was a sense of popular unity, of generosity, pride, perhaps even virtue, and a *racial inclusiveness* which permeated the country and was celebrated. The fact that this inclusivity was achieved partly by projecting on to the Queen and royal family the nation's dis-content is not relevant here. What is significant is that at its heart lay the acknowledgement and acceptance of the love affair and possible marriage of Diana, the people's princess, with a foreigner: an Arab and a Muslim no less. In this instance, British xenophobia seemed as much in decline and out of favour as the royal family. Dodi was made welcome – was even loved – by the people because he made Diana happy.

The tragedy is that there was no opportunity to consolidate this racial reconfiguration. Maybe a child of Diana and Dodi, a mixed-race half-sibling to the future king, would have done the trick. It would certainly have confirmed Britain's new sense of self and would have made internationally manifest changes that are already increasingly visible in every conurbation in the country. The modern rainbow nation, with Diana as its queen, would have been not just a multicultural nation where different groups exist side-by-side but a post-colonial one where the descendants of the colonizers can no longer be distinguished from the descendants of the colonized, where cultural and racial differences are transformed by their interaction and merger with each other: where sexual desire and intermarriage produce a new generation of racially indeterminate Britons. It is precisely because this utopian vision – this fantasy – is so appealing to so many, and yet at the same time so subversive, that the conspiracy theories, which have continued to circulate in the West as well as in the Arab world, have had such an extensive reach. The rumours have varied in their detail and emphasis and some have been more plausible than others. Their interest lies not in their relationship to the 'truth' but as evidence of the texture of popular myth. The most frequently recurring theme has been that Diana was pregnant and that she and Dodi were about to marry. It is because of this, it is said, that 'the establishment' instructed its secret agents to murder the couple (Fisk 1997). The phantom pregnancy can be read in this account as a symbol of a new and longed-for, yet also dangerous, union. The rumours are fantasies of cultural reconciliation.

Diana and Dodi may be dead, but they have not been eliminated from the popular imagination. What we saw played out in the brief and intense period following their death was a scenario in which racial difference was both highly visible and at the same time part of the taken-for-granted face of modern Britain. In this context a serious romance between a white English princess and a North African millionaire was noted as a controversial step, yet at the same time was widely accepted as part of the everyday life of the end-of-the-century cosmopolitan nation. A cynic could argue that, like Barthes's photo of the Negro soldier saluting the French tricolour (Barthes 1972), the visibility of blackness in Britain today merely confirms the whiteness of the national consciousness. On the other hand it may also signal a much more radical transformation in the cultural identifications and fantasies of the people.

Notes

An earlier version of this article entitled 'Diana, Princess of Others: The Politics and Romance of "Race"' was published in *Planet Diana: Cultural Studies and Global Mourning* (ed) Re:Public, Kingswood, New South Wales: University of Western Sydney, 1997.

1 Nancy Cunard, daughter of London society figure Lady Emerald Cunard, had a long relationship with Afro-American Henry Crowder during the late 1920s and early 1930s (and other blacks it is alleged) but, because of the social disapproval of her mother and the British public, she and Crowder lived mainly in France and New York (Chisholm 1981). Edwina Mountbatten, granddaughter of Jewish financier Ernest Cassell and wife of the King's cousin Lord Louis Mountbatten, is supposed to have had a brief affair with the

celebrated African-American actor Paul Robeson in the 1930s (though their respective biographers disagree about this, see Morgan 1992, Mountbatten's official biographer, and Duberman 1989) and a much longer one with Jawarharlal Nehru in the 1940s and 1950s (though again there is disagreement between Morgan and Nehru's biographers J. Adams and P. Whitehead 1997). The point is that until very recently, although affairs are likely to have been known about and even countenanced within the immediate social circles of those involved, public denial was required in order to protect status and respectability. For a longer discussion of the romance of difference and cosmopolitan modernity at the beginning of the century, which bears on these issues, see Nava (1998).

2　Both Nancy Cunard and Edwina Mountbatten had large numbers of lovers but this information was not in the public domain during their lives.

3　There was also a very high proportion of black and brown faces among the crowd outside the hospital in Paris to which Diana was taken. It seems that there also she had made an impact on those who experienced themselves as outsiders.

4　The British boxing champion and celebrity of Yemeni origin. The name Prince was adopted by deed poll.

5　The sympathetic tone in this passage from the *Express* is undermined somewhat by the use of 'Moslem' rather than Muslim, the preferred term among British Muslims.

6　Richard Littlejohn's phrase in the *Daily Mail*, 4 September 1997.

7　Mohamed Al Fayed, Dodi's father and owner of Harrods, received, according to his spokesman, sixty thousand messages of condolence. There was certainly plenty of visible evidence of sympathy in the bouquets left outside Harrods.

8　See Christopher Hitchens's documentary *Diana: The Mourning After*, Channel 4 (UK), 27 August 1998.

9　Despite the tendency for Kensington Palace and Harrods to recruit the more dissenting supporters, it must not be assumed that those outside Buckingham Palace were straightforwardly monarchist and deferential. They appear as much as any other sector to have contributed to the ground swell of discontent about the failure of the Queen to speak to the people.

10　An articulate young black woman interviewed by television reporters outside Kensington Palace on the day after the accident expressed her support in the following terms: 'Diana meant a lot to me. She was one of the members of royalty that the nation identified with most. The fact that she did a lot of work for charities really touched my heart. Although I'm not really a royalist I felt compelled to come here this morning to leave these flowers for her. I'm just completely shocked. It's just so absurd that the best one of the lot had to go first.'

11　This point has been explicitly and consistently confirmed by members of the charity groups who knew Diana personally.

12　Stories of Diana's abandonment by her mother when she was a child have circulated widely and are assumed to have had an impact on her adult life. Similar patterns of relative motherlessness as well as identification with the marginalized were experienced by the historical figures referred to earlier, Nancy Cunard and Edwina Mountbatten, but one must of course be wary of reducing their adult identifications to these childhood events.

13　On the programme, Bashir seemed to be of Afro-Caribbean origin. His appearance was significant because most viewers had not seen or heard of him before.

14 Diana declared these her favourite photos of herself in her interview with *Le Monde* the week before she died. This was also the interview in which she attacked the British press for the way it harassed her.

15 In the months after the death, and especially after his public confrontation with Diana's mother in Paris, Mohammed Al Fayed's reputation declined still further but that story cannot be embarked on here.

16 Four months after the accident the American magazine *Vanity Fair*, already being sued for libel by Mohamed Al Fayed, published a detailed portrait of Dodi from which he emerges as an insecure man with an alleged coke habit who 'spent recklessly in pursuit of love and status'. The author argues that the Dodi who emerged in the days after his death bore little relation to the 'reality' she uncovered in the course of researching her article (Bedell Smith 1997).

17 Dodi's lifestyle suggests that he was not devout. Mohamed is married to a Finnish woman and there is no evidence that she has converted to Islam.

18 This description is Michael Cole's, Mohamed Al Fayed's spokesman.

19 There is a longer tradition of defiance against the protocols of society, as I have already pointed out. Divisions within the aristocracy during the First World War between xenophobic conservative Tories and cosmopolitan modernizing Liberals who were relatively unconstrained in their sexual behaviour or 'decadent' as they were described at the time have been documented by Hoare in his account of the Maud Allan 'cult of the clitoris' trial (Hoare 1997). See also Bland 1998.

20 See e.g. Littlejohn in the *Daily Mail*, 4 September 1997.

References

Adams, Jad and Whitehead, Philip (1997) *The Dynasty: The Nehru–Gandhi Story*, London: Penguin and BBC Books.

Barthes, Roland (1972) 'Myth Today', in *Mythologies* London: Jonathan Cape.

Bedell Smith (1997) 'Dodi's Life in the Fast Lane', *Vanity Fair*, December.

Bland, Lucy (1998) 'Trial by Sexology? Maud Allan, *Salome* and the "Cult of the Clitoris"', in L. Bland and L. Doan (eds) *Sexology in Culture*, Cambridge: Polity Press.

Chisholm, Anne (1981) *Nancy Cunard*, Harmondsworth: Penguin.

Crosbie, Paul (1997) 'Playboy Outsider who Took On Diana' *Daily Express*, 1 September.

Cunningham, John (1997) 'Dodi Al Fayed – Obituary', *Guardian*, 1 September.

Duberman, Martin Bauml (1989) *Paul Robeson*, London: Bodley Head.

Fisk, Robert (1997) 'Arab World Gripped by Conspiracy Theories', *Independent*, 12 October.

Hall, Sarah (1997) *Guardian*, 1 September.

Hencke, David (1997) 'Interview with Ann Clwyd MP', *Guardian*, 11 September.

Hoare, Philip (1997) *Wilde's Last Stand: Decadence, Conspiracy and the First World War*, London: Duckworth.

Jacques, Martin (1997) 'Ancient and Modern', *New Statesman*, 5 September.

Monckton, Rosa (1997) 'My Friend Diana', *Guardian*, 8 September.

Morgan, Janet (1992) *Edwina Mountbatten*, London: Fontana.

Nava, Mica (1998) 'The Cosmopolitanism of Commerce and the Allure of

Difference: Selfridges, the Russian Ballet and the Tango 1911–1914', *International Journal of Cultural Studies*, vol. 1, no. 2.

Pukas, Anna and Gallagher, Ian (1997) 'A Nation Weeps for its Queen of Hearts', *Daily Express*, 1 September.

Roberts, Glenys (1997) *Daily Mail*, 1 September.

Streeter, Michael (1997) 'The Best Fundraiser in the World', *Independent*, 1 September.

8

MOURNING DIANA, ASIAN STYLE

Jatinder Verma

In the early hours of a late-August morning, as I lay in a motel bed on the outskirts of Liverpool, I heard an urgent knocking on the door. It was one of my actors. A large man. Full of bonhomie. The kind of actor who turns a performance tour into a pleasant adventure, almost a holiday. His face this morning was a curious mixture of excitement and pain. 'She's dead', he said. 'Who?' 'Princess Di.' 'They've killed her', we blurted simultaneously, and held each other's hands.

We were on tour with a tragic tale of love from India. It was a play about a princess who chooses to marry a commoner, and is killed by her doting father to preserve 'face'. The play had just finished a stint in one former slave-port, Liverpool and we were on our way to another ex-slave-port, Cardiff. As we travelled down the motorway that morning, incessant Radio 4 coverage vied with chats about our next gig. Every half-hour, it seemed later, there'd be a snippet of news interrupting our plans – news that served only to reconfirm our conviction of a conspiracy. The security guard travelling with Diana and Dodi Al Fayed was in a coma – Surprise, surprise! we chorused. A white car had been seen in front of Dodi's moments before the fatal crash – See, see! we shouted.

Why had the sense of a conspiracy instinctively gripped our imaginations? And why, Asians all, did we care? Perhaps it is an excess of the epic in our imaginations. Was not the beautiful, proud Heer, the jewel of the Punjab, poisoned by her own uncle on the eve of the wedding she desired with her cowherd-lover, Ranjha? Life confirms Story, for us. Or at least, gives some meaning to its perfidiousness. Making Occasions out of its twists and turns. And we do love Occasions. Opening a shop, buying a new car – whatever, provides a reason to congregate. And death, along with wedding, offers the greatest Occasion of all.

Death is a collective forty-one-day period of mourning, for a start. The idea of holding emotions in check is anathema. After all, Yama, the God of Death, demands no less an honour than to be acknowledged for his labours.

And so we wept. Openly, loudly. At the railings of Kensington Palace. At Buckingham Palace. Along the funeral route. We flocked to town halls to sign our names in the register of condolences. We travelled from Leicester to London, to pay homage to the mountain of flowers and add our own small bouquets.

This, for me, was the most startling aspect of the mourning for Diana: the stridently visible presence of Asians. Why so many mourning, insinuating their presences into every television picture? Why so many willing to give their tuppence-worth of thoughts on Diana? Why, now, did so many come out of the wings to share centre-stage with white England? Well, she *was* a friend of Imran Khan and Jemima. She *was* seen, in a salwar-kameez, with a dupatta appropriately covering her head, holding an Asian baby in a Lahore hospital. She *was*, at the end, with Dodi Al Fayed whom perhaps, if Yama had not been so hasty, she'd have married. Or was it, more simply, that we Asians – of whatever gender – are suckers for blonde aristocrats (it helps if they are beautiful as well)? There is, I suspect, some truth in all of this. Diana certainly was the first of the English aristocrats to be seen to cuddle black babies without any visible discomfort. She seemed actually to like it. And her choice of friends certainly appeared to cross boundaries of race. While her blonde hair personified her whiteness. White, as empire taught us, is Purity, Goodness – above all, is Power. That is how the colour came to be experienced by Asians at the dawn of empire, and how it was legated to successive generations. White was generic power, in the way (I presume) black was generic servitude, premodern for white English people. For the first fourteen years of my life, growing up in East Africa, I encountered a total of three white people, whose faces I still remember. Despite over thirty years of life in England, I still have to make a conscious effort to discern, for example, family resemblances amongst white people I know. The intuitive perception is a kind of bleaching: they all look the same. Diana had made herself stand out from the crowd.

Yet another legacy of empire is the ambivalent attraction to white skins for non-whites: thanks to the continued domination of Europe through its cousin, the United States, whiteness continues to exude value. A source both of envy and aspiration as well as indifference and mistrust. The non-European world is having to grapple with the white mask on its black skins. Empire, if it had one dynamic, it was a universalizing tendency. Opera is high culture and, all over the world, music theatre is to be judged by it. Shakespeare is the greatest playwright. England is the home of theatre. Huge generalizations, given value by the force of technology. As Hilaire Belloc once famously satirized:

Whatever happens we have got
The Maxim gun and they have not.

The rules of the game are laid by this dominant culture; it can cheat, cut corners at will, but the rest of the world is always found wanting in its understanding of the rules. And moral crusades are launched against transgressors – as witness the attitude to Saddam Hussein. And yet, we subscribe to the myth of white superiority: judging ourselves against its standards. Much of contemporary Asian theatre practice in Britain is driven, for example, by the desire for acceptance by Them. And our practice is judged according to their criteria. Reviewing my recent production of *Exodus* (on the migration of Asians from Kenya to Britain in 1968), a critic from *Time Out* pronounced upon my company's need immediately to sign-on the renowned voice coach Cicely Berry, who happened to be in the audience, to lend clarity to the actors' voice. This neatly sidestepped the points that (*a*) the text of the play was a negotiation across four languages – English, Swahili, Punjabi and Gujarati – and that (*b*) the predominantly Asian audience was enthusiastically engaging with the production text. Was the critic, perhaps, intimidated by the feeling of being a minority in her own home city? What she was certainly doing was to appropriate to her frame of reference and consign to the periphery what she could not understand. Far from encountering the Other in her midst, she was dismissing the encounter. And, in so doing, she was following in the footsteps of a tradition that goes back to the foundations of the empire: the world outside England is to be understood on England's terms and none other. That is the 'level playing field' that English diplomats of late are so fond of citing.

Another explanation for why so many Asians mourned Diana lies in the structure of Asian languages. Imbedded in these languages is a hierarchical sense of the world. Our languages instil a sense of deference, allowing us to modulate sentences according to whom we are speaking to or about. The honorific has a sacrosanct place in the world as it comes to us through our languages. This structure of language goes some way to explaining our instinctive response to royalty in general, whether actual or assumed. Fathers are never addressed with the familiar 'you'. The closest approximate in English would be 'thou'. This structural principle is extended to all deemed to be 'above' oneself – because of age or position. In other words, Asian languages are Shakespearian – royalist at heart, with an automatic sense of respect for power. Witness, for example, the easy deification of the Nehru dynasty as much as Bollywood superstars in India. The structure of Asian languages does not allow for choice in granting respect – though, humans being what they are, one can always feign respect! (As an aside, this also goes some way towards explaining the 'wily Oriental' epithet given by early English travellers and administrators to Asia.)

It is not incidental that such languages gave voice to some of the most powerful female characters in literature. Beatific Sita, who dutifully followed her husband into exile and stoically resisted the loving advances of her kidnapper; vengeful Draupadi, who provided the moral justification for her husbands to annihilate their cousins in the *Mahabharata*, shampooing her hair in the blood of her tormentor; malelovent Kali, with a garland of male heads adorning her neck. Regal Mother, powerful Mother, dangerous Mother. These mythic characters had, in recent times, their living manifestation in Mrs Gandhi. Diana neatly fitted into this iconography. Was she not a mother abused? Did she not zealously guard and defend her children?

That being said, Asians in Britain are also assailed – if not exactly invaded – by another language, English, and other sets of experiences, the most profound of which is the sense of ambivalence towards England. It's a 'home' in the sense of where one lives and earns the means of livelihood, but not quite 'home' in the sense of a comforting space – a condition I term 'Binglish'. Binglish for me denotes more than modes of speech. If language is a way of structuring the world, then Binglish more accurately reflects the fractured world – the overlapping world – that is modern England; where English vies with a whole host of languages in our cities and towns. This is amply demonstrated in the works of the current masters of English literature – Salman Rushdie, Vikram Seth, Rohinton Mistry. Binglish represents a flirtation with English: what Salman Rushdie has called 'a different sort of noise in English'. And, quite literally through our stomachs, we are all, in England today, undergoing Binglish experiences: vindaloo, biriyani, kebab, curry, bindi, salwar, bhangra, fatwa, henna . . . words and concepts from other lands are infusing our sensibilities through our stomachs.

And yet, despite the contemporary Binglish experience, Asians remain minor actors (if not now, mercifully, hidden completely from view in the wings). This sense of being, at one and the same time, both visible and invisible is inherent in the contemporary Asian experience in Britain.

Perhaps it was this ambivalence that we saw echoed in Diana: a princess, but not quite of the blue-blood Windsor variety. A princess who was a rejected wife; and, being rejected, had reinvented herself as an ordinary woman, trying to raise her children and get some happiness herself. A princess who chose to bare all to an Asian journalist (Martin Bashir) in the famous *Panorama* interview. Someone, in other words, who – constantly dogged by the media – echoed our own sense of being frustratingly English. A princess in search of a home. As an Outsider, Diana received more respect than as the mother of the future king. It seemed that here, but for the accident of skin colour, was someone who understood what it meant to be left out of the club – indeed, who chose to taunt at every opportunity the very club of which she'd been a radiant member. As a hallowed critic once commented on a Shakespeare production by me, 'in the case of Jatinder Verma's production of *Troilus and Cressida*, I feel an attack of blimpish nationalism coming on: damned outsider gatecrashing the club, doesn't know the rules . . . Eventually, if not quite yet, the club will have to find room for it,' (Irving Wardle, *Independent on Sunday*, 3 October 1993).

Instinctively, the Outsider is aware of the dangers of flirting with the club: one can only be a member on *its* terms. Any transgression, and the punishment is final. This is what many of us felt was the real story behind the crash that killed Diana. This goes beyond rationality, of course; but it matters little. Diana now belongs to us, thanks to Yama. We can attach any significance we choose to her life.

Of some facts of her death, however, there can be little doubt: her funeral visibly brought Britain into the late twentieth century: a Britain that was undoubtedly multi-coloured, multi-tongued and multi-faith. She – an emblem of imperial hauteur – had in her life stooped to lift a black baby and cuddle it in her arms; stooped to accept a garland of marigolds and a bindhi on her forehead; stooped to cover her head with a chunni; stooped to hug her child on returning from a trip; stooped, as if to say, 'I, too, am one of you'. In death, Diana became an icon for all that Britain could yet become: at ease with its multiple cultures and races. A grief shared is like a meal shared, affecting the stomach where the senses reside.

And yet, I cannot help reflecting how very quickly our stomachs were betrayed – almost at the point of inception. Throughout the long week of the funeral, while our eyes and ears were assailed by the sheer presence of 'other' Britons, while Asians and other ethnics shared, in effect, centre-stage, they remained singularly absent as pundits on our media (with the minor exception of myself on Channel 4 news!). It was as if we could give vent to our grief, but not comment on it; remain bit-part actors, brought on for their colour, but not ones meriting a write-up. The media that had created Di had, it seems, not caught up with its stomach. It steadfastly refused to admit into its portals these other voices of Britain that had equally legitimate claims on Di. Rather like the house of Windsor which had for so long appeared to shut the door on Di.

So, in the end, in Princess Diana's death, we were confirmed in our ambivalence with England: offered a brief glimpse of the club before the doors were shut.

As a postscript, there was an echo of a feeling I had in 1981, when Charles and Di had married. I'd thought then how extraordinary it would be if Charles were to marry an Asian. Following Di's death, I think about her and Dodi. An English aristocrat marrying not only an Asian but a Muslim to boot! What a symbol for the New Britain. Would it have made a material difference to the discrimination faced by Asians in general and Muslims in particular? Perhaps, given the nature of this story, exchanging rings with Dodi would have only confirmed Di's outsider status, cast out of the pale.

Heer, the legendary beauty of the Punjab, had won the right to marry her cowherd-lover Ranjha from across the River Chenab. At one point, when being forced into a marriage with another, she'd defied the officiating priest: 'Ranjha and I were married in the eyes of God. Will you go against God's judgement?' The priest had relented before her fierce gaze but her uncle, seeming to relent to the wedding of her choice, had poisoned her cup of wine as Ranjha rode resplendent on a horse to claim his Heer. Diana, by all accounts, was happy on her last night. A ring had been given. The lovers died before they could cross the river to a new abode.

On the day of the funeral, we were on the road again, this time taking our play to yet another former slave-city, Bristol. As a gesture of respect, the company felt we should seek our audience's indulgence for a minute's silence before the performance began. The audience, however – which was very mixed – was in the mood to see us perform, take centre-stage. It declined our moment's silence, urging us to get on with the performance. Which was in Punjabi, Urdu and English. We were centre-stage.

That, finally, is how I would choose to see Princess Diana.

9

CELEBRITY AND THE POLITICS OF CHARITY

Memories of a missionary departed

Arvind Rajagopal

Our beloved Mother went home to Jesus suddenly at 9:30 tonight.
The cause of her death was acute left-ventricular failure. We ask
all to pray for the repose of her soul.
(Sister Nirmala, Missionaries of Charity, 5 September 1997)

The city lost its Nobel laureate, as the Yugoslavia-born Mother,
who made the city her home, had long become its glowing spirit.
(*Statesman*, Calcutta, 6 September 1997)

It is rather lovely to think that Mother Teresa, who was very
friendly with Diana, should have gone so soon to join her.
(Cardinal Basil Hume, head of the Roman Catholic Church
in England and Wales, *The Times*, 6 September 1997)

On 5 September 1997, Mother Teresa died of heart failure in Calcutta. Only
a few days before her death, she had offered condolences for the death of her
friend Princess Diana. The death of Mother Teresa just days after Diana's
fatal accident gave rise to reflections both in India and in the UK on their
similarity as figures of compassion and caring whose death could ever only
be untimely (e.g. Ghose 1997: 6). In many ways it was a curious juxtaposi-
tion: the so-called Saint of the Gutters paired with the woman who, among
other things, symbolized high fashion, and the exaltation of the body not as
an instrument for good works but as a thing in itself, of beauty and frailty.
The former was a Nobel Peace Prize winner, a nun who had devoted nearly
seventy years of her life to the order she had founded, the Missionaries of
Charity, that ministered to the poorest of the poor, mostly in the (former)
Third World. Fame of course constructs its own equivalences, but these are
not innocent; they indicate a way of refiguring national celebrity within

126

global relations of culture and power. Diana appeared like an ordinary individual, a princess whose many flaws only brought her closer to the Britons who sought to identify with her, whereas Mother Teresa was in many ways like a Third World potentate, appearing to be a paragon of virtue, on a level far above the people whom she served, and thus lacking popularity as such. Presenting these two figures togther offers a synthetic global vision of celebrity embodying compassionate virtue, obscuring the very different contexts they were located within, and naturalizing the inequality between them.

Charity, especially publicized charity, involves a harmonious relation between giver and receiver, and can thus be understood as one face of power, representing it as it would like to be seen, in a benevolent aspect. The construction of these women as figures of caring and charity thus form an implicit gendered counterpoint to a more coercive conception of power. These representations can hence be understood by placing them in a broader context, in which the modern state acts to rule coercively over its subjects while at the same time undertaking a pastoral function of nurturing and caring for individual citizens. The problem of simultaneously exercising these two very different kinds of power, which is 'the welfare state problem', Foucault points out, involves the 'tricky adjustment' between political power operating on legal subjects and pastoral power exercised over live individuals (Foucault 1989: 67). He offers a way of thinking about their co-presence in his essay on governmentality.

In his arguments on the emergence of governmentality, that is, the transformation of governance from an art to a science from the medieval to the modern era, Foucault highlights four changes as being central. There is a shift from the focus on the territory of the ruler to the people and things under his domain. Second, the mode of intervention into society is determined not by the ends of the ruler himself, but rather, by the aim of enhancing the convenience of his subjects, with the economy becoming the model of government. In this process, the family (signalled in the root word *oikos*/*oikonomie*) ceases to be the model of government, and instead becomes an instrument through which government acts. Finally, population becomes the category through which the art of government recentres the theme of the economy on a different plane from that of the family. In contrast to sovereignty, whose purpose is the act of government itself, population now becomes the end of government, to be taken into account in all of the government's knowledge and observations for effective governance. Proper governance now entails a sensitivity to the extremities of the points of the application of power, and an attention to the economic exercise of power rather than to simply illustrate the sovereign's might. Like older state structures, but with categories that help overcome the blocks posed by the models of the family and territory, the modern state seeks to be both individualizing and totalizing (Foucault 1991: 87–104). To the group of relations and techniques that allow these relations of power to be exercised, Foucault gives the name 'governmentality' (Foucault 1997: 156).

The media constitute a crucial location for the exercise of governmental power, i.e., power that is not exclusively coercive and regulatory, but as well productive, and experienced as enhancing. That is, the media are a site where technologies of domination intersect with technologies of the self, where techniques used to direct and control the behaviour of individuals are modified by and work through techniques that individuals adopt of their own accord, to pursue ends they deem worthwhile and desirable for themselves, and as capable of realizing their ideals.[1] Previously, how ordinary people thought and felt in daily life was not something that political power concerned itself about, and moreover the prevailing forms of communication provided a certain insulation from such concerns. Modern communications render it difficult to maintain such a compartmentalized mode of governing society, and instead present 'a whole series of subtle fabulations' which can have the effect of 'directing the behaviour of people in such a way that others' behaviour can have no negative effect on us later' (Foucault 1997a: 157).[2] That is, the media can exercise a productive rather than a repressive form of power, shaping desirable images that people seek to emulate, and thus at least partially bridge the gap between state power and citizenry.

In this chapter, I argue that we can read Diana and Mother Teresa as figures reflecting differently configured patterns of governmentality, and as offering insights into the tensions contained in such a project. If the British empire established a rule of colonial difference between citizens at home and subjects abroad, between individuals with equally constituted rights and those defined *en masse* as civilizationally and racially inferior, this historical set of distinctions remains discernible in the forms in which power continues to be exercised. In the figure of Diana and in the public responses to her death, we observe the fashioning of a set of bodily practices (or technologies of the self), e.g., of the acknowledgement of pain and suffering, of the irreducible and incommunicable character of this pain, of the sensation of one's body as the precious and precarious vehicle of one's life projects, that requires nurturing and care. The entrepreneurial character of a neoliberal regime, and the scaling back of state welfare form the context for these practices, with the latter perceptible both as resistance and as enacting an ethic of individual responsibility. What was prominent in the reactions to Diana's death was the vivid sense of bereavement expressed by individuals from across the social spectrum, suggesting the extent of popular identification with her, and the convergence of a range of individual understandings and practices.

What was noteworthy in the figure of Mother Teresa, by contrast, was the denial of individuality, including Mother Teresa's own, and her relegation of the suffering, the poor and the dying to an anonymous category requiring to be saved by missionary activity. Mother Teresa of course achieved prominence as a negative symbol of Third World poverty, working in a city (Calcutta, the first capital of British India) seen as a privileged instance of urban blight. As such, the context for her coming to prominence was the failed developmental state, whose presumed indifference to its subjects stood in implicit contrast to the imagined protectiveness of the welfare state. The response to Mother Teresa's death was then largely from state officials and heads of foreign states, with the poor themselves present literally in police escort.[3] The kind of self-identification witnessed with Diana in the UK reflected a definite historical relationship between the state, the media and the public, with the media acting as a kind of critical go-between element, representing popular desires in ways that sought to negotiate with dominant cultural understandings. This was not possible in the more state-dominated media in the Indian context, as I explain below.

If what was interesting about Diana's death was the depth and intensity of the grief it provoked from the British public as a whole, the death of Mother Teresa was interesting for what it did not provoke. The Indian public was largely indifferent to the event, something strange indeed considering she had evidently devoted her life to its most disadvantaged sections. The laudatory accounts of Mother Teresa in the press, both in India and abroad, and of the huge state funeral held for her paid little attention to this absence; the Indian press for its part simulated the appearance of public grieving.[4] I will argue that in fact, Mother Teresa was more important as a figure of compassion and caring for the West, as an emblem for its own concern for the world's poor, and that this was a conceit that the Indian state could not challenge without attracting international opprobrium. Although it is not the whole truth about her, Mother Teresa could equally have been represented, as by Christopher Hitchens for instance and as I will elaborate below, as a canny propagandist for whom the suffering of the poor was a means for Catholic proselytizing rather than an injustice to be erased (Hitchens 1995). For the Western press, Diana's life was an ongoing saga guaranteed to win audiences; it was the sense of empathic identification the public expressed with her privileged and compassionate but ultimately tragic life that was most prominent. Two figures that represented strikingly different relationships between states and their publics came to reinforce the media images of each other in death.

The story of Mother Teresa offers a sustained series of contrasts to Diana's own life and death. Mother Teresa appeared as a 'successful' example of self-abnegation and charitable works, of ascetic devotion to the cause of the suffering poor. Against this was Diana's own more distressed royal life: her determinedly self-assertive and pleasure-seeking behaviour against the deadening routines of palace convention; her unwillingness to adopt the rigid formality required of her; her need to receive and to give what she called

'TLC', tender loving care; her refusal to settle for the familiar role of cuckolded consort and her flamboyant assertion of her sexuality; her struggles with self-definition in the wake of her marital separation and the emergence of a new public persona, as advocate of unconventional causes outside the usual royal charities (banning landmines, AIDS). Diana's overwhelming popularity was partly a result of the intimacy she could effortlessly establish with others, no doubt, and testimony to the rare quality of empathy she possessed. At the same time, the public character of her personal difficulties, from Charles's infidelity to her retaliation, and her growing estrangement from the House of Windsor, made her a royal figure with a singularly unauthoritarian aspect. Her tribulations spoke to a new emotional culture of self-definition that worked against and on the strength of acknowledged victimhood and suffering rather than one that measured public virtues and private failings on different registers. Her willingness to reveal her battles with herself (e.g., her eating disorders) and her environment thus made her a role model of a different sort, a celebrity situated within the establishment, in a sense, but one who was marginal too, by her own declaration flawed and vulnerable, and thus in a category all by herself.

Diana appeared in many ways as a figure mediating and reflecting essential tensions in the larger society. Most immediately there were the traditions of Britain's royal family, unbending before an increasingly demanding public and still unaccustomed to the experience of modern publicity, invoking moribund conceptions of privilege in its attempt to protect itself from the masses. There was the hangover of the imperial past, with an older generation retaining strong notions of Britain's place in the world, and corresponding ideas of the kind of conduct befitting the British, as opposed to a generation for whom decolonization itself was not within living memory, and to whom nationalist assertion sat more uneasily with experiences of de-industrialization, domestic unemployment and racial tension. The unbending propriety characteristic of an earlier age that was obedient to colonial forms of decorum contrasted with the more casual and direct attitudes affected by a younger generation, which could not take comfort in quite the same myths of domestic or public harmony. The relationship between private and public was slowly being transformed, with a new, dimly discernible set of norms emerging. If personal behaviour appeared less repressed, and more intimate, individualized codes of address and comportment became prevalent, the security of earlier understandings and guarantees about public life were simultaneously being eroded. More entrepreneurial and market-oriented standards increasingly took the place of the commitments of the welfare state, ushered in by Margaret Thatcher, who emphasized a combination of British pride and harsh discipline. Diana was in a sense the counterfoil and indispensable accompaniment to Thatcher, then, the ex-nanny counterbalancing the woman who took on the challenge of dismantling the 'nanny state' (Schama 1997: 139).

The contrast with Mother Teresa could not be greater. Mother Teresa's work highlighted the existence of millions who were poor and uncared for, and her own fortitude in devoting herself to such people, forgotten or ignored by their governments and fellow citizens. Her own life seemed to exist on this single dimension, however, as a model of ascetic piety and altruism, about which little else was known or indeed was required to be known. She was to all intents and purposes a saint, indeed she could well be a candidate for beatification by the Church.

With Diana, there was an emphasis on her own corporeality, on her desirability and vulnerability, and the mysterious ability of her body to condense and represent so much more than herself: royalty as well as its discontents, and a broad cross-section of its adoring and suffering subjects, and the generational changes experienced across them. Where the "nanny state" had declined to fulfil its charge of attending to the tribulations of its individual subjects, declaring this to be a matter of their own responsibility, celebrity stepped into the breach, as a figure of popular desires as well as of the unattainability of these desires, as a vehicle for the unacknowledged hopes and humiliations of the majority.

In the case of Mother Teresa, on the other hand, there was a denial of the body, even a glorification of its denial, and an understanding of service in terms of charity and of ministering to the all-too-visible bodies of the poor, of the display of their suffering, of physically emaciated bodies, and so on. Simultaneously, what was highlighted was the benevolent intent of the provider of charity, and a complementary effacement of the recipient's personhood: the poor were the stage on which the drama of good works was enacted, and the concern of the benevolent was proclaimed.

Now, a model of charity is simultaneously a model by which power chooses to represent itself, in this case, as diligent, dedicated and self-effacing. But in the context of India, where social welfare is subordinated to state-determined needs of 'national development,' the relevance of this particular model is qualified by the fact that the benefactor here was not the state but a private person, highlighting the inadequacies of prevailing development programmes. Small wonder then that it was in the West that Mother Teresa's growing beatitude was most energetically affirmed, as symbol of Third World misery, and the west's own denunciation of it. How much misery was alleviated by Mother Teresa was not the question, as the *Times of India* argued in its editorial obit. The effective scope of social work done by Baba Amte and others, little known outside India, was 'considerably greater'; what was important, the editorial pointed out, was the sincerity and feeling that Mother Teresa epitomized (*Times of India*, 8 September 1997).

The following quotation from a piece by the correspondent of the London *Times* in Delhi, Christopher Thomas, illustrates some of the perceptions

surrounding Mother Teresa, although it misinterprets them in a characteristic way:

> India was confused by Mother Teresa. It honoured her work while
> secretly hating it. Her Missionaries of Charity nuns made Calcutta
> an international byword for urban vileness and cruelty, and an
> embarrassed nation felt compelled to shower awards on her.
>
> It will never allow her like again. Now that she is dead, India
> will wonder once more at the foreign-born Roman Catholic who
> scoured rubbish tips for discarded babies and retrieved the dying
> poor from the pavements, contributing to Calcutta's excessively
> evil reputation. The politicians who honoured her resented her the
> most; it was their incompetence and venality her work exposed,
> yet it is they who will shout loudest in tribute today. This was the
> paradox of Mother Teresa's influence: she was not always liked but
> was impossible to criticise or control, enabling her to weave into
> the centre of political and bureaucratic power when she needed
> something.
>
> (6 September 1997)

Thomas plays on a familiar stereotype, of Third World corruption and
inhumanity to the poor, against the heroism of the foreign-born Roman
Catholic crusader. It is necessary to detach the figures of the state and the
public from 'India', however, and to consider their possible relations to
representations of Mother Teresa separately.

The public in India as expressed in the press is to a considerable extent a
ventriloquism of the state, that is, the values expressed in press coverage
tend to express state interests, and to define the boundaries within which
news is categorized and conceived, and editorial control exercised. This is a
result of the cultural and political dominance of an English-language press,
something the recent growth in indigenous language news media is
beginning to change.[5] It is a carry-over of British colonial rule, which
was hostile to the independent press, regarding it as irresponsible and
mischief-making.[6] The Western experience of a rational-critical public,
developing in a structured opposition to state authority, did not then obtain
in India. Instead, the state itself was the venue for public expression,
courtesy of the British colonial government. With the party leading the
Indian national movement forming the first independent government, the
terms of political contestation, and also of social inquiry in an incompletely
modern society, again became questions internal to the state. The agenda of
national development came to exercise a prerogative over other priorities. As
a result, the hybrid social phenomena characteristic of uneven development
tended to be understood through a state-centric lens. In addition to this
crucial politico-cultural influence, explicit state controls over the press are

also maintained, but through resource-allocation rather than censorship, in terms for example of government advertising.[7] As a consequence, law and order tends to be the dominant news frame in the coverage of social issues, hence obscuring the precise meaning and significance of actual events in the news. This was illustrated in news coverage of Mother Teresa, in the write-ups and obituaries on her. The point is not to discover the reality behind the public myth of Mother Teresa, or to argue that the coverage on Diana was in some sense superior in its veracity to that on Mother Teresa. Rather, it is to situate historically the kinds of media representations constructed and to relate these representations to distinct forms of governmental power.

For the Indian state, Mother Teresa represented something of a political dilemma, drawing international attention to domestic social problems, and providing an implicit rebuke to the government's limited success in its developmental efforts. The slightest hindrance to Mother Teresa's work from the state could have provoked an international outcry, and embarrassed bureaucrats sensitive to their reputation with international agencies and foreign governments. She was therefore exempt from the summary treatment an independent do-gooder would have received from the Indian state, which maintained a jealous relationship to its subjects in this respect. Popular responses to her were more equivocal, broadly, because of the limited character of the charitable work performed, and the ways in which they were carried out. A brief account of Mother Teresa's life and work make clear the extent to which caring and compassion, even if used by her as a description of the order's work, are terms that can easily be misunderstood. A systematic denial of individuality, and a preference for austerity to the extent that it was imposed on unwilling recipients, characterized their approach. In the case of Diana, there was a continuity of bodily practices between herself and her admirers and mourners, as what united them was a sense of shared or similar experience. With Mother Teresa, there was a sharp break between herself and those she served, and a monological relationship between the Missionaries of Charity and the poor, wherein the poor were more or less mute victims to be 'saved.'

In 1950, the Missionaries of Charity was set up in Calcutta, twenty-two years after Mother Teresa arrived in India at the age of eighteen.[8] Her fame was established with a December 1969 BBC film produced by Malcolm Muggeridge, followed by a 1971 book (largely a transcript of the film), *Something Beautiful For God*. A priest who worked with her for many years commented later that Mother Teresa was 'made by the media', and that without it she would be a little nun working with a few other nuns (*Guardian Weekly*, 14 September 1997). Muggeridge's own very public attempts to come to terms with religion made both the film and the book an unusually engaged account, and the unalloyed idealization of Mother Teresa set the tone for future reportage, with a pious and adoring approach to its subject (Muggeridge 1971).[9]

By 1975, the Missionaries of Charity had established thirty-two Homes for the Dying, sixty-seven leprosariums and twenty-eight children's homes around the world. Advancing to a new country did not of course mean that nothing remained to be done in the countries where the Missionaries of Charity was already working; in fact the capacity of most of the homes was modest. Rather, attaining a global presence was seen to be important in itself, perhaps just as the Catholic Church itself had a global presence and stood for a powerful set of universalist goals.

Leading medical opinion was not always in favour of the results of Mother Teresa's work. Robin Fox, editor of *The Lancet*, writing about a visit to the Missionaries of Charity's Home for the Dying in Calcutta, criticized the unavailability of powerful analgesics and what seemed like cavalier treatment of the sick. Mother Teresa preferred 'providence to planning', and thus refused to adopt the simple algorithms used in primary health care even in India, to help untrained staff diagnose illnesses and prescribe drugs. Thus one young man was thought to have meningitis but in fact died of cerebral malaria, a matter that a blood examination could have clarified. 'If you give money to Mother Teresa's home,' Fox wrote, 'don't expect it to be spent on some little luxury' (Sebba 1997: 136). He was referring to an electric blender that had been gifted to the centre, to purée food for those with mouth and throat cancer, who had difficulty in swallowing. The nuns had rejected the blender as being against their philosophy. '[W]hat shocked me most', he said in an interview, 'was the insistence of simplicity to the point of discomfort. Clearly there are many things which could make a patient comfortable and yet keep the conditions consistent with those to which the poor were accustomed' (Sebba 1997: 136). He concluded his article in *The Lancet*: 'Along with the neglect of diagnosis, the lack of good analgesia marks Mother Teresa's approach as clearly separate from the hospice movement. I know which I prefer' (Sebba: 1997: 137).

Suffering was the object of her attentions, but it gained its meaning not at the earthly level, and certainly did not organize relief work as a matter of eliminating pain and providing pleasure. Suffering was proof of the Lord's continued presence amongst humankind, and as such commanded their ministration. It was not the pain of souls on earth as such that the Missionaries of Charity sought to alleviate; the transcendental act of salvation in heaven was the one that mattered. The body in this conception was a proving ground of piety, to be exhibited as exemplary of one's own capacity for asceticism and pain. Thus Mother Teresa, operating a multi-million-dollar charity in Calcutta, worked out of a small room with no fan or air-conditioner, accumulating large amounts of money but seemingly indifferent to this achievement and drawing no commensurate benefit from it, and apparently with little idea of precisely what was being accumulated.

Few charities can have attracted the kind of support Missionaries of

Charity did. Organizations like Catholic Relief Services, Miserior, Swiss Aid and the Vatican's own support system contributed to the 755 homes Mother Teresa established in 120 countries. One estimate of the Missionaries of Charity's holdings was as high as $200 million for its Calcutta account alone (*India Today*, 22 September 1997). Christopher Hitchens estimated its total annual receipts worldwide to be in the tens of millions of dollars (Hitchens: 1995: 78). Contrasted with these munificent holdings, the scale of any particular operation of the Missionaries of Charity was niggardly indeed, and represented a determined Franciscan effort to hold fast to their vow of poverty rather than to address the challenge of poverty itself.

Any large-scale attempt to 'save the heathen' was of course politically hazardous, facing as it did the prospect of local opposition on religious or nationalist grounds. Mother Teresa's work in India was missionary work, but this was a 'missionary of charity' rather than one of conversion. In this sense it represented an adroit adaptation to altered historical circumstances, to an age of decolonization and nationalist assertion, to the steadily changing character of religious authority, and to that of the Church in particular. As a Catholic nun of European origin, working mainly but not exclusively in the non-Western world, there was unavoidably a colonialist tinge in the reception of her work, perhaps intensifying the identification of those who knew of her in the West, but capable of provoking the opposite reaction in countries like India. There were those who saw missionary activity as inherently dubious, operating under the cloak of good causes to add to the growing army of Christian converts worldwide, no doubt capable of lending their strength to some future anti-national insurrection. The Hindu right and its supporters, a growing body in India, were notable for this view.[10] But for those sympathetic to the possibility of progressive forms of Church activity too, Mother Teresa's interventions in India, compromised as they were, were objectionable in their refusal to challenge the inegalitarian character of the Church in India. Indian Christianity, dominated by upper-caste converts, has resisted the reformist currents emanating in the wake of Pope John XXII's Second Vatican Council, as for example with liberation theology, and chosen instead to work entirely within and alongside a brutally repressive caste order.[11] As such, the kind of tendencies Missionaries of Charity represented were in concordance with those of the Church in India, deeply political in its avoidance of political conflict.

It might be said that the reaction to Diana's death would have been less surprising if it had been occasioned by that which was observed at Mother Teresa's, and vice versa. The Indian government clearly had to generate a response adequate to the international outpouring of sympathy from heads of state and from dignitaries. First, in Calcutta, no mean city in terms of population, the West Bengal state government declared a state holiday to 'allow' its employees to attend the funeral. Then, presumably as apprehensions about the adequacy of the crowds grew, a request was made to all employers to grant a paid holiday to workers in all private businesses, including factories and shops, so that they could 'observe Mother's last journey' (*Statesman* 1997c). Still, the leading Calcutta newspaper, the *Statesman* noted, with a careful lack of exactitude, that 'tens of thousands' were present at the funeral procession. Newspaper photographs showed pictures of solitary mourners: a girl sniffling here, a wreath-bearing nun there. It was reported that more than five hundred security personnel would be deployed in and outside the Netaji Indoor Stadium complex, where funeral services were conducted, and nearly four thousand others, including commandos, would be deployed all along the five-kilometre route of the funeral procession (*Statesman* 1997c). Taken together with the number of official guests, including the nuns, which was about two thousand, the size of civilian mourners must have been small indeed. At the burial service itself, apart from two thousand nuns, officials and dignitaries present, we are told there were 'scores of people' who braved a drizzle, and crowded into Mother House, where hymns were sung and rituals were conducted by Cardinal Sodano (*Statesman* 1997d).

Observers felt that the grief on display at the funeral was limited, to say the least. Members of an ABC television crew expressed surprise 'to see the people disappear so fast' once the cortège had moved on. Two workers from Delhi's St Mary's Church expressed dismay at the 'lack of sympathy in the crowd. It looks more like a little fair,' one said. A British woman who witnessed Diana's funeral described those mourning Mother Teresa as 'less overwhelming' (*Times of India*, 15 September 1997). Some of the poor who did try to pay their last respects were deterred by the well-groomed appearance of the mourners. Asha, a beggar based in Park Street and Esplanade in Calcutta, was reported as saying, 'How can I in my tattered clothes stand together with these people. They will feel offended.' Shamsher, from Kidderpore, had already been turned away by the police, but on his next attempt was embarrassed at his own appearance, and was reported as saying, 'See so many *sahibs* have come. How can I stand in my dirty and smelly clothes next to them?' (*Statesman* 1997a). If the poor were not present in large numbers in the crowds, the state government ensured that they would be there none the less. A convoy of vehicles carrying 170 people was to follow the funeral cortège, bearing among others, a cross-section of 'the poorest of the poor' (*Times of India*, 13 September 1997).

The press conference with Sister Nirmala, Mother Teresa's successor, was revealing not only in the extent of the suspicion towards the Missionaries of Charity, concealed in most of the reportage. In addition, lacking the poise and the experience of her predecessor, Sister Nirmala, in her maiden appearance before reporters, fumbled enough to allow reporters to challenge the prevailing official account of Mother Teresa, with questions about the mission's accounts, allegations of conversion of the poor to Christianity, and criticisms of the order's lack of engagement with poverty-alleviation (*Statesman* 1997b). Some of the interchanges went as follows:

Hasn't your order received tainted money?
'I am not aware of it. It's all God's love.'
There must be some donor whom everyone knows is corrupt and the order must have knowingly taken help from such donors.
'It hasn't been done until now.'
What's the Missionaries of Charity's annual turnover? Is there any auditor?
'I have no idea. We have an auditor. But I am not worried about money matters.'
Don't you think the order needs to change with time, especially when it comes to family planning?
'No, I don't think so.'
. . .
Sister Nirmala iterated [*sic*] Mother Teresa's assertion that 'poverty is beautiful.'
'We want the poor to use poverty in the right way.'
What is the right way?
'Acceptance, content [*sic*] and the trust that God will provide. Not moan and groan about poverty.'
She continued: 'Poverty is a gift of God and so is riches. Share it (she referred to the latter).'
Why doesn't the order try to root out poverty, instead of just helping the poor?
Sister Nirmala [said she] left poverty-alleviation programmes to the government.
What would happen if the poor became rich?
'We will lose our jobs,' she replied.
Sister Nirmala was without words for a few seconds when the media referred to allegations of conversion of the poor to Christianity in the order's homes.
But she recovered and asserted: 'We encourage Hindus to be better Hindus and Muslims to be better Muslims. But if they seek help spiritually, we help them.'
How many have sought such 'help' till now?
She could not provide any figure.
Sister Nirmala had no clear idea about the participation of the poorest of the poor in tomorrow's funeral procession. 'They will be there,' she said, but she couldn't specify where they would be.

The aggressive questions, fielded haplessly by someone who had never addressed a press conference before, presented a very different picture of the Missionaries of Charity from the adulatory image conveyed in standard press coverage. Imputations of the receipt of tainted money, indifference to family planning and to women's own concerns, and allegations of converting the poor dominated the story. There was an aestheticization of poverty that seemed to be explained by the order's own dependence on poverty for its livelihood, rather than on a desire to ameliorate poverty as such. And finally, there was the suspicion that the poor themselves would not necessarily be present in substantial numbers at Mother Teresa's funeral, thereby underlining the question of precisely who Missionaries of Charity's ultimate beneficiaries were.

The report was a critical one, though the title was misleadingly bland: 'It is all God's love: Sister Nirmala.'[12] It is interesting that so stark a contrast between a news report and the public image of a celebrated organization did not provoke further inquiry. In this case, however, the report remained an isolated note in what was a chorus of simulated grief in the press coverage.

The extent to which any charitable work Diana performed influenced her popular reception was probably exceeded by her significance as a zone of empathic convergence, which then spoke to a different kind of charity and a different form of governmental power. The multiple uses of her body, as a body of high fashion, as a sexualized figure, as a hurt single mother and so forth, allowed individuals a variety of subject positions in their identification with her. In the popular response to Diana's death, we saw the symptoms of a highly governmentalized society, albeit one insufficiently attentive to the needs of individuals. These contradictions were registered and symbolically transcended in the media, as a spectacle of mourning created the impression of a nation at one with itself in its grief.

The kinds of bodily practices evidenced in the case of Mother Teresa, the impersonality and self-abnegation with which she pursued her good works, on the one hand, and the objectified way in which the bodies of the poor themselves were ministered to on the other hand, harkened back to a Dickensian conception of charity, with a consequent lack of popular identification with Mother Teresa. The Missionaries of Charity's apparently selfless model of work treated the poor as a ground from which to pursue their agenda rather than addressing the needs of the poor as such. This approach addressed the drawback of a developmental state that conceived the needs of the population *en masse*, while reproducing the lack of a discriminating application of power in the prevailing political culture. The merging of such disparate celebrities in one trope of charity represents, no doubt, a sentimental response to the problem of poverty, whether therapeutic or material. As such, it is an interesting cultural symptom of the way in which media images can straddle diverse and unequal societies in one global regime of representation.

Notes

1 In this context, see Foucault's discussion of technologies of the self (Foucault 1997b: 181).

2 Foucault concludes this passage, which is not about the media as such, 'And this is the field of governmentality' (Foucault 1997a: 157).

3 See below.

4 Mother Teresa was thus only the second private person accorded a state funeral in India, the first being Mahatma Gandhi (Mukherjee 1997: 1).

5 In this chapter, I will discuss only the English-language press, since it is most in tune with the forms of reportage of events in the Western world, and thus offers an appropriate index of comparison with British accounts of Diana or Mother Teresa. Understanding the interaction between the English and indigenous-language press is crucial, however, in assessing the larger significance of the press and its relationship to Indian politics. See Chapter Four in my *Politics After Television: Hindu Nationalism and the Reshaping of the Indian Public*, Cambridge, forthcoming, for a discussion of what I call a 'split public', which was important in the recent development of Hindu nationalism.

6 The independence movement existed as an articulate domain of politics for the educated middle classes, to be sure, but it was through Gandhi's religiocultural forms of mobilization that it became a mass movement. The kinds of politics that developed in this process, and their relation to the notion of a modern public are thus in dispute. See, e.g., Sandria Freitag, 'Contesting in Public: Colonial Legacies and Contemporary Communalism', in David Ludden (ed.) *Contesting the Nation: Religion, Community and the Politics of Democracy in India*: Philadelphia: University of Pennsylvania Press, 1996: 211–34.

7 A strict regime of newsprint controls was abolished in 1995, and was an important means of government control over the press. Changes in the culture of the press in the wake of liberalization will obviously take some time to manifest themselves.

8 My account is taken mostly from Sebba 1997.

9 Even as Muggeridge's book came out, Mother Teresa's peculiar vision of charity was generating astonishment and resentment in the subcontinent. Immediately after the 1971 war in Bangladesh, on 14 January 1972, she announced that she was going to Bangladesh, with ten other nuns, including Sister Margaret Mary, whose family came from Dhaka (then Dacca). Pakistani troops had raped some four thousand women in Bangladesh, according to a Catholic relief organization, Caritas; other estimates of women raped went as high as two hundred thousand. But although Mother Teresa's intention was to help these women, she herself admitted that few women were coming forward to ask for their help. Given the Missionaries of Charity's steadfast opposition to abortion, which was what most of the women presumably wanted, this was perhaps not surprising. Germaine Greer, after talking to relief workers, later reported that Bangladeshi women who had complications associated with late pregnancy, caused by a combination of physical abuse and malnutrition, as well as women who had miscarried, were simply turned away by Mother Teresa's nuns. Furthermore, all the babies that were sent away for adoption, Greer reported, were sent by Missionaries of Charity to Catholic homes: Germaine Greer, *Independent* Magazine, 22 September 1990, cited in Sebba (Sebba 1997: 93–4). The new Prime Minister of Bangladesh, Sheikh Mujibur Rehman, did set up a Rehabilitation Board for Affected Women, which organized abortion services for women five months pregnant or less.

10 Thus Ashok Singhal, general secretary of the Hindu right Vishwa Hindu Parishad (World Hindu Council, or VHP), denounced the Nobel Prize award to Mother Teresa as part of a Christian plot to convert Hindus in India. He criticized the Nobel Prize given to economist Amartya Sen for good measure, claiming that Sen's interest in improving the literacy rate in India was similarly missionary-inspired. *The Hindu*, 28 December 1998.

11 Christianity in India, like other religions in the subcontinent, has absorbed the caste system into itself, so that converts tend to be identified by their caste of origin, and to retain many if not all of the accompanying advantages and disadvantages. Missionaries saw such a compromise as necessary if they were to persuade upper castes to convert, to assure them that they would not lose status in the majority society. If the lowest caste groups sought to overcome the overwhelming prejudice and stigma imposed by a Hindu ritual order by embracing Christianity, they often found themselves doubly disadvantaged after conversion. On the one hand, the Church marked them as untouchable Christians and denied them the right to share space with upper-caste converts, whether in church services or in the cemeteries. On the other hand, they lost the government-mandated quotas of jobs and seats in educational institutions because they were deemed to have left the Hindu fold, and thus to have left untouchability behind. See James Massey, 'Ingredients for a Dalit Theology', in *Indigenous People: Dalits, Dalit Issues in Today's Theological Debate*, New Delhi: ISPCK, 1994: 339; also Sathianathan Clarke, *Dalits and Christianity: Subaltern Religion and Liberation Theology in India*, Delhi: Oxford University Press, 1998: 41–2, and B. Kailasam, *The Twice Discriminated: Dalit Christians in Tamil Nadu*: Video, MFA Thesis, Department of Film, University of Iowa, 1987.

12 *The Times of India* carried an account of the press conference on the same day that corroborated several details of *The Statesman*'s report. Shikha Mukherjee, '"We Will All Lose Our Jobs"', 13 September 1997.

References

Foucault, Michel (1989) 'Politics and Reason' in *Michel Foucault: Politics Philosophy Culture. Interviews and Other Writings 1977–1984*, trans. Alan Sheridan and others, ed. Lawrence Kritzman, New York and London: Routledge.

Foucault, Michel (1991) 'Governmentality', trans. Pasquale Pasquino, in Graham Burchell, Colin Gordon and Peter Miller (eds) *The Foucault Effect: Studies in Governmentality*, Chicago: University of Chicago Press.

Foucault, Michel (1997a) 'What Our Present Is', trans. Lysa Hocroth, in Sylvère Lotringer (ed.) *The Politics of Truth*, New York: Semiotext(e).

Foucault, Michel (1997b) 'Subjectivity and Truth', transcribed and ed. by Thomas Keenan with the assistance of Mark Blasius, in Sylvère Lotringer (ed.) *The Politics of Truth*, New York: Semiotext(e): 171–98.

Ghose, Saswaty (1997) 'Two Funerals and a Resurrection', *Statesman*, 14 September.

Guardian Weekly (1997) 'Inspiration to the World', editorial, 14 September.

Hitchens, Christopher (1995) *The Missionary Position*, London: Verso.

Muggeride, Malcolm (1971) *Something Beautiful for God*, London: Collins.

Mukherjee, Shikha (1997) 'All Set for Mother Teresa's Last Journey', *Times of India*, 13 September.

Namboodiri, Udayan (1997) 'Difficult Legacy', *India Today*, 22 September.

Schama, Simon (1997) 'Diana National, Diana International', in Brian MacArthur (ed.) *Requiem: Diana, Princess of Wales 1961–1997: Memories and Tributes*, London and New York: Pavilion Books and Arcade Publishing.

Sebba, Anne (1997) *Mother Teresa: Beyond the Image*, London: Weidenfeld and Nicolson.

Statesman (1997a) *Statesman* News Service, 'When Rich and Pauper United', 8 September.

Statesman (1997b) *Statesman* News Service, 'Paid Holiday', 13 September.

Statesman (1997c) *Statesman* News Service, 'City Braces for Final Farewell to Mother', 13 September.

Statesman (1997d) *Statesman* News Service, '"Saint of the Gutters" Laid to Rest', 14 September.

Thomas, Christopher (1997) 'Legacy of Admiration and Resentment among Calcutta's Elite', *The Times*, 6 September.

Times of India (1997) 'Teresa of the Poor', editorial, 8 September.

10

MOURNING AT A DISTANCE
Australians and the death of a British princess

Jean Duruz and Carol Johnson

While Britons slept, on the other side of the world, Australians were awake and following the unfolding news reports on the extent of Diana's injuries and whether she would survive them. Our viewing, like our subsequent mourning, was at a distance but our very distance provided not only different but, in this case, privileged insights into the global phenomenon that was mourning Diana.

In an increasingly multicultural and post-colonial Australia, the lives of British princesses do not have the same significance for political institutions as Diana's death proved they can still have for British ones. Unlike in Britain, Diana's life and death did not gel with the agenda of a major political party. Nor did the public outpouring of grief over her death have implications for debates about national identity or the 'feminization' of politics as it did in Britain. For us, Diana was predominantly an international media icon, whose story could be appropriated by a wide variety of groups and individuals. Sometimes these responses had particularly Australian overtones, on other occasions they did not. The groups claiming an affiliation with Diana themselves often had transnational identities, for example as 'mothers' or as 'queers'. What was one theme in British responses, that is Diana as an embodiment of media 'excess' and 'surfeit' – a 'living simulacrum . . . a copy without an original, a multiple personality with no "real" Diana to which her public could turn' (Wilson 1997: 140), became the main form of public appropriation of Diana in Australia. The lack of a clear government or institutional discourse facilitated multiple appropriations.

By contrast, Beatrix Campbell has argued that the sexual politics of Diana's treatment by the royal family, particularly by her husband, the future king, contributed to a new wave of republican sentiment in Britain, despite attempts by the Labour government to harness her death to the cause of modernizing the monarchy (Campbell 1998). That was not the case in Australia, where the sexual politics of Diana's life and death took other

142

forms. Liberal (i.e. conservative) Prime Minister, and monarchist, John Howard was anxious to distance Diana's death from the monarchy, claiming that 'our responses to and the emotions caused by these tragic events have absolutely nothing to do with the attitudes we may have about the role of the monarchy or the royal family in our society' (*House of Representatives Hansard*, 1 September 1997: 7191). Labor Leader of the Opposition and republican Kim Beazley agreed by default, saying that he was surprised by how much he missed Diana given that 'issues affecting the British royal family are not the first thing on my mind every morning' (*House of Representatives Hansard*, 1 September 1997: 7192).

A *Bulletin* Morgan poll showed that support for a republic had increased to fifty-three per cent of respondents, a three per cent increase on the previous high point in November 1994 and a six per cent increase on a poll taken the previous June. Twenty-five per cent of female respondents and seventeen per cent of male respondents said that they thought less of the royal family after the death of Diana. However, the important point is that eighty-eight per cent of respondents 'said that Princess Diana's death made no difference to whether they would vote for a republic or not' (*The Bulletin*, 16 September 1997: 16–17; Morgan poll, finding no. 3018). Undoubtedly Diana's death did have some influence on attitudes to the royal family and to republicanism but a three percentage point increase over a previous high suggests that the impact was not particularly significant. Indeed, Beazley's parliamentary condolence speech suggests that a common republican response was to miss Diana as a person, a supporter of good causes, a mother and a media icon rather than as a member of the British royal family. Downplaying the royal connection became some republicans' ultimate revenge.

Howard too played down her connections with royalty seeing Diana much more as a beautiful, stylish woman who was an object of intense fascination and a performer of good works (*House of Representatives Hansard*, 1 September 1997: 7191). Diana's sexualized persona and media icon status did not mesh with Howard's agenda of reinforcing comfortable 1950s femininity. Nor did her support for marginalized groups such as the victims of AIDS, her fights with the royal family, or her love for a Middle Eastern, Muslim boyfriend gel with his political agenda of reassuring conservative, male, heterosexual Anglo-Celtic voters terrified of change (see Johnson 1997).

Howard's agenda in respect to social inclusiveness and the cultural significance of the British monarchy was precisely the opposite to Blair's. Blair depicted Diana as being representative of a transformed, socially inclusive, late-twentieth-century monarchy and a caring society. Howard wished to use the monarchy as a symbol of nostalgia, certainty and continuing Anglo-Celtic dominance in Australia's increasingly multicultural society. In fact, as Mandy Thomas's study of Vietnamese Australian responses shows, understandings of Diana's life and death were being mediated through a wide range of cultural meanings (Thomas 1997). None the less, Australian Labor could not use a member of the British royal family to endorse social diversity because to do so would not only undermine the republican cause but would also privilege Anglo-Celtic identifications above other ethnic identifications. Diana's positioning was therefore very different in Australian and British political discourse. Furthermore, her supposed significance often boiled down to her media profile. Prominent republican businesswoman Janet Holmes à Court remarked that, if Diana had lived, 'she probably would have been an asset to the monarchist cause in Australia' because of her media status. Diana had been transformed 'into an international celebrity . . . largely due to her ability to manipulate the media' (*Sun-Herald*, 2 November 1997: 55).

The nearest the Australian gender politics of Diana came to an institutional or party-political form was in debates over the public image and media treatment of female politicians. Diana, as a female media icon straddling the public and private spheres, came to represent a touchstone for Australian female political figures with a high media profile. Some of these figures seem more appropriate than others. Diana Simmonds's (1998) book, *Diana the Hunted*, was launched by Cheryl Kernot, who also endorses the book on the back cover. Kernot, often ironically known as 'Saint Cheryl', is a high-profile, left of centre political figure – a consummate media performer and former leader of the Australian Democrats who defected in a blaze of publicity to join the Australian Labor Party. Kernot's private life, particularly a relationship some twenty years ago with one of her ex-school-students, has been subject to intense media scrutiny. While her presence at the book launch was an example of a sympathetic comparison with Princess Diana, other comparisons between the two have been more hostile. Media commentator Helen Verlander complains that 'Big-haired blondes can get away with a lot, whether they be princesses or politicians'. Verlander goes on to argue that 'the image of Kernot has a lot in common with that of the late Diana, Princess of Wales. Both were/are Teflon princesses – blonde and glamorous with big hair. They have both demonstrated the ability to say or do virtually anything without any blame ever sticking to them' – including, in Kernot's case, fundamentally betraying the political party she led (*Australian*, 6 January 1998: 1).

However, at least Kernot is a long-term advocate of social tolerance and diversity. More surprising perhaps has been the association of Diana with Pauline Hanson, the enormously controversial, and highly sexualized, face of right-wing populism who has helped to stir the Australian race debate with her statements against multiculturalism, government benefits for Aboriginal people and Asian immigration (Johnson 1998). Paul Sheehan, himself one of the populist writers in the race debate, says that 'right from the start' the political phenomenon of Pauline Hanson 'was propelled by a ferocious level of attention from the media, which accorded her the news status of a redneck Princess Diana' (Sheehan 1998: 155). De-Anne Kelly, a sympathetic MP from a rival party, acknowledges the comparison in terms of media attention but sees Hanson's response as totally different from Diana's. Kelly writes that when she first met Hanson: 'She'd had a terrible time. She'd been disendorsed, she'd lost her privacy, but she didn't run and cry; she was no Princess Di. She put up with all the personal barbs and never responded in a personal way – never, ever. And people respected her for that' (*Canberra Times*, Panorama section, 27 June 1998: 12). Meanwhile, Hanson's supporters seem happy to call Hanson 'our princess' while also comparing her to Queen Boudicca and feminist television icon Xena the Warrior Princess (*Sun-Herald*, 7 June 1998: 5).

However, it is not just the degree of media attention that the two are seen to have in common. Critical media commentators have dubbed Hanson 'the People's Politician' and 'The Princess of Wails' – thereby playing on Diana's and Hanson's apparent vulnerability as well as Hanson's appeal to those unhappy with the current direction of Australian society (*Australian*, 20–1 June 1998: 22). The combination of vulnerability and sexuality is seen to be particularly crucial. Noting the proximity of Diana's death and Pauline Hanson's electoral success in the Queensland state election, Shelley Gare writes that 'even as the scent of victory is still flaring in our Pauline's pug nose, the first bonking rumours are spreading . . . Of all the qualities a women must have to become an icon, a haze of sexuality – overt, covert, concocted or otherwise – is indispensable. So is the quiver of vulnerability' (*Australian*, 20–1 June 1998, 22). Other commentators also emphasize the comparisons in terms of vulnerability. According to feminist historian Miriam Dixson, 'if a woman is potent, playing the game means she does well to also be sweet, suffering and vulnerable . . . Di had a wonderful mix of it, and so does Pauline Hanson.' Prominent feminist company director Wendy McCarthy makes a similar point: 'What you are getting with Di and Hanson is the appeal of their vulnerability. They're prepared to relate in these domestic female homespun ways, and encouraging people to think that's enough' (cited by Gare, *Australian*, 20–1 June 1998: 22). It is noticeable that: sexuality and vulnerability are traditional feminine attributes in combination, rather than attributes that subvert conventional conceptions of femininity. Diana is not being extolled as a feminist icon here – someone who overcame her status as wronged prince's wife and bulimia victim to become a prominent figure supporting AIDS victims and calling for the abolition of landmines – but as the exact opposite.

However, once one moves beyond issues of vulnerability and sexuality, the comparison between Hanson and Diana seems particularly perverse given their opposing positions on issues of social diversity and the fact that Diana was not an elected politician. A far more obvious British comparison for Hanson is that made by journalist Diana Simmonds, coincidentally the author of *Diana the Hunted* (as well as two best-selling lesbian romance novels). Simmonds has argued that the gendered, derisory way in which Hanson is treated by the media and opposing parliamentarians is remarkably similar to the way in which Margaret Thatcher was treated, and sees it as a common response to prominent, but highly controversial, female politicians (*Bulletin*, 30 June 1998: 30). Thatcher too was known for her homespun references to groceries and balancing the household budget. Whichever comparison is most appropriate, the association between Diana, Kernot and Hanson accords Diana a political status that she was not accorded in life. In Australia, Diana's political status has been derived not from the republican debate or, as the Hanson comparison shows, from her position as a supporter of social diversity, but from her position as a prominent female media icon. Any prominent female public figure with sexual allure who receives intrusive media attention is likely to be compared to Diana – whatever their politics and whatever the commentator's attitudes to Diana or to the woman being compared with her. The references are just as likely to be favourable as unfavourable, a point which once again displays the multiple readings of the life and death of Diana.

The politics of grieving were also positioned differently in Australia. In Britain, public outpourings of grief were seen to be undermining traditional conceptions of British national character (the stiff upper lip) and heralding the coming of a more caring, feminized, post-Thatcherite society, associated with the Blair Labour government (*The Times* 1, 4, 5, 6 September 1997; Wilson 1997: 140–3). Indeed, Blair was subsequently called upon to defend the public outpouring of grief following Diana's death from right-wing accusations that it was an 'emotionally correct', 'fake sentimentality ' (BBC News, 19 April 1998). However, mass displays of emotion did not have the same political significance in Australia given that public expressions of grief are probably far more usual in Australian than in British culture. For example, it is not particularly unusual for relatively macho Australian politicians, such as former Labor Prime Minister Bob Hawke, to cry openly during emotional interviews or public speeches. In Diana's case, Liberal (conservative) Prime Minister Howard extolled 'the outpouring of emotion and sadness from so many people within the mainstream of our society' as evidence of 'the continued force of the human personality in a world that is meant to be increasingly depersonalised' (*House of Representatives Hansard*, 1 September 1997: 1791). Since the 'mainstream' in Howard rhetoric represents the forces of conservatism, opposed to 'political correctness' and 'special interest' groups, Howard is here endorsing the process of mourning as a legitimate manifestation of common humanity and popular grief.

The subversive politics of mourning, Australian style, was to take other forms, such as the outpouring of grief by white Australians during 'National Sorry Day' for the 'stolen generations' of Aboriginal children – children

Fig. 10.1 Johnathon Yolanduy, of the Gupapungu clan, holds a wreath for Diana during a traditional funeral in Arnhem Land, Northern Australia. Photo courtesy *Northern Territory News*

forcibly taken from their families to be inculcated into white Australian values. Then the federal government refused to make an official apology or endorse the public expression of grief which formed part of the larger reconciliation process between colonial settler and Aboriginal Australia. None the less, several hundred thousand ordinary white Australians signed Sorry Books, wore Sorry Ribbons, participated in public 'Sorry' events, or made their own personal statements (such as some Adelaide bus drivers who changed their bus destination signs to read 'Sorry'). Similarly, it was Sorry Day, rather than grief over Diana's death, that led to accusations regarding a feminization of Australian politics. The conservative Minister for Aboriginal Affairs denounced male Labor politicians who wept in Parliament while reading accounts of the stolen children as 'wimps' (*Sydney Morning Herald*, 27 May 1998).

While Diana died the year before National Sorry Day, journalist Tess Lawrence claims that Diana was 'aware of things such as the stolen generation' and 'felt she might have been able to do something to build the bridge between black and white' (*New Idea*, 27 September 1997: 9). If so, Diana was displaying considerable hubris, given the complexities of the reconciliation process, and the need for it primarily to involve white Australian beneficiaries of Aboriginal genocide and dispossession. None the less, she could bridge the gap between white and black sufficiently for Aboriginal Australians to also mourn her death. On Milingimbi, one of the very remote Northern Territory Crocodile Islands, members of fourteen language clans living on the island united to hold an Aboriginal funeral for her. As part of the traditional mourning process, women exchanged 'Diana stories' (*Northern Territory News*, 9 September 1997: 27).

As we shall see, the ability of ordinary Australians, from diverse backgrounds, to tell 'Diana stories' was an important part of the process of mourning Diana. The following section explores more personal meanings and appropriations of Diana's death.

Telling Diana stories

Almost a year after Diana's death, the Australian press announces the resale of her 'old bachelor pad in South Kensington' (*Sun-Herald*, 7 June 1998: 60). This is to strike a chord in memory for the authors of this piece. As travelling Australians, we are occasional guests of friends who live in the block of mansion flats that includes Diana's former 'pad'. So, now we are tempted – retrospectively, and from a distance – to reinstate a homely connection with Diana. Here Diana becomes not only that figure of youth, innocence and (moneyed/titled) femininity, awkwardly posing for press photographs in the early months of 1981, but also a lead player in our own fiction of domesticity and neighbourliness. Diana, we might imagine, is the wholesome bachelor girl downstairs, sharing her three-bedroom flat with girlfriends, working in a nearby kindergarten and shopping during weekends on Old Brompton Road. (In fact, we never met her, though other residents claimed they had.) So, for a moment, at the intersection of memory and fantasy, we reposition Diana in 'our' adopted local. Here Diana becomes domesticated, and intimately known.

Claims of continued intimacy and, hence, grief at its sudden loss echo in the personal tributes published by the Australian media during the week following Diana's death. For example, Cathy de Vriend says: 'From the moment I saw her on TV there was some sort of connection . . . I used to copy her hairstyles and dress like her. I loved the way she helped people. She wasn't afraid to touch Aids patients or anything like that. She was a wonderful mother and I really admired her for that' (*Age Online*, 7 September 1997). So, simultaneously, Diana is paraded as glamorous star, miracle worker, mother. As one woman mourns and remembers another, multiple identities of femininity are on offer, to be raided in the name of intimacy and 'connection' ('I saw her . . . I used to copy her . . . I really admired her . . .'). Furthermore, that blissful state of 'knowing Diana' as a spectacular, highly mediated, imaginary figure pre dates de Vriend's meeting the 'real' Diana at St Vincent's Hospital, Sydney, in 1996, and constitutes an already sense of connectedness that the brief meeting could only confirm.

Presumably, the greater the feelings of 'connection', the greater the grief. It is here that the gendered forms of grieving are worth unravelling. At the time of Diana's death, the Australian press comments on the significance of this event for women, in particular. 'A lot of our female staff were deeply affected', reports George Bedwani, general manager of three major Sydney hotels. 'We called in grief and trauma counsellors to help the staff deal with it' (*Who Weekly*, 22 September 1997, 42). 'I didn't know her' says commentator Zoe Carides, an actor and journalist, and astonished by the extent of her own weeping. 'But like the rest of the world I felt I did . . . I take my kid to school the day after, and the other mothers are talking about it. We discover we all had the same reaction. A lot of our mothers had called, and we'd been grateful for their unashamed grief, which gave licence to our own' (*Sydney Morning Herald*, 6 September 1997: 1–2). Meanwhile, six months after the funeral, David Salinger, a Sydney trichologist, reports treating women patients suffering from hair loss, as well as weight loss 'as a result of trauma associated with the death of Diana' (*Sydney Morning Herald*, 16 January 1998, Stay in Touch section, 1). Tears, trauma, bodies in shock – is this iconic femininity under threat, its losses to be mourned?

Certainly, in Australia, as in Britain, the extent and depth of feeling that Diana's death arouses catches many by surprise. Father Tony Doherty, Dean of St Mary's Cathedral in Sydney, confronted with tearful parishioners, telephoning for grief counselling, comments: 'There's a lot we're grieving for that we don't understand' (*Australian*, 4 September 1997: 7). Zoe Carides, on the other hand, is less puzzled: 'I know who she'd slept with

... I knew she'd suffered that familiar female curse – an eating disorder. She, like me, was a mother; she, like me, was a good one, if slightly unconventional about it. For God's sake, we were almost the same age' (*Sydney Morning Herald*, 6 September 1997: 1). Knowing Diana, she implies, was the same as knowing oneself.

Nevertheless, despite women's 'tears for a shared life and a shared loss' shed while with mothers, with female friends, and with friends as young mothers, Carides returns to the question of the gendering of grief: 'A woman friend told me today that all the women at her work were deeply sad but the men were not as affected. Indeed a male friend of mine said it was like coming home to find the couch had gone – a shock but not devastating' (*Sydney Morning Herald*, 6 September 1997: 2).

Of course, Carides is not denying examples of male grieving, especially those beamed to us via global television networks in the days after Diana's death, and during the heart-stopping solemnity of her funeral. Nevertheless, Carides muses, 'perhaps she [Diana] did mean more to women' (*Sydney Morning Herald*, 6 September 1997: 2). Alternatively, is Diana simply to be reduced to an unexpected absence in the furniture – an almost taken-for-granted fixture in the narrative of everyday life? In contrast to the figure that attracts high mourning for quintessential femininity, Diana is now reworked as a 'shocking' object of disruption to our familiar routines and practices. Ultimately, like the couch, she is expendable, or at least, replaceable.

Consider this, for example, as a replacement scenario – a local simulacrum of Diana's funeral. About six months later in Sydney, a young policeman is stabbed to death in the course of duty. During the 'extraordinary public mourning that his death aroused', crowds lined the streets and 'tossed proteas, daisies and gladioli onto the roof of the hearse' and 'struggling for some way to mark . . . [their] appreciation of the 28-year-old officer, broke into applause'. Meanwhile, the image of the policeman's beautiful, young widow with her two small children is a poignant one, and 'there were many in tears, or fighting them back, among the [police] honour guard flanking the [family]' (*Sydney Morning Herald*, 6 March 1998: 1). Masculinity, mateship and service . . . fatherhood, widowhood and the vulnerability of children . . . senseless, violent and premature death – there are endless possibilities here for local re-enactments.

However, not all women (or men either, for that matter) want to weep. Kate Legge, a Sydney journalist, confesses to some bewilderment at the spectacle of the 'world . . . in mourning' and at the 'extravagant grief' expressed for Diana. In a mirror-image opposite of Carides's account, Legge is astonished by the performance of a babysitter crying for a week, or enquiries at the school gate about how she herself was 'coping' ('"With what?" I asked'). She then turns to her female friends for confirmation of 'feeling disconnected from the cult of Diana'. Legge concludes:

We did not identify with her or see her as a symbol of modern women, juggling home, family and job. She was beautiful, stylish and glamorous, and performed her civic duties with exceptional success, but she lived on another planet, far removed from ours – a world of butlers, valets, palaces, psychics, pop stars, paparazzi, and 'people'. And if her life wallpapered our lives, we managed to maintain a distance and resisted developing an unhealthy obsession with her image.

(*Australian*, 12 September 1997: 13)

So, in contrast to those claiming to 'know Diana', Legge readily disavows such knowledge. For her, Planet Diana is a Baudrillardian simulacrum, a world of mirrors constantly reflecting the excesses of Hollywood-style glamour, wealth, passions and 'personalities'. There is little to be learnt here for narratives of everyday Australian femininity in the late 1990s and its complex negotiations of 'public' and 'private' positioning. Curiously though, despite this emotional distancing from the global Diana romance, Legge at the same time resituates Diana in homely territory, reconfiguring this fantasy figure as mundane and domesticated. As the 'wallpaper' of our lives, Diana is simply *there* – a novelty at first, perhaps, a distraction, but ultimately 'fading into the woodwork'.

At the end of the day, perhaps it is the television set that presents an even more obvious motif for Diana's presence in the everyday life of Australian living rooms? Legge continues: 'People talk about Charles and Di and Wills and Harry and Dodi as if they were personal friends, as if we own them – a common occurrence in the global village, where we are better acquainted with Cindy and Cher . . . than neighbours or relatives' (*Australian*, 12 September 1997: 13). Intimacy then has become a virtual intimacy, tied to a particular mode of looking. From the familiar spaces of our homes, we can witness a star performance on a global scale. Meanwhile, we exercise the skills of 'knowing' – the textual practices of reading the screen that ensure legitimate membership in late twentieth-century spectatorship. Of course, in this performance of virtual knowing, one is not obliged to choose between competing figures of Diana – Diana the Domesticated, Diana, Queen of Hearts or Diana, Star of the Stage and Screen. Meanings of Diana are flexible indeed. Simultaneously, references to the local, the homely, the material 'stuff' of everyday life and the reassuring presence of mothers, can be incorporated along with their very opposites – the global, the virtual and the production of femininity as spectacle. At home with television, we find our 'connection' to Diana is assured.

To change the focus to a different repertoire of Diana stories, it is time to leave the comforts of suburban living rooms for the night life of cities. Despite images of the sunshine of an early autumn morning in London, for

Australians, the funeral of Diana was at night – or rather, our viewing of it occurred at night. Furthermore, it was Saturday night – the traditional night of frenzied activity for inner-city venues in larger cities, the high point in trading for pubs, clubs, bars, games arcades, restaurants, theatres and cinemas. However, this Saturday, the press reported, was quite different. In Melbourne, for example, there was an eerie silence and stillness in many of the dance clubs. 'It was a very strange night', says Patrick Dromi of Inflation Nightclub, where patrons eschewed the dance floor for the television. 'It was clear what people wanted to do, and that was to watch the funeral' (*Who Weekly*, 22 September 1997: 42).

Mourning, however, requires 'proper' watching – 'proper' behaviour at the shrine of television or in other spaces of everyday life. For example, a week after the funeral, 'Cameron', a member of the Sydney gay community, claimed he was 'extremely proud of my fellow queers' when the host of a drag show, attempting to tell Princess Diana jokes, was 'hissed and booed till she gave up'. The writer continues: 'I am not a Royalist, but Princess Diana deserves respect from us. If it were not for Di the straight community would still be scared of touching people with HIV/AIDS . . . Shame on the person who forgets' (Letter to the Editor, *Capital Q Weekly*, 1997: 6).

Here Diana's royal identity is to be exchanged for her identity as icon of humanitarianism, an identity that is able to cross boundaries of class, gender, ethnicity and sexuality to connect with identities that are marginalized and 'deviant'. Meanings of nation, state or monarchy then have little place in these identifications of Diana as angel of mercy, or in these calls, on behalf of the collective, to observe due respect. Instead it is in the name of 'queerness' that 'Cameron' (via Internet) rallies 'fellow queers' to 'think about who they are . . . and the charity work . . . [Diana] did for us when no other well known person would' (Letter to the Editor, *Capital Q Weekly*, 19 September 1997: 6).

Once again, however, not everyone is touched, not everyone wants to watch. Hermione Quirke, a columnist for *Lesbians on the Loose* [*LOTL*], describes attending a gay venue on the night of Diana's funeral, an occasion advertised as an opportunity to 'join others in remembering and grieving Diana'. Nevertheless, while 'the sea of gay men around the television swells', the writer reflects on how little acknowledgement is given to the labour and caring of ordinary women, and how infrequently this community expresses its grief. In this context, the writer sees mourning Diana not only as an act of excess but almost one of obscenity:

> But now I am expected to mourn the loss of a straight woman who lived a life of extraordinary privilege and who dared to touch a man with HIV. How is it that we are grateful for so little? . . . And why do we devalue our own grief for those we have met, have talked to, have known, have loved but have lost, by embracing the

carefully crafted images of Diana – the People's Princess, the
Queen of Hearts and now, the most mythical (and profitable) of
all her incarnations, the Lady of the Lake.

(*LOTL*, October 1997: 13)

In contrast to 'real' people and 'real' personal losses, Diana can only appear
as a fabrication, a commodity, a monumental distraction from a community's political projects.

A month later, other readers from the lesbian community responded. 'I
found the article an insult' wrote one. '[Diana] may have been born
privileged and into high society but she chose to give herself to the
less fortunate and I believe she was sincere' (Letter to the Editor,
LOTL, November 1997: 16). Another accused the author of the article
of hypocrisy for attending the gay venue as an act of grieving, but failing
to express her own 'misguided thoughts and opinions at that time' (16).
So, while the figure of Diana becomes an icon of mourning for members of
gay and lesbian communities – a 'queer' appropriation, in fact, of heterosexual femininity – it is also a figure that is in dispute. Contested
meanings of Diana and their significance for collective identity produce
not only diverse and multiple appropriations of the Diana myth but also
competing moments of refusal and dissent.

The telling of Diana stories continued. However, it could be claimed that
this telling had both a transnational and a peculiarly Australian flavour. In
Australia, the figure of Diana did not have the same institutional role as in
Britain, nor was it incorporated into a party's political agenda. Hence,
mourning Diana's death did not involve redefining the people's space in
the same way as in Britain. This mourning did not constitute the 'official'
speaking of nationhood, multiculturalism and the erasure of difference, as it
did in Britain. Instead, in Australia, the people – individuals, groups,
members of transnational communities such as 'indigenous people',
'women', 'mothers', 'queers' – had spaces to tell their own Diana stories,
without an orthodox 'public' discourse acting to marginalize and suppress
them. Likewise, despite the flood of syndicated material from the international media, there was a diversity of local media stories. Indeed, mourning
was less managed, less mobilized, more diffuse and open to other 'connections'. Of course, this kind of 'nineties' storytelling will continue, but its
focus is less certain. Meanwhile, at a distance, and positioned before the
shrine of television, we await a new performance and retell the unhappy
ending to a very nineties' fairytale.

Once upon a time, in the green countryside of England, lived a little
girl called Lady Diana. Her father, Lord Spencer, was a rich farmer.
They lived in Park House on the royal estate of Sandringham, next
door to the holiday home of the Queen. The grand old house was

surrounded by gardens and orchards, and forests and fields, which in summer were yellow with ripening corn.

(Stammers 1997: 1 – Australian children's storybook account of Diana's life and death)

Acknowledgements

Our thanks to Ann Curthoys and John Docker for some wonderful dinners discussing Diana.

References

Campbell, Beatrix (1998) *Diana, Princess of Wales: How Sexual Politics Shook the Monarchy*, London: Women's Press.

Johnson, Carol (1997) 'Visiting the Margins: Revenge, Transgression or Incorporation – An Australian Engagement with Theories of Identity', *Theory and Event*, no. 3 1. (Johns Hopkins electronic journal) http://128.220.50.88/journals/theory_&_event/v001/1.3johnson.html

Johnson, Carol (1998) 'Pauline Hanson and One Nation', in Hans-Georg Betz and Stefan Immerfall (eds) *New Politics of the Right*, New York: St Martin's Press: 211–18.

Sheehan, Paul (1998) *Among the Barbarians: The Dividing of Australia,* Sydney: Random House.

Simmonds, Diana (1998) *Diana the Hunted: Assassination! Fascination! Australia's Love–Hate Affair with the Royals,* Leichhardt: Pluto.

Stammers, Kay (1997) *Princess Diana: A True Fairytale*, Port Melbourne: Lothian.

Thomas, Mandy (1997) '"Beautiful Woman Dies: Diana in Vietnam and in the Diaspora"', in Re:public (Ien Ang, Ruth Barcan *et al.*) (eds) *Planet Diana: Cultural Studies and Global Mourning*, Kingswood, New South Wales: Research Centre of Intercommunal Studies, University of Western Sydney, Nepean: 149–54.

Wilson, Elizabeth (1997) 'The Unbearable Lightness of Diana', *New Left Review*, no. 22: 136–45.

11

I'D RATHER BE THE PRINCESS THAN THE QUEEN!

Mourning Diana as a gay icon

William J. Spurlin

Before Diana's death, I prided myself in being rather smug about anything particularly royal. I found the Windsors an incredibly dull lot striving to maintain a sense of substantive purpose in the world by hopelessly clinging to outdated trappings of monarchy – ritualized ceremonies, the Queen's Christmas broadcast, stuffy public appearances, ostentatious palaces, shallow pretensions of happy family life. Frivolous Charles trying desperately to be taken seriously, dowdy Elizabeth, cranky Philip, Fergie's careless flaunting of royal wealth, and Diana without a single O level – except for Prince Edward, long rumoured to be gay, the Windsors had little appeal for me.

Diana's death in 1997 forced me to look at her again, critically this time. A good deal of my earlier cynicism for the other royals had been heightened to contempt following their reaction to Diana's death; recall, for instance, the Queen's uptight, almost angry, scowl upon first returning from Balmoral after Diana's death as she inspected the floral bouquets scattered in front of Buckingham Palace left in Diana's memory, an expression of displeasure that seemed to say, 'Who made this mess?' Though I didn't pay much attention to Diana's life when she was alive, I became rather morbidly addicted to news reports about her death, and later, to the television narratives about her life. Like many others, I, too, visited the British Consulate in New York in the days before Diana's funeral – waiting in a long queue that wrapped around the block as if a new box-office hit film had just opened, struggling to etch thoughtful words in the elegant black leather condolence book once my turn finally came, trying not to be noticed as I turned back the pages to glimpse at what others before me had written, chatting with tearful mourners, some British, some American, some from other parts of the world, and, with my partner, laying down our own small bouquet of orange daylilies, yellow daisies and violet chrysanthemums whose colours, along with others on the already flower-enshrined sidewalk, captured the balmy September afternoon sunlight just outside the austere Third Avenue building. Why was I suddenly 'hooked' on Diana when the system of which she was part and, for most of her life, valued, seems so repressive to gay people – patriarchal family life enmeshed in primogeniture, obligatory heterosexual marriage and procreative sexuality tied to the production of heirs, the suppression of one's desires for the good of the family, the monarchy, and the state, and rigidly prescribed gender roles that reinvent and help sustain oppressive binary oppositions?[1]

Is it possible for Diana to be a gay icon? I had once hoped that it would be Edward who would provide the initial queer trajectory for (re-)reading the current royal family; ironically, I have come to believe, it was Diana who did that and much more.[2] Her own sexual identity is not at issue; rather, it is her monumentality that enables resistant and critical rereadings. For me, Diana's death captured and reshaped her image in my mind, so much so that she nearly became more mythic than real. During most of her adult life, except for that brief period following her separation from Charles, the queer aspects of Diana's image were difficult to ascertain as they were often socially obscured by official images of her connections to royalty. Diana's betrothal to Charles, her wedding, the birth of the heir and the spare, her official functions as Princess of Wales, her divorce, and even her attempts to find happiness outside of the realm of Buckingham Palace positioned her in some relation to the royal family (and therefore in relation to its personification of heteronormativity, at least in the present age) even as she tried to escape it. These events served, initially at least, to camouflage who Diana was, or could be, to her many audiences, and the ways in which her life could be read through multiple, sometimes contradictory, trajectories. This does not imply, of course, that icons, in this case gay icons, whatever their sexuality, need to be dead to fascinate; obviously such is not the case with contemporary living icons like Bette Midler, Liza Minnelli, Madonna, or Barbra Streisand, to name a few, who, in their own way, signify as 'gay', and/or as 'lesbian', and/or quite possibly as 'queer', whether through camp, through taking on the persona of the 'bad girl' or through their status as 'diva', all in ways that Diana clearly did not. If we consider a cultural icon as that legible grid on to which our fantasies, desires and aspirations are projected as a means to their conscious expression, given her brief life, I believe that it is predominately, though perhaps not exclusively, after her death that queer identification with Diana's life, as it has been (and continues to be) represented, could occur, not identification with her actual life, which was knowable only to a relatively small circle of family and close friends, but her life *as depicted*, as represented. Diana becomes fixed in our systems of reference, but, as Wayne Koestenbaum points out, an icon is more of an *idea* than a person; sometimes the icon and actual person converge, sometimes they do not (Koestenbaum 1996: 4). We respond to Diana, then, as signifier, which we try to fix as it circulates in culture, whereas its signified remains endlessly deferred. But similar to other cultural icons, strategies of identification with the admired person are often so intense that the distinction between self and Other becomes blurred. How then might Diana be read queerly?

Wayne Koestenbaum's work on Jacqueline Kennedy Onassis has helped to set an important precedent for studying cultural icons, especially the ways in which they are created, represented and read, and sustained largely through the various apparatuses of the modern media. He writes:

> We called Jackie an icon because she glowed, because she seemed ceaseless, because she resided in a worshipped, aura-filled niche. We called Jackie an icon because *her image* was frequently and influentially reproduced. . . . We called Jackie an icon because her story provided a foundation for our own stories, and because her face, and the sometimes glamorous, sometimes tragic turns her life took, were lodged in our systems of thought and reference, as if she were a concept, a numeral, a virtue, or a universal tendency, like rainfall or drought.
>
> (Koestenbaum 1996: 4; emphasis added)

What is interesting is not only the similar way Diana can be interpreted as a (gay) icon but the parallel ways in which both women functioned as icons. Though Jackie was often conferred token royal status in the United States as the 'Queen' of the new Camelot that characterized the Kennedy campaign and carried over into JFK's years in the White House, the actual lives of Jackie and Diana, being a generation apart, were lived quite differently. At the same time, it must be acknowledged that the time between John F. Kennedy's assassination and Jackie's own death in 1994 allowed a more significant period for Jackie's life to be represented while she was alive. But it is possible to think about the representations of Jackie's and Diana's lived lives in parallel ways. For example, after President Kennedy's assassination in 1963, Jackie no longer held a legislated public or political position (Koestenbaum 1996: 137) except as a former First Lady; similarly, following her divorce from Prince Charles in 1996, Diana relinquished her status and rank within the inner circle of the royal family (though she maintained her other titles) – yet both women went on to possess legitimacy more fully *in their own right*. Though widowhood and divorce respectively brought both women closer to the status of private citizens, they remained in the public eye, still able to transcend the domain of the familiar and everyday. Once 'on their own', the need to represent them, to see their lives depicted, became more intense than when they held their 'official' positions. In other words, their status as icons, as cultural signifiers, is marked by an *over-determination* that exceeds and is not reducible to their signified positions through which they became public figures in the first place. Never did the now infamous paparazzi follow Diana more than when she was separated and later divorced from Charles, and while Jackie deliberately sought privacy after the JFK assassination, and more so after the death of Aristotle Onassis, she became even more of an enigma to the American imagination and to audiences worldwide. Their connections to being First Lady of the United States and Her Royal Highness, the Princess of Wales, cannot be totally severed from Jackie's or Diana's status as cultural icons; indeed, we could even proffer that Jackie 'came out' at the JFK Inauguration in 1961 as did Diana at her wedding twenty years later as these respective events made their titles official and forever secured their celebrity positions. But their capacity to signify culturally is not reducible to those originary social positions. For this reason, I must extend Koestenbaum's point about Jackie to include Diana when he suggests, quite insightfully, that Jackie (like Diana) is 'remembered not so much for what she *was* but for what she invoked and catalyzed' (Koestenbaum 1996: 272).

Yet, in looking back from our present perspective, especially in the case of Diana, their monumentality is evident even in their official capacities, prior to the JFK assassination, prior to Diana's separation and divorce from the Prince of Wales. In looking at photographs of the two couples, it is Jackie and Diana who dominate the photographic space in spite of the fact that it was their husbands who held the higher, more powerful social position. It is almost as if the materiality of the bodies of these two women physically operate somehow to refute the subordinate, feminized role socially constructed for them as wives of 'important men' like the President of the United States and the heir to the British throne; Jackie's and Diana's bodies exude an energy that claims the camera's centre. Along these lines, Koestenbaum describes how Jackie was able effortlessly to upstage JFK in his dark suits, his rather sleepy look, his gaze away from the camera in contrast to Jackie's sleek outfits (in fuchsia suits, her signature pillbox hats, her sleek 1960s hairdos), her direct gaze at the lens, 'a body that wants to move and to act, rather than be photographed or emblematic' (Koestenbaum 1996: 118).

In photographs of Diana and Charles together, one notices a more gradual claiming of the centre of photographic space by Diana, in that early photographs of the couple, as Sir Roy Strong has pointed out, were carefully controlled (i.e. constructed) images of what the Palace conceived a Princess of Wales should look like – for the most part, the romantic English rose look, downcast face and eyes and dressed in 'billowing tides of soft diaphanous fabrics' (Strong 1997: 133). From the time of her marriage until the birth of her second son, we see Diana largely as the shy and demure wife trying *not* to be at the camera's centre, though its lens seems more obsessed with her than with her husband. Even in the photo of the newlywed couple honeymooning at Balmoral in August 1981, Charles stands, fully decked in Scottish kilt, while Diana is seated behind him, holding his hand. Though

Charles is erect, towering above and occupying more physical space in the photograph than his wife, our gaze nonetheless reverts to Diana. Most of her biographies indicate how uncomfortable she was in front of the cameras, especially in those early years, yet, in spite of suffering from bulimia at the time, she, similar to Jackie, unselfconsciously and effortlessly upstages her husband in his drab suits or full military garb (or kilts, as the case may be!). Koestenbaum, in speaking of Jackie and JFK, interestingly notes that prior to the 1970s, when gay male standards of beauty began to enter the mainstream media, as in the Calvin Klein ads, male escorts of famous women need not have been attractive; a double standard existed which demanded that the woman be beautiful but forgave the man his physical flaws (Koestenbaum 1996: 144–5). Though Koestenbaum is speaking of JFK, the same seems to be true for Diana and Charles in the 1980s and early 1990s; Charles's body appears as uptight, rigid and aloof, most likely according to royal protocol. It isn't that Charles simply isn't physically attractive; his body exudes desexualization, as well as a lack of charisma, in stark contrast to Diana's. During the couple's first official visit to Wales in 1981, when each would take a side of the street to greet the crowds, audible groans could be heard from the spectators on the side of the street chosen by Charles, thereby expressing their disappointment at not being able to see Diana up close, a trend which would continue as Diana's popularity grew, much to the consternation of Charles and his family. But in the early photographs of Diana and Charles, despite attempts of the Palace to place Charles more in the limelight as the Prince of Wales and future king alongside his decorous wife, the photographic space, including that occupied by Charles, is organized around Diana. Like Jackie in photos with JFK, Diana is the Barthesian *punctum*. In contrast to the *studium* of a photograph, which Roland Barthes describes as the cultural, conscious participation 'in the figures, the faces, the gestures, the settings, the actions' (Barthes 1981: 26), the *punctum* pricks, ruptures, pierces the *studium* (Barthes 1981: 26–7); while the *studium* refers to the political and historical contexts surrounding the photograph, the photographic *punctum* is absolutely personal – it changes our reading, it overwhelms us and causes us to *linger*. Photographs play an important role in constructing cultural icons in the contemporary world. As Susan Sontag reminds us: 'The camera makes reality atomic, manageable, and opaque . . . to see something in the form of a photograph is to encounter a potential object of fascination. . . . Photographs, which cannot themselves explain anything, are inexhaustible invitations to deduction, speculation, and fantasy' (Sontag 1977: 23). Diana, photographed with Charles, pierces, ruptures, and perhaps wounds the fantasy of the picture-perfect heterosexual couple; the spectator's attention seems drawn invariably to her, not to Charles and what he, and his family, stand for, as if there is a gap between Diana's represented image in the photo and her more or less 'real' life, which, to most of us, is largely unknowable. And on that grid, our own desires, fantasies, thoughts and feelings for her are projected, which, in turn, render Diana her status as cultural icon.

Around the mid-1980s, some time after the birth of Prince Harry, in resistance to the sanitized image the Palace wanted portrayed of the Princess of Wales, Diana wilfully discarded the romanticized English rose look with her soft pastel fabrics and high necklines and became not only more fashionable but glamorous; Diana became a more contemporary, worldly woman in tailored, custom-made designer suits, sleek sleeveless evening gowns, and dazzling hairstyles that radically revised her image as she joined 'the ranks of the international glitterati' (Strong 1997: 133), very similar to the ways in which Jackie's outfits and hairdos stood out in stark contrast to the First Ladies who preceded her. In photos of the period leading to her divorce, and in those in the period between her divorce and her death, whether in the breathtakingly beautiful formal poses captured by French photographer Patrick Demarchelier (many of which appear on covers of her biographies), in those of her hugging people in need, or in photos wearing simple cotton shirts and jeans while campaigning for the abolition of landmines in Angola and Bosnia, Diana, similar to Jackie, 'disorganizes the 2-D flatness of a photo' (Koestenbaum 1996: 239); she emanates a sense of presence, especially in these later photos, that *pricks* the spectator, giving the snapshot its *snap!* quality.

Of course one cannot take the Diana/Jackie comparison too far; Jackie, largely through Koestenbaum's readings of her, provides a salient lens from which to begin to read Diana as icon, opening up several matrices, as I will discuss shortly, through which to read Diana's iconicity queerly. While both women epitomized the system of celebrity in contemporary culture; one crucial difference is that Jackie tried to avoid public attention as much as possible, which, ironically, made her image more sought, more enigmatic. Jackie, as Koestenbaum notes, seemed more detached from her celebrity (Koestenbaum 1996: 284), while Diana clearly did not. Diana was part of the 'globalized, electronically connected culture' (Appleyard 1997: 165), which, unlike Jackie, she often used to her own advantage, whether as a forum for confessional (as in her BBC *Panorama* interview with Martin Bashir in 1994), as a means to highlight her charity work and the causes she felt deserved wider attention, or to complain about unscrupulous media intervention in her personal life. So while Jackie played a more unintentional role in fashioning herself as a cultural icon by deliberately avoiding public attention and scrutiny, Diana, one might surmise, sometimes consciously, sometimes not, played a more proactive role in shaping her own iconicity. Certainly the recent deaths of both women, only three years apart, help to point to important parallels in terms of how they are received and interpreted as cultural icons as I have tried to show. And surely the images we have of both women will remain in circulation and remain more or less fixed as the various social and cultural contexts that surround and read their images move on and change. But, at the same time, we must remember that, as I have already mentioned, their lived lives are not necessarily reducible to their iconicity, just as Diana as icon and Jackie as icon are not reducible to each other.

But the question remains of the more specific status of Diana as a gay icon. And this is where I think her iconicity, while sharing similar qualities with that of Jackie's, differentiates itself and develops in ways that Jackie's did not. First, let me mention that we must resist the easy temptation to read Diana's iconicity queerly simply because she touched and spontaneously hugged AIDS sufferers, many of them gay men, without gloves and without restraint. Such a reading not only patronizes her and trivializes her commitment to candidly addressing the social issues, particularly homophobia, surrounding AIDS and HIV infection, it also further demeans the lives of those already devastated by the disease. Quite un-Diana-like, it is a reading that merely tokenizes the Other, holding people marked by difference at bay, at arm's length (as opposed to Diana's physical embracements), without any genuine understanding (or interest) in the ways in which they are positioned in the world, which is very often at the fringes of hegemonic social formations. Indeed, the question to ask is why Diana, or anyone else, would *need* gloves to touch or to hold someone with AIDS. The patronizing gesture which I criticize also carelessly misreads her struggle as a mother of a future king to shape a more relevant monarchy that does not simply stand on ceremony, bask in royal tradition and remain aloof and distant from its subjects. When Diana took her son William to the hospital to visit her friend Adrian-Ward Jackson, who was suffering from complications from AIDS and eventually died, her purpose was not to present him with the spectacle of AIDS. Because the person who was HIV-infected and suffering was someone whom she knew and for whom she cared deeply, Diana effectively disrupted (for William, and perhaps for others) the simplistic correlation of the spectre of illness and decay with death related to AIDS, providing a formative opportunity for William not only to develop compassion and empathy for those who suffer but to think deeply about the specific medical, social, and political complexities that exist at the nexus of AIDS. Donald Spoto has acknowledged that her involvement with AIDS charities and her closeness to AIDS patients led to criticism that she was 'bowing to gay propaganda' (Spoto 1997: 63), and Andrew Morton, in *Diana: Her True Story*, points out that her counselling of AIDS patients often met with hostility and anonymous hate mail (Morton 1997: 171); yet, in defending Diana from such attacks, both Spoto and Morton sanitize her commitment to AIDS by reducing the specificity of the disease to a concern for illness in general. The lack of an antihomophobic position in most biographical work on Diana fails to explore how hostile responses to her involvement with AIDS reveal contempt for those (like Diana) who do not feel or act the way it is felt they should feel or act towards others whom society holds in contempt.

I mention this because I also think it provides a useful lens to begin framing the question as to how one might consider reading Diana's iconicity queerly. Her representativeness is significant to gay men and lesbians not because she hugged AIDS victims without wearing gloves, but because this was one of several ways in which she crossed social and political boundaries. On one level, Diana's glamour, her social status, her jet-set lifestyle, her indulgences in pleasure and her naughty indiscretions align her closely with Jackie O. And we must acknowledge that, like Diana, Jackie also did some boundary crossing of her own by breaking away from oppressive family relations in refusing the role of the mourning widow her in-laws had constructed for her, and by marrying, much to the chagrin of the Kennedy family, Aristotle Onassis. Koestenbaum reads the signifier 'O' of 'Jackie O' as 'Oh my!', as if we are in shock at her conduct in that she provokes open-mouthed awe (Koestenbaum 1996: 156). Jackie's independence of mind, her transgression of conventional cultural norms held for a former US First Lady that were mired in the memory of her husband, duty to her children, and remaining chaste ('in the closet', sexually speaking), at least in the public eye, all of which served to efface her own desires, certainly have resonance for lesbians and gay men. Though we may use Jackie as a point of reference for talking about Diana as a (gay) icon, Diana went much further. While Jackie remained aloof like most of the British royal family today, Diana *flaunted* it – not her wealth and her privileged position as did Fergie, but her beauty, her weaknesses and vulnerabilities, her compassion for others. Unlike the other Windsors, Diana didn't merely gaze out at the world but moved effectively through it. Yet one cannot go so far as Spoto who claims that because Diana mixed freely with many different kinds of people, she stood for a new classless society which the world sees as the fruit of democracy (Spoto 1997: 105). This is no more than utopian; Diana did show us her vulnerabilities, which seemed to make her more human, yet she remained nonetheless an aristocrat, leading a life that was by no means classless or 'common'. But she did help revise the way we see, and are told to see, the British royal family, and she effectively shattered the myth of the Windsors as emblematic of heteronormative family life. As Morton points out, Diana's struggles within the royal family made her realize that she did not want to hide behind the conventional mask of monarchy to the extent that conventional royal life anaesthetizes individuals from the world (Morton 1997: 205) outside its very visible, and clearly demarcated, borders. As she resisted the self-serving ideology of royal protocol, scapegoating by the royal family for its own problems with public relations, psychological abuse and emotional neglect from her husband, and, ultimately, attempts of the royal family and Palace courtiers to silence her, gay men and women watched Diana grow assertive. Indeed her *queer* 'coming out' was not her wedding but was in her creation of multiple subject positions to inhabit rather than merely accepting those already appropriated for her.

It would be similarly utopian to assume that, at some point, Diana simply became a self-determining subject, transcending ideological influence from the monarchy in particular and from her privileged class position in Britain and elsewhere. An important turning point that enabled her to cross social and political boundaries effectively was her own more critical reading of the interaction of ideological pressures in her life and her own subjective existence. Her resistance, following Paul Smith's work on subjectivity, was possible through her readings both of the ways in which she was implicated in systems of power and ideology and the disturbances and contradictions in and among the multiple subject positions she held (P. Smith 1988: xxxi, xxxv) as princess, as (single) mother, as woman, as philanthropist, as citizen, as celebrity, to name a few. She becomes emblematic for queers not through her sexual identity but metaphorically, through what Catharine R. Stimpson, in speaking of lesbianism as a political position, has eloquently described as 'that invaluable way of being in, with, and against the world' (Stimpson 1990: 377).

More specifically, Diana crossed the boundaries of gender. In the early years of her marriage, she performed, and was expected to take on, the role of obedient, docile wife and dutiful mother. Spoto writes that during her courtship with Charles, the Queen saw value in Diana's shyness which seemed to indicate submissiveness (Spoto 1997: 54). Yet when it became evident to her that the marriage was collapsing, and when the royal family and its spin machines closed ranks against her, characterizing her as irrational, hysterical, and unreasonable, once again (de-)feminizing her as one who had lost 'proper' gender, Diana refused to go away quietly. Joan Smith and others have written how royal women have traditionally been expected to relinquish personal satisfaction for the greater good of the monarchy (as was the case with Princess Margaret, who had to give up a marriage proposal from Peter Townsend who was divorced) (J. Smith 1997: 155). Refusing the gender(ed) expectations to be dutiful and to sacrifice personal happiness for the greater good of an institution that demonized, abused and nearly demoralized her, Diana spoke out publicly, with an unusual blend of eloquence and defiance, about Charles's infidelities and his indifference to her bulimia and depression during most of their marriage. The contestation of regulatory regimes of gender is often central to queer politics to the extent that the social abjection of homosexuality, read as damaged or failed gender, is reworked into political agency and defiance. Such contentious practices, as Judith Butler's work has illustrated, open up critical spaces to retheorize relations between gender and sexuality beyond the causal and reductive ones posited by heteronormativity. The proliferation and persistence of gender identities that do not adhere to the 'norm' through which bodies, genders, and desires are naturalized expose the limits of the cultural intelligibility of gender and help open up subversive matrices of gender dis-order within that very (heterosexual) matrix of intelligibility (Butler 1990: 17). Butler is clear in her later work that cross-gendered identification is not the only paradigm for thinking about homosexuality, but one among others (Butler 1997: 146); while Diana did not go so far as to make a cross-gender identification, her refusal to cite the gender norm nonetheless, I would argue, links her to queerness, though such a refusal may not appear to be obviously subversive. As Alexander Doty reminds us in *Making Things Perfectly Queer*, queerness, in interpreting mass culture, can be read as 'a quality related to any expression that can be marked as contra-, non-, or anti-straight' (Doty 1993: xv).

In *Bodies that Matter*, Butler indicates that gender norms operate by requiring the embodiment of certain ideals of femininity and masculinity almost always tied to the idealization of the heterosexual bond (Butler 1993: 231–2). Diana's wedding and her production of two heirs certainly were gender(ed) performances, nearly theatrical in their cultural representation, that enhanced the social idealization of heterosexuality in the strongest sense of the word, given the almost impenetrable bonds between femininity, hegemonically conceived, and the subject position of princess. But at the same time, Diana's later refusal to only limit herself to royal ideals of femininity, and her disavowal of the concomitant relations of discipline and regulation that accompany them, enabled a reformulation of gender, a redeployment of the categories of the dominant culture, and operated oppositionally. Her decision, and her subsequent actions resulting from it, reveal another failure of heteronormativity, which insists on fixed notions of gender and sexuality, to legislate its ideals fully. Through becoming more assertive, by publicly accusing her husband of infidelity and insensitivity, and by eventually moving out and into the world instead of simply receiving it, Diana didn't transcend royalty, or the monarchy as a political institution, but she did socially transform the role of princess and the archaic gender and family norms that attend it. Similar to queer performativity, Diana's life, especially after her marriage, both contained *and* exceeded the heterosexual matrix. As Butler sums up:

> Performativity describes this relation of being implicated in that which one opposes, this turning of power against itself to produce alternative modalities of power, to establish a kind of political contestation that is not a 'pure' opposition, a 'transcendence' of contemporary relations of power, but a difficult labor of forging a future from resources inevitably impure.
>
> (Butler 1993: 241)

Closely related, Diana's life and memory work as a potential site of identification for queers not only because both are a critique of the British establishment, as Clive Aslet has noted (Aslet 1997: 159), but because her life and her memory also work more specifically as critiques of normalizing regimes, including that of the nuclear family, which serve the interests of patriarchal power. While she remained a dedicated and loving mother until the end of her life, and while she was sexually straight, Diana was able to expose the dysfunctionality of the Windsors, shatter their pretence to serve as a healthy model for family and domestic life, and effectively collapse the myth of her so-called 'fairytale' marriage to Charles. Her relationship with Dodi Al Fayed, who was also part of her children's lives, enabled not only the redeployment of gender norms insofar as she unapologetically enjoyed sexuality outside of the confines of marriage and procreation, both of which are legibly inscribed in her position as princess, but also showed the world the ways in which it is possible to realign one's affectional and familial bonds in meaningful ways beyond those dictated by convention, by biology or by marriage – a narrative which is so familiar to contemporary gay and lesbian life.

There has been speculation that, had she lived, Diana might have married Dodi Fayed. Perhaps so. But could it be possible that the happiness many of her friends report that she found with Dodi, and on her own after her divorce, came out of the fact that she and Dodi were not bound by marriage? I cannot agree with Spoto's seemingly racist and misogynistic implications about the Diana/Dodi relationship, that is, that Diana 'had *so recently* selected a *Muslim* playboy for the object of her affections' and that 'her subsequent marriage to a *man of color* would have outraged class-conscious Buckingham Palace even more than her maverick charitable causes and her earlier love affairs' (Spoto 1997: 188–9; emphasis added). One wonders who else would have been outraged besides the Palace, and one cannot help but invoke, once again, Jackie and the admonishment directed towards her for marrying Aristotle Onassis 'so soon' (i.e. five years!) after the Kennedy assassination. But, in considering the normalizing forces that organize and regulate heterosexual marriage and family life, I am not so sure that Diana would have married again, and if she did, given her unhappy first marriage, she would certainly not have done so as an act of retaliation against the royal family. Perhaps she had 'selected' Dodi simply because she loved him, because he, too, had reciprocally 'selected' and loved her. But I think Diana was more subversive (and more queer) as single. Indeed, the period between her divorce and her death was the most interesting in her life as she became a public figure in her own right.

Remarriage would have most likely represented a regression for Diana, a return, perhaps, to the metaphorical closet, where her desires for pleasure, for achieving good in the world, for personal fulfilment outside of the marriage might have been subordinated through the demands of married life. Obviously the Palace was somewhat aware of this; hence, the orchestration and redeployment of the fantasy of heteronormative life as it arranged Diana's funeral, with her former husband and ex-father-in-law following the funeral cortège (together with Princes William and Harry and her brother, Earl Spencer) to Westminster Abbey.[3] Fortunately, this did not obfuscate our memory of Diana as colourful, defiant, glamorous, and having a bite. From a queer perspective, at a time when the signifier 'family' seems stubbornly lodged to the heterosexual nuclear family and legitimated only by marriage, Diana's stature and her realignment of familial bonds have helped to create a tear in the social conflation of heterosexual marriage with family life. Eve Sedgwick has written about the need for more inclusive understandings of family:

> in order to project into the future a vision of 'family' elastic enough to do justice to the depth and sometimes durability of nonmarital and/or nonprocreative bonds, same-sex bonds, nondyadic bonds, bonds not defined by genitality, 'step'-bonds, adult sibling bonds, nonbiological bonds across generations, etc. At the same time, . . . a different angle . . . onto the family of the *present* can show this heterosexist structure always already awash with homosexual energies and potentials, even with lesbian and gay persons, whose making-visible might then require only an adjustment of the interrogatory optic, the bringing *to* the family structure of the pressure of our different claims, our different needs.
>
> (Sedgwick 1993: 71)

Diana's life, whether consciously or not, provided that angle and put pressure on the revered and often static definition of family, which helped to open it up and make it more susceptible to other configurations including same-sex bonds. And the extraordinary blend of energy, dignity and defiance with which she accomplished this is part of the pleasure we take in reading icon Diana queerly.

Many gay men and lesbians identified with Diana's struggles to break away from the narrow confines of 'appropriate' gender behaviour imposed on her by her birthright (royal women do not go to rock concerts in leather pants!), by marriage and by patriarchal family relations, all of which exerted keen pressure on her to become something she clearly did not want to be – in her case, an emblematic Windsor without voice or subjective agency. In the last part of her marriage and in her brief life afterwards, similar to Jackie, yet played out very differently in her own lived experience, Diana resisted inhabiting subject positions that inhibited the expression of her desires, and, in so doing, found new ways to create alternative affectional and familial bonds while keeping the traditional family ones that meant most to her (her sons). Through working hard to overcome bulimia, depression, intense alienation, an unhappy marriage and family life, and other personal difficulties, Diana won the respect and admiration of most of the world. However, this last stage of respect, indeed of admiration from the world at large, for overcoming what often appear to be insurmountable odds, has yet to be realized by lesbians and gay men for the continual struggles we face – this, perhaps, is a fantasy, a hope, a desire, that I project on to the grid of Diana's life and memory in the hope that one day it will.

Notes

1 The binary oppositions pertaining to gender are not only oppressive because they impose fixed gender roles on such royal titles as prince/princess, duke/duchess, etc., but also because each dyad is not really a 'true' opposition since the masculine term in each is given the higher social value.

2 I use the term 'queer' to denote an oppositional political praxis which operates against normalizing ideologies in general (e.g. race, gender, class, nationality) *in addition to sexuality*. This is an especially important distinction in the context of a discussion of Diana, who identified as sexually straight, but, as I shall argue, functioned as politically queer. The use of the term also helps to resist what Phillip Brian Harper has referred to as sexual identity 'as a primary identificatory principle, uninflected by the pressures of other subjectivizing factors' (Harper 1997: 26). When I refer to Diana as a gay icon, I am writing from a more personal position in terms of how she signified for me and possibly, though not universally, for gay men. Reading Diana as a gay icon will intersect, at various sites, with lesbian positions (related to the critiques of gender and conventional marriage her life and memory evoke), and I have attempted to indicate such intersections by using the more inclusive term 'lesbian and gay' in some contexts, 'queer' in others, while recognizing that 'lesbian and gay' cannot always be used interchangeably as if lesbians and gay men always stand on the same political ground.

3 Similarly, at her own request, Jackie was buried in Arlington Cemetery next to JFK thirty-one years after his assassination. Perhaps this was an act of atonement to a public highly critical of her subsequent lifestyle and remarriage following Kennedy's death. But this act of burial, intentional on her part, did reinscribe Jackie back into heteronormative family relations. Diana's death, on the other hand, was the result of an accident and could not possibly have been foreseen, but I think she would have been appalled by the return to the pretence of family normativity on the part of the royals through having the Prince of Wales and the Duke of Edinburgh walk with her sons and brother in the funeral procession. Nonetheless, both acts, by Jackie, and by those who arranged Diana's funeral, point to the strong heteronormative pressures to attempt to frame the memory of these women within the confines of their marriages even though they had ended through JFK's death and through remarriage (for Jackie) and through divorce (for Diana).

References

Appleyard, Bryan (1997) 'A New World, a Goddess, a New Kind of Heaven', in Brian MacArthur (ed.) *Requiem: Diana, Princess of Wales 1961–1997: Memories and Tributes*, New York: Arcade Publishing.

Aslet, Clive (1997) 'The Legacy', in Brian MacArthur (ed.) *Requiem: Diana,*

Princess of Wales 1961–1997: Memories and Tributes, London and New York: Pavilion Books and Arcade Publishing.

Barthes, Roland (1981) *Camera Lucida: Reflections on Photography*, trans. Richard Howard, New York: Hill and Wang.

Butler, Judith (1990) *Gender Trouble: Feminism and the Subversion of Identity*, New York: Routledge.

Butler, Judith (1993) *Bodies that Matter: On the Discursive Limits of 'Sex'*, New York and London: Routledge.

Butler, Judith (1997) *The Psychic Life of Power: Theories in Subjection*, Stanford: Stanford University Press.

Doty, Alexander (1993) *Making Things Perfectly Queer: Interpreting Mass Culture*, Minneapolis: University of Minnesota Press.

Harper, Phillip Brian (1997) 'Gay Male Identities, Personal Privacy, and Relations of Public Exchange: Notes on Directions for Queer Critique', *Social Text* vol. 15, nos. 3–4: 5–29.

Koestenbaum, Wayne (1996) *Jackie Under My Skin: Interpreting an Icon*, New York: Penguin.

Morton, Andrew (1997) *Diana: Her True Story – In Her Own Words 1961–1997*, London and New York: Michael O'Mara Books and Simon and Schuster.

Sedgwick, Eve Kosofsky (1993) 'Tales of the Avunculate: Queer Tutelage in *The Importance of Being Earnest*', in *Tendencies*, Durham: Duke University Press.

Smith, Joan (1997) 'Unusual Normality, Jetset Glamour', in Brian MacArthur (ed.) *Requiem: Diana, Princess of Wales 1961–1997: Memories and Tributes*, London and New York: Pavilion Books and Arcade Publishing.

Smith, Paul (1988) *Discerning the Subject*, Minneapolis: University of Minnesota Press.

Sontag, Susan (1977) *On Photography*, New York: Doubleday.

Spoto, Donald (1997) *Diana: The Last Year*, New York: Crown Publishers.

Stimpson, Catharine R. (1990) 'Lesbian Studies in the 1990s', in Karla Jay and Joanne Glasgow (eds) *Lesbian Texts and Contexts: Radical Revisions*, New York: New York University Press.

Strong, Roy (1997) 'An Icon for the Meritocratic Age', in Brian MacArthur (ed.) *Requiem: Diana, Princess of Wales 1961–1997: Memories and Tributes*, London and New York: Pavilion Books and Arcade Publishing.

12

DIANA BETWEEN TWO DEATHS

Spectral ethics and the time of mourning

Adrian Kear

The narrative is genealogical but it is not simply an act of memory. It bears witness, in the manner of an ethical or political act, for today and tomorrow. It means first of all thinking about what takes place today.

(Derrida 1995: 35)

If he loves justice at least, the 'scholar' of the future, the 'intellectual' of tomorrow should learn it and from the ghost. He should learn to live by learning not how to make conversation with the ghost but how to talk with him, with her, how to let them speak or how to give them back their speech, even if it is in oneself, in the other, in the other in oneself: they are always *there*, specters, even if they do not exist, even if they are no longer, even if they are not yet.

(Derrida 1994: 176)

The ethical injunction voiced in the spectacular events following the death of Diana appeared at the time to take the form of a simple demand: a demand for *justice* (Critchley 1997). A famously wronged woman, the icon of her age, had just died wrongly, her life once more smashed to pieces by the furious pursuit of cultural capital. To many her untimely death seemed to evidence the cruel injustice of unjust times: her battered body became the *corpus delicti*, the indisputable proof that the time itself was out of joint and that something now had to be done to set it right. As Diana disappeared into the underpass between life and death, her image re-emerged from the other side more powerfully radiant than ever before. Her famous face haunted every frame of media coverage thereafter, as if the spectre of Diana was returning from the beyond to articulate a demand for justice that went way beyond the need for a right and proper response to her death. As a result, the semblance of private grief countenanced by the royal family paled into insignificance against a public expression of mourning that appeared to mobilize this repeated demand for justice into a renewed desire for *change*.[1]

Diana's 'cultic' role in what Walter Benjamin once termed the 'phantasmagoria' of consumer capitalism (cited in Diamond 1997: 145) seemed to enable her ghost to rattle the chains of contemporary cultural politics with uncanny vigour. The Diana who inhabited the spectral economy of media speculation surrounding the events of her death appeared to articulate with great clarity the spectre's long familiar injunction: remember me and learn to live *ethically*. The spooky 'aura' emanating from her 'aristocratic' face made her apparition seem doubly enchanting, summoning up both an 'involuntary memory' of past injustice 'veiled by the tears of nostalgia' and a 'unique manifestation' of the 'perceptibility' of the future. This 'auratic' quality seemed to disinter a spectral discourse of immanent potential, in which the image of Diana looked back and forwards in time simultaneously (Benjamin 1969: 186–8). Of course, there was always the possibility that this was a phantom rhetoric originating from that phantasmatic space between life and death where nothing is ever what it appears to be, just another structuring illusion from the sententious repertoire that 'always feigns to speak like the just' (Derrida 1994: xviii). And yet its promise of *futurity*, echoing the Enlightenment invocation to make today different in respect to yesterday, seemed an irresistibly ethical way out of a culture of creeping cynicism,[2] notwithstanding the warnings of age-old theatrical irony that it may merely be another conjuring trick of a duplicitous ideology.

There seemed to be a strange *punctum* to the photographs of Diana in circulation at the time of her death that was experienced by the viewer as less of a trick than a 'prick' (Barthes 1993: 27). There seemed to be something invisibly *moving* about them that could be seen to amount to a stimulus to action. They appeared invested with an ability to both retain and return the viewer's gaze – even though the haunted eyes within them had long since lost their ability to look with anything but the 'mirrorlike blankness' of the strangely 'familiar regard' (Benjamin 1969: 190). Their depth of focus – taking in the gaze to a vanishing point beyond which there appeared to be nothing – simply served to bring their reflective purpose even closer to the surface. The viewer seemed able to perceive something *intimate* in them, something secretly interior. Through this contradictory 'magic of distance', Diana's face seemed to possess a peculiarly 'tragic concision' in which viewers were able to see something close to them expressed (Benjamin 1969: 191). The 'auratic' quality of these portraits was accentuated by the media's ceaseless circulation of them at the time of her death as 'effigies' directly designed to stand in for the dead Diana. Despite their clearly 'cultic' role in the hauntological economy of the postmodern 'phantasmagoria', they appeared to perform a 're-enchantment' of the cultural sphere in which the effigy 'Diana' held in tension the coextensive potentiality of political recuperation and social change.[3] This spectral Diana appeared to embody a dazzlingly contradictory image of 'dialectic at a standstill', formed in a moment 'when that which has been and the Now come together in a flash as a constellation' (Walter Benjamin, quoted in Diamond 1997: 209). The dislocating effect of the collision of these temporalities in the 'dialectical image' served to realign the viewer's perception of the 'continuum' of contemporary history through the disjunctive experience of a 'now-time' which seemed to raise the spectre of the possibility of change (Diamond 1997: 145–7).

Diana's overexposed existence seemed freeze-framed in the 'now-time' of the temporality of the image, her *being-there* jarring with the uncanny awareness of her *having-been-there* (Barthes 1977: 44), her face confronting the security of the 'this has been' with the spookiness of the 'this will be' (Barthes 1993: 96). Each time she was shot and captured in the imprint of the image there appeared to be a recognition that this was a repetition of events that were yet to come. Every image seemed to configure and confirm Diana as always-already dead, catching her imprisoned in the tortuous temporality between two deaths – symbolic and real. Through her ambivalent relationship with the camera, Diana lived 'a life that is about to turn into a certain death, a death lived by anticipation, a death that crosses over into the sphere of life, a life that moves into the realm of death' (Lacan 1992: 248). Perhaps this was nowhere more clearly evidenced than in the security camera footage of her leaving the Ritz Hotel on her way to the fateful crash. As Diana comes through the revolving doors she looks and moves as if she is dead already and yet she appears to be hastening to her 'second death' (Lacan 1992: 298). The perpetual replaying of this scene in 'now-time' video format creates a conjunction between the viewer's awareness of the subsequent events and Diana's already acknowledged anticipation of them. The revolving doors seem to be in perpetual motion, with 'Diana' returning time after time to repeat the scene of her prior death. Therefore Diana remains, at least in effigy, in the hauntological media apparatus between life and death. Even more uncannily, perhaps, this living-dead 'Diana' appeared to open up a spectral space between the knowledge of 'this has been' and the certainty of 'this will be' – the indeterminate 'this ought to be' in which, Michel de Certeau insists, 'we have something to do' (cited in Read 1993: 90).

The injunction to mourn Diana appeared to be addressed precisely to this unspecified 'we.' A double articulation seemed to be in place here: to the extent that the revenant 'Diana' incorporated an ethical injunction delivered as a perceptual return from 'the beyond', 'we', those of us still 'here', were incorporated as the witnesses to the demand for justice, our very *being-there* requiring that we become its agents of execution.[4] The 'we' thereby operated as an interpellative mechanism of *inclusion*, in which we were transformed into 'a community in mourning', hailed as the performative effect of an indisputable injunction to act. In the face of the death of Diana 'we' came to see mourning as our ethical responsibility. This recognition of responsibility for and before the other, which, Levinas argues, even extends to being included in 'the event' of the other's death, appeared to be nothing less than the assumption of intersubjective responsibility for the future: 'The other is the future. The very relationship with the other is the relationship with the future' (Levinas 1989: 44). The death of the other, then, is clearly an event 'the scholar of the future, the intellectual of tomorrow' has a duty to speak to. Doing justice to the dead provides the dramatic language of the discourse of futurity, the key to the performative enunciation of an ethical 'enlightenment to come' (Derrida 1994: 90).[5] But, as Levinas stipulates, 'the future that death gives, the future of the event, is not yet time. In order for this future . . . to become an element of time, it must enter into a relationship with the present' (Levinas 1989: 45). In other words, the future must be *mediated*.

The spectre appears to occupy such an immanently intermediate space – the hauntological in-between – that enables it to traverse the historical, the ontological and the futural in order to 'spectralize' the present (Derrida 1994: 51). This ghostly temporality produces an uncanny synchronicity in which the remembrance of things past coincides with the performance of things to come in the production of a familiarly tragic reverberation in the continuous present.[6] The images of Diana beamed around the globe on the event of her death thus functioned as more than a simple *momento mori* of a troubled existence. They effectively spectralized the public domain and appeared to testify to 'the presence of the future in the present' (Levinas 1989: 45). Despite the fact that these images were in themselves stand-ins – both for the real live Diana and for the reels of film confiscated at the scene of her death – they effectively stood in for, and mediated between, the spectre and the spectator. The face of Diana, radiant beyond reality, brought the spectator face-to-face with the uncanny image of the Other. In the transition from the ontological to the hauntological, in the liminal realm of the still living dead, Diana had been transformed into an altogether Other 'Diana'. There was self-evidently something in 'Diana' other than Diana herself,[7] and this indeterminate surplus enabled her to occupy an intermediary space in which to articulate an *excess* of meaning.[8]

Semantically speaking, Diana herself was profoundly empty. She did not need to possess some magical subjective content or mysterious individual quality to be able to become a locus of phantasmatic investment and political mobilization. Indeed, it was precisely her quintessential emptiness that enabled her image to host a multiplicity of contradictory demands and sustain the illusory promise of their successful resolution. The 'auratic' impact of 'Diana' resided in the 'magic of distance' created between her image and affect (Benjamin 1969: 191) – a playing space across which a series of projective identifications and introjective interpretations could be made to make Diana meaningful. The isolation and solitude captured by the famous scene of Diana sitting in front of the Taj Mahal appeared to be an index of her distance, her difference from others. The fact that Diana could appear to be so alone in front of an enraptured global audience provided the key moment in her construction as a tragic figure, living at the edge of the social beyond the established limit between life and death (Lacan 1992: 272). She stood in front of the world's most famous mausoleum – a monument to interminable grief and lost love[9] – exposed to the vicissitudes of judgement. In the assumption of the intrusive eyes of the public gaze she looked an abused woman locked into a loveless relationship and entombed within an archaic institution. Her face seemed to bear a set of encrypted codes as complex and arcane as the text embedded in the structure of the marble buildings, a palimpsest upon which no end of interpretative identifications could be performed. She appeared to countenance multiple layers of buried meaning, giving glimpses of lost loves and traumas past that dare not speak their name. 'Diana' seemed to act as an 'enigmatic signifier' pointing to the materiality of loss without being able to signify its content directly (Murray 1997: 10). The empathetic audience seemed to recognize this genre and imbue her performance with the polysemic meanings of their own multifaceted pain.

This was the moment that appeared to define 'Diana' – which redefined Diana as melancholia incarnate – and re-inscribed her beauty as the effect of a specifically *tragic* judgement. 'The beauty effect', Lacan argues, 'derives from the relationship of the hero to the limit' (Lacan 1992: 286). Diana both fascinated and distanced the spectator through her occupation of the limit zone between two deaths, and her apparent desire to cross the limit – to cross the limit of desire – posited her beauty 'at the very point of transition between life and death' (Lacan 1992: 297). Like the tragic actor endowed with the task of embodying the dead and giving them back their voice, the spectral 'Diana' appeared to act as a ghostly goodwill ambassador able to speak both *for* and *with* the Other. The echo-effect that spoke to us through her effigies repeatedly announced that it was somewhere in-between, the ambivalent representative of an invisible host. Behind the mask of Diana's famous face there appeared to reside an uncannily undecidable some*thing*.[10] This presence could be felt without being seen, as if it was observing without being observed. The haunting quality of Diana's visage seemed to reside in this incorporation of the Other's gaze, her image's ability to move being the effect of simultaneously concealing and revealing the invisible movements within. The face of Diana might therefore have functioned as a kind of representational fetish, a visual contortion or ideological distortion which, when observed from a suitably obtuse angle, reveals a remarkably different meaning to that immediately available to view. Indeed, the performance of an *anamorphic* interpretation of 'Diana' might clarify the contradictory representations of her life and deaths, revealing in turn the range and complexity of their performative effects.[11]

Looking back, it now seems that there was a distinctively theatrical exchange in the events enacted at the time of Diana's 'second death' (Lacan 1992: 298). The actorly effigy 'Diana' appeared to be a surrogate for the imagined community's fabrication of a temporal loop between a reconstructed past and an anticipated future, a stand-in on the tragic stage whose death provided the occasion to act out a phantom ethics of *necessary illusion*.[12] This intermediary 'Diana' acted as the protagonist in events whose very 'eventness' suggested that they went beyond the boundaries of a discretely dramatized duration, as if the participants were 'not actors of their own volition, but rather conduits for a phenomenon . . . older than their awareness of themselves' (Sloterdijk 1989: 88). The spectator appeared to witness the reappearance of something approximating the Dionysian passion of the *physis* – the ritual re-enactment of the trauma of separation and individuation – within the mediatized frame of a global performance event. The postmodern screen seemed transformed by the projection of an inexorably split scene in which the Diana events appeared as an intertextual space somewhere between contemporary reality, historical drama and anachronistic mythology. Their simultaneity produced an uncanny synchronicity in which the temporality of 'the event' appeared displaced from the ground of ontology into the undecidability of a hauntological fantasy or 'primal scene' (Lukacher 1986: 24). As in the theatre, a willing suspension of disbelief enabled this true illusion to have a scale and significance greater than it would otherwise appear to possess. An empty space was opened up to be filled out by a symbolic surrogate – a chimerical apparition possessing a necessarily 'negative' magnitude[13] – able to bridge the gap between now and then: the phantasmatic 'Diana' whose apparent loss was experienced as a traumatic temporary return to an *atemporal* reality.[14]

Within the boundaries of this specifically theatrical representation of the tautological 'primal' scene, it becomes clear that 'Diana' existed as a symbol of the lack and loss experienced in the exigencies of everyday life, a moving hauntological index pointing to real ontological trauma. 'Diana' appeared to give body to a range of unknown or unacknowledged losses, to become an allegorical figure for their unresolved effects – and *mourning* Diana seemed a form in which to act out their multiple meanings on a 'universal' stage. The widespread identification with 'Diana' that appeared to cross the otherwise seemingly stable categories of identity – gender, race, sexuality; nation, culture, class – might have been less of an identification with what she stood for than a indication of what she stood-in for: something akin to the *primacy* of pain. This is not to say that she was herself a 'universal' figure – the timely embodiment of some timeless truth – but rather a phantasmatic space in which multiple, conflicting, contradictory identifications could be incorporated. The spectral 'Diana' simultaneously configured narratives of bodily possession and physical dispossession, of class privilege and social alienation, of imperial power and post-colonial deterritorialization. She appeared to enable projection of the coextensive possibilities of gender liberation and romantic recuperation, of sexual freedom and heterosexual normalization. She left an impression crossing international borders and social formations, reconfiguring cultural boundaries and intersubjective relations. In 'Diana' we saw the prime representative of the *contemporary* cultural processes through which 'fantasies are increasingly immediately externalized in the public symbolic space; the sphere of intimacy is more and more directly socialized' (Zizek 1997: 164). The spectre of Diana appeared to occupy the space of a sublime object traversing the ideological field, floating between imprecise positions and indistinct ideas.

During the theatricality of Diana events, however, the meaning of her name became more pinned down.[15] The immeasurably variegated, differentially structured forms of pain – the effects of social power as much as personal injury and subjective trauma – seemed to be condensed and displaced by a new universalizing discourse of 'compassion'. Diana herself was certainly no stranger to this reterritorialization of the landscape of suffering, frequently the performer of a 'sympathetic gesture' which served to extend the process of vicarious feeling 'for oneself through and as the other' (Butler 1993: 100). Indeed, her brother's dramatic funeral speech was at pains to draw attention to the fact that her compassionate work stemmed from her own sense of injury and *hurt*, and it was the deflection of this that enabled her to identify with others. The attempt to overcome an overwhelming feeling of worthlessness, he said, led her to invest more and more time in worthwhile causes – notably those of the oppressed and dispossessed victims of war and social injustice – with the obvious objective of trying to make herself feel worthy, 'worthy of love'.[16] Diana's famous capacity to love seemed to be an indication of her own lack, and it was through this simple gesture of giving something that she did not have that she herself appeared to become loved (Lacan 1994: 104). Confronted with this desire for something in them which they themselves did not have, the people Diana loved could only reciprocate the gesture and offer her their lack – 'returning only *love*' (Bozovic 1994: 77).

A similar process seemed at work in the identifications made with her at the time of her death, in which the desire to be loved was articulated as love for Diana. 'The people' appeared to identify their lack in her, to relate to Diana as the metaphorical embodiment of love itself. To love Diana therefore appeared to *demand* love, and even those of us who did not identify with her could identify with this, with both the *need* and the expressions of the people articulating it. This seemed to incorporate even those of us who deliberately disidentified with Diana and distanced ourselves from the Diana events, enabling us to become invested in the visible need for change that went beyond the ability of the simple 'demand of love' to formulate. As a seemingly literal enactment of 'the metonymy of the discourse of demand' (Lacan 1992: 293), mourning Diana appeared to provide the dramatic language in which to articulate the 'excessive' meanings of *desire*, and a theatrical form in which to represent them. At every stage of this theatrical event a double articulation appeared to echo through the work of mourning. The drama that took place on the public stage – the action in full view, said out loud and perfectly intelligible in itself – seemed to point to an inexorably 'other scene' being played out simultaneously, unknown to the spectator, through the 'chain-like mode' of 'unconscious logic' (Green 1979: 28–9). The metonymic performance of mourning 'Diana' seemed to enable the performers to act out losses that could not be grieved, to allegorize the fantasy at work in the profoundly *melancholic* structuring of identity (Butler 1993: 234–5).[17]

The signifier 'Diana' appeared to function in this performance as 'the instrument by which the missing signified expresses itself' (Lacan 1993: 221). Her (in)corporeal form played host to the haunt of ghosts inhabiting the full range of traumatic primal scenes, from social disruption and subjective destitution through to individual despair and historical dislocation. The temporally excluded and symbolically repudiated existence of these spectres made their presence able to be felt but not seen, leaving the spectator somehow floating in between the mourning of 'Diana' and some ineluctably melancholic and unrecognizable 'other scene'. In the initial stages of the show a multifaceted range of cross-category mourners were clearly articulating a multiplicity of the 'discontents of the culture' (Lacan 1992: 150) which they believed she too felt, feeling she believed in them. Looking through a glass darkly at the image of Diana, they saw their lack in her loss, identifying their innumerably different and inevitably conflicting senses of political dispossession with her expression of individual lack. The long duration of the performance of mourning 'Diana' appeared to make these differences present but at the same time to conflate them into a shared, unilaterally inflected *national* grief in which all the participants believed in the same thing (Zizek 1993: 201–2) – The Diorama of Love. The incorporative inclusivity of the Diana events meant that those of us watching, even those of us who felt we did not for a single moment believe in any of it, seemed to have 'what we truly believe' enacted for and in front of us by others (Zizek 1997: 120). The act of repudiating the illusory significance of the events simply served to reveal a vicarious investment in both the action and the actions of the people performing them. The articulation of demands for 'real political action' or 'strong social values', for 'class war' or 'multicultural cohesion', configured 'the people' and 'the nation' as objects of phantasmatic belief and displaced desire as well as the agents of its operation.

The metonymical linkage of the language of love and the desire for change enabled 'Diana' to function as the signifier holding together the ideological domain. 'The Queen of Hearts', 'the People's Princess' seemed to condense the complexities of social injustice into a sliding scale of human pain and to compress the multiple possibilities of political activism into the uniform design of singular 'compassionate' action. The complex identifications through which the things being mourned in 'Diana' – including those things being mourned by not mourning her – seemed to matter much more than Diana herself ever could. And yet these in themselves appeared to be overtaken by the irresistibly negative energy of 'the whole Diana thing' – a phantom politics which appeared to enjoin the phantasmatic 'promise of the manageability of unspeakable loss' (Butler 1993: 209) to the service of some terribly *nationalistic* fantasy. This was perhaps encapsulated in the incongruous image of the coffin containing the body of a woman who opposed the production of landmines in Britain and their placement in the foreign fields of post-colonial countries being paraded past London's monuments to imperial power on a British military gun-carriage. The effect of this performative recuperation was to resituate 'Diana' firmly within the discourse of political authority – that something in Diana more than herself being the very stuff of *majesty* able to engender intransigent belief (Zizek 1991: 254– 5). Revisiting the scene of mourning, we come face-to-face with Diana in the faint traces of the neat handiwork holding together the threads of cultural power. Her spectre appeared to reappear in order to enable these invisible stitches to disappear, the hauntological substitute effectively 'suturing' the ideological supplement. 'Diana' acted as the 'vanishing mediator' in the performative construction of New Britain, a self-effacing performer whose image remains buried in the fabric of its ideological folds (Zizek 1989: 195). Whilst at the time it may have seemed that she authored the processes of 'Dianaization' and embodied what it meant, in retrospect it is clear that her memory and name acted *retroactively* as the 'articulating principle' of a new hegemonic formation (Laclau and Mouffe 1985: 113). As the measured inflections of Tony Blair's funereal reading of 1 Corinthians 13 made clear, through 'Diana' there was now in place a silent pact in which political belief, ethical action and compassionate love appeared to abide together. After all, 'of these three, the greatest *is* love'.[18]

The funeral performances seemed to deliver an anamorphic catharsis of the emotions expressed earlier in the week's dramatic action. They appeared to stabilize the 'disturbing oscillation between seeing and feeling' (Diamond 1995: 153) that was characteristic of the mourning process, and clarify the effective meaning of 'Diana' without the distortion and disorder of visible pain. The formalization of mourning on the public stage seemed to translate Dionysiac suffering into Apollonian structure, during which the performativity of loss was displaced into the performance of grief. The funeral represented the final stage of a process in which the public performance of mourning was rearticulated towards the performative production of 'the public.' The affective power of its address appeared to reside in its ability to provide 'an Apollonian embodiment of Dionysiac insights and powers' (Nietzsche 1956: 56). The mass of people assembled in the extended ampitheatrical auditorium around Westminster Abbey appeared to represent a new political constituency demanding recognition. This was perhaps most clearly expressed by the sudden and spontaneous applause that accompanied Earl Spencer's accusatory speech, in which doing justice to the name of the dead Diana seemed once more to coincide with a more general demand for social justice. The enraptured crowd made it echo through London like the effect of a collective cathartic shudder – a visceral experience of feeling the invisible presence that was summoned by his incantation of the spectral 'Diana'. The instantaneously collectivized audience appeared to respond to Spencer's demands as the recognition of their desire, and yet, as if touched by the primordial power of the big Other, seemed to seize that moment to rearticulate them as their desire to be recognised as worthy of the Other's desire. The otherwise immanent potentiality of this mobilized mourning appeared to become cathected to a recuperative dynamic of political obedience, in which the demand for justice converged with the authority of the enunciation of pure demand. At this moment the loss of the phantasmatic 'Diana' seemed to necessitate an unmediated encounter with the desire of the Other, to speak to it face-to-face, to find out what it wanted to see and confront its apparently unmitigated determinacy. But the cathartic shudder of this *coup de théâtre* also enabled a clarifying premonition or recognition of the gap or lack in the Other, of the terrifyingly impossible vacuity that waits to be filled by ideological fantasy (Zizek 1993: 237). Therefore, a further double movement of ideological processes seemed in progress during this transitory moment of anamorphic perception. It appeared to witness the effective recuperation of the ethical injunction into the reformation of social stability, to testify to a concomitant resurrection of political certainties, and yet at the same time to offer a haunting glimpse of the efficacy of whatever lay 'beyond' the terms of the demand. This chink in power's psychic armoury seemed to be opened by the question that otherwise appeared to perform the task of interpellation – 'What does Diana want?'[19] – with the signifier 'Diana' at once looking to reflect desire and to deflect it into ideology.

The injunction to mourn Diana seemed to set in play her transformation into the signifier of 'the relationship of man [*sic*] to his second death, the signifier of his desire, his visible desire' (Lacan 1992: 298). Mourning 'Diana' appeared to enable a temporal anticipation of the possibility of *freedom* that 'authentic' being-towards-death brings (Heidegger 1962: 308) alongside a traumatic recapitulation of the imprisoned primal scene. 'Diana' seemed to function as 'desire made visible' (Lacan 1992: 268), and the manner of her demise appeared to mark the shift from desire into drive – driving desire down the long tunnel 'in the direction of the triumph of death' (Lacan 1992: 313). Diana's act of dicing with the motorcycled furies of the paparazzi seemed to literally enact her desire to escape the interminable space between two deaths and to anticipate their desire to rip her to pieces in the process. However, it would be a mistake to argue that the desire that inhabited the final action of this 'tragedy' was a consummation of the ultimate desire for death itself. The tragic hero, Lacan argues, embodies ethics by not giving way as to their desire but rather by following it through inexorably to the end (Lacan 1992: 323). Drive may appear to overtake desire en route, but desire never finishes prematurely; desire never comes to an end. The ethical act is therefore one that keeps desire alive with a tragic fidelity to the fragmentary experience of social identity, testifying to the continued presence of hauntological spectres disturbing the fragile structure of ontological reality (Zizek 1997: 213–14). It appears to bring about a contradictory moment of revelation in which coming face-to-face with the Other instigates the startling recognition that 'the Other is others' and institutes a stark realization of intersubjective responsibility (Levinas 1989: 246). The end that death brings seems to secretly set in motion an endless metonymy in which desire necessarily irrupts through the discourse of demand into a strangely articulated *ethical* desire for 'change as such' (Lacan 1992: 293).

The answer to the question 'What does Diana want?' seemed to be writ large in the faces of her two uncannily similar sons. Her brother's funeral oration spoke of her desire to see their 'hearts sing free' – and their personas would now have to bear the weight of Diana's legacy. The Spencers, Diana's 'blood family', would take up the responsibility of maintaining the *jouissance* of public mourning by ensuring constant protection of her image and continued identification with the immortality of her desire (Irigaray 1985: 219). As the direct inheritors and uncannily familiar incarnations of their mother's look, the Princes William and Harry entered the popular imaginary as the new sublime objects of an ideologically refashioned monarchy. Through this matrilineal progeny the narrative remained open for the construction of a new hegemony, with Diana's desire, like her image, seemingly living on in perpetuity. But perhaps the enduring element of this mythology will be the way the image of the revenant 'Diana' spectralized the injustices of the past and brought us face to face with the possibility of an *ethical* futurity. To grasp hold of this memory 'as it flashes up at a moment of danger' might be precisely 'to articulate the past historically' and thereby nurture 'the spark of hope' through which 'even the dead' may appear illuminated (Benjamin 1969: 255). 'History decomposes into images, not narratives', Benjamin wrote, and likewise there now remains 'nothing to say, only to show' (cited in Diamond 1997: 146).[20]

Notes and asides

1 This formulation is, of course, dependent upon Lacan's distinction between 'need, demand and desire' in which the excess meaning that extends 'beyond' whatever need the demand is able to articulate is metonymically displaced into the realm of desire. In other words, 'desire is nothing more than the metonymy of the discourse of demand' (Lacan 1992: 293).

2 The embedded references are to the Enlightenment's attempts to make ethical praxis the basis of the rational organization of social life, as articulated in Kant's essay 'What is Enlightenment?' (1992). The exposition and extension of this essay forms the fertile ground of a crucial debate about the direction of modernity between Michel Foucault (1984) and Jürgen Habermas (1985, 1986, 1987). See also Sloterdijk (1988, 1989) for a detailed contemporary rearticulation of the project of Enlightened modernity.

3 Throughout this essay quotation marks are used to distinguish between the ontological Diana (the woman who lived the life) and her ghostly hauntological counterpart (the 'Diana' of phantasmatic investment and imaginary construction). The notion of 'Diana' as an 'effigy' is indebted to Joseph Roach's suggestive use of the term in which its 'similarity to performance should be clear enough: it fills out by means of surrogation a vacancy created by the absence of an original'. He argues that 'performed effigies – those fabricated from human bodies and the associations they evoke – provide communities with a method of perpetuating themselves through specially nominated mediums or surrogates: among them actors, dancers, . . . statesmen, celebrities . . . and especially, by virtue of an intense but unsurprising paradox, corpses' (Roach 1996: 36).

4 Kantian ethics always appears to enunciate the question of justice from the perspective of an Absolute condition, whose demands emanate from the ineluctable, noumenal 'beyond' of the Law, which remains inaccessible to the phenomenal world. According to Kant, this limitation is, however, a necessary condition of the operation of human judgement, the ethical imperative to act in accordance with an Absolute universality. In other words, this 'beyond' is effectively more tropological than topographical: it functions as an incorporated space, an *internal* domain (see Zizek 1993: 83–124). However, as Zizek later explains, there is a terrifying immediacy about the Kantian concept of 'transcendental freedom' that exists in the space between ethics and aesthetics as 'the unthinkable direct intervention of the noumenal into the phenomenal' (Zizek 1997: 239). In its irruption the terror of the Sublime is unleashed as an ethical force (See Copjec 1996).

5 'The future is not described, it is not foreseen in the constantive mode; it is announced, promised, called for in a performative mode' (Derrida 1994: 103).

6 Walter Benjamin's ruminations on the *Trauerspiel* (Benjamin 1985) also echo here: the mourning plays enacted to remember a royal martyr might indeed return to haunt modernity's resolutely historical perspective. As Michel Mafessoli suggests, 'the marginalization of the aesthetic within the finished perspective of *history* may be replaced by the centralization of the aesthetic within the post-historical perspective of *destiny*. In the former, things are only valued to the extent that they conform to the workings of an evolutionary mechanism: drama in its etymological sense (*dramein*); in the latter, each thing is valued for itself, since it is a signifying element of an *organicity*, an organic whole: hence the *tragic*, which is the mode in which we are living today' (Mafessoli 1991: 18).

7 This outline formulation of 'Diana' resonates with the Lacanian concept of the *objet petit a* – the object here (other) standing in for (the Other) – which confers upon the subject the illusion of ontological consistency and formal reality. In his reading of *Hamlet*, Lacan provides a sustained account of the position of the *objet petit a* in relation to the temporal work of mourning (see Lacan 1982).

8 This excess is, of course, *desire*. (See note 1 above.)

9 The Taj Mahal (started 1631, completed 1653) was built as the tomb of the Princess Mumtaz Mahal by her lifetime lover Shah Jahan, Emperor of All India. Its incredible architecture was both a monument to their love and a monumental exercise in creating heaven on earth according to the descriptions of the Qur'an and the predictions of Sufi mysticism. Whole chapters of the Qur'an are inscribed on the marble walls and across the sarcophagus at the focal point of the mausoleum. The image presented a clear disjunction between this pre-colonial tale of love and Diana's post-colonial melancholia, as well as reappropriating the Taj Mahal back into the image-repertoire of colonial occupation and imperial domination.

10 This might be precisely 'The Thing' that Lacan locates as 'the beyond-of the-signified' (Lacan 1992: 54). The Lacanian 'Thing' always remains 'fundamentally veiled' and becomes apparent only as a 'veiled entity' (Lacan 1992: 118). 'The Thing' is experienced only as an affective 'it hurts' and is simply impossible to imagine, a terrifying emptiness given only transient positivity by the signifier that appears to mask it (Lacan 1992: 121–5). The filling out of the place of 'The Thing' by the signifier is, Zizek argues, central in the construction of cultural identities and, in particular, nationalist formations. The signifier that takes the place of 'The Thing' – 'Nation' ('Diana'?) – is a tautological vacuity whose very power resides in its emptiness: 'the whole meaning of the thing turns on the fact that "it means something" to people' (Zizek 1993: 202).

11 *Anamorphosis* is a term Lacan borrows from visual representation to differentiate between the eye and the gaze to explain how 'the domain of vision has been integrated into the field of desire' (Lacan 1994: 85). His famous reading of Holbein's *The Ambassadors* makes use of the visual anamorphosis in the centre of the image – the death skull which appears at first as a squashed disk in the pattern of the carpet until looked at from an acute angle – to conceptualize psychoanalytic anamorphosis as a process of clarifying the stains or blots on the horizon of the subject's desire. In an interesting formulation of a specifically *theatrical* anamorphosis, Ned Lukacher explains the term as 'Lacan's figure for the way in which we "feel" seeing, for the way we feel seeing as an invisible materiality, like feeling the gaze of an other without seeing the other's eyes' (Lukacher 1989: 876). This is not very far removed from Derrida's concept, also derived from Shakespeare, of 'the visor-effect', in which the *appearance* of the revenant introduces 'a spectral asymmetry' which interrupts the synchronicity of spectrality despite the fact that 'we do not see who looks at us'. In this temporal 'anachrony' the power of the spectre's injunction is experienced as a demand for obedience to an *anterior*, atavistic law (Derrida 1994: 6–7).

12 The term deployed here is derived from Nietzsche and expresses perfectly a quintessentially *theatrical* ontology (Sloterdijk 1989: 80). It reverberates with the theatrical logic of his aphorism in *Truth and Lie in an Extra-moral Sense*, that 'truths are illusions about which one has forgotten that this is what they are' (Nietzsche 1976: 47). Epistemological coherence and ideological cohesion

equally require a willing suspension of disbelief – in both the illusion and the illusion that the illusion is 'an illusion'. This is precisely what Zizek develops in his concept of the 'ideological fantasy' (Zizek 1989: 33). Borrowing from Lacan's phrasing, 'the real supports the fantasy, the fantasy protects the real' (Lacan 1994: 41), he argues that 'far from being a kind of dreamlike cobweb that prevents us from "seeing reality as it effectively is", fantasy constitutes what we call reality' (Zizek 1993: 118–19). This idea is what he terms 'the fundamental thesis of Lacanian psychoanalysis': that the common sense understanding of 'reality' is tenable only by maintaining the exclusion of some traumatic 'Real' (See below, note 14). Furthermore, it enables him to argue that 'This is probably the fundamental dimension of "ideology": ideology is not simply a "false consciousness", an illusory representation of reality, it is rather this reality which is to be conceived of as "ideological" . . . supported by "false consciousness"' – i.e. the consciousness supported by the phantasmatic protection of the 'Real' (Zizek 1989: 21). As such, 'What they ["the people"] overlook, what they misrecognize, is not the reality but the illusion which is structuring their reality, their real social activity' (Zizek 1989: 32). Echoing Nietzsche, Zizek argues that 'the illusion is therefore double: it consists in overlooking the illusion which is structuring our real, effective relationship to reality' (Zizek 1989: 32–33).

13 The Lacanian *objet petit a* is precisely such a negative form – something standing for nothing, giving body to a lack, making present a void. As Zizek explains 'the basic premise of the Lacanian ontology is that if our experience of reality is to maintain its consistency, the positive field of reality has to be "sutured" with a supplement which the subject (mis)perceives as a positive entity, but is effectively a "negative magnitude" (Zizek 1997: 81).

14 This atemporal reality corresponds to the metapsychological concept of the Real, which, in Lacan's famous triadic formulation, is that which cannot be symbolized i.e., addressed directly at the level of the symbolic. In other words, the Real remains inaccessible to what is, in commonsense terms, 'reality'. Moreover, it is itself constituted as the effect of what has been excluded and expelled from the symbolic structure (the phenomenal realm of things-as-they-appear-to-be), hence the famous phrasing 'whatever is refused in the symbolic order, in the sense of *Verwerfung* [foreclusion], reappears in the real' (Lacan 1993: 13). As Zizek pithily puts it, 'The Real is therefore simultaneously both the hard, impenetrable kernel resisting symbolization *and* a pure chimerical entity which has in itself no ontological consistency' (Zizek 1989: 168). The Real thus appears to exist in an undecidable temporality – a primal scene – that is both a retroactive effect of a failure of symbolization and an *a priori* condition of the symbolic structure. To this extent, the Real is a *performative* construct, whose dynamic defines the traumatic event as 'a point of failure of symbolization, but at the same time never given in its positivity – it can be constituted only backwards, from its structural effects. All its effectivity lies in the distortions it produces in the symbolic universe of the subject: the traumatic event is ultimately just a fantasy-construct filling out a certain void in the symbolic structure and, as such, a retroactive effect of this structure' (Zizek 1989: 169). Acting out, Lacan argues, is a similarly phantasmatic response to a chimerical trauma 'equivalent to a hallucinatory phenomenon of the delusional type that occurs when you symbolise prematurely, when you address something in the order of reality and not within the symbolic register' (Lacan 1993: 80).

15 The allusion here is to the Lacanian construct of the *point de capiton*, or

'quilting point'. This is the location of the signifier that appears to fix the otherwise deferred meaning of the signifying chain: 'Everything radiates out from and is organized around this signifier, similar to these little lines of force that an upholstery button forms on the surface of material. It's the point of convergence that enables everything that happens in this discourse to be situated retroactively and retrospectively' (Lacan 1993: 268). In other words, the signifier at the quilting point *performatively* enacts the *capitonnage* or 'quilting' of the meaning of a discursive formation. Zizek's development of this concept with a specific emphasis on its political performativity makes it clear that the importance of the signifier as a proper name is its ability to stabilize and give authoritative meaning to a specifically *ideological* domain (Zizek 1989: 101–3).

16 In Lacanian terms, the desire to be 'worthy of love' is the desire to be the object of the Other's desire. The demand for love is precisely the articulation of desire *as* desire: that which always misses its object, over or undershoots itself as it tries to reach 'beyond' its apparent meaning, needing more than words can say (Lacan 1992: 294).

17 Identity can be seen to be a melancholic structure in that, in order to maintain subjective consistency and illusory integrity, the ego has to repudiate or foreclose those identifications that enabled it to come into being (see Kear forthcoming). The psychic mechanism by which it achieves this 'magical resolution of loss' is the anti-metaphorical *fantasy of incorporation*, which internalizes the lost or foreclosed 'object' within an artificially constructed unconscious or 'crypt' (Abraham and Torok 1994: 110–15). This fantasy is to be sharply distinguished from the *process of introjection*, which compensates for the loss of a love object by gradually introducing the desire associated with it into the ego. Whilst introjection enables the subject to come to terms with loss through a work of *mourning* that transforms aspects of the other into the self, the fantasy of incorporation functions to deny the loss as such, to effectively preserve the other as other within the *melancholic* self. Incorporation therefore both marks and masks the failure of introjection and the loss itself, with the 'crypt' functioning as 'the place in the psychic apparatus where the secret is buried' (Abraham and Torok 1994: 157). The phantasmatic 'crypt' is thus the site of the internment of the desires excluded from introjection into the ego and foreclosed from signification in the Symbolic (see Kear 1997: 256–60). The secret cannot be spoken of, but, in order to be a secret, must to some extent be shared and may even be metonymically *shown*. The incorporated secret is more properly a secret *primal scene* that implicates a whole cast of characters in the fantasy of incorporation (Derrida 1986: xix). The scene and its actors are kept alive inside the Real so as to prevent its trauma being repeated 'in reality'. In other words, the corporeal subject plays host to incorporated guests who lodge in the Real – the cryptic residence of the living dead – and enact a spectral 'internal hysteria' (Abraham and Torok 1986: 21). As Derrida succinctly puts it, 'Ego = Ghost. Therefore "I am" would mean "I am haunted"' (Derrida 1994: 133). If melancholia is the product of the fantasy of incorporation and mourning the enactment of the process of introjection, it follows that 'melancholia makes mourning possible' (Butler 1997: 170). Furthermore, mourning enables the subject simultaneously to perform the introjection of the desire attached to the lost object and to act out allegorically the failed introjection of the hauntologically 'primal' scene and the continued trauma of originary loss.

18 It is worth noting that Blair's reading itself conflated love and charity,

preferring the former translation so that the other meaning could still resonate within it. By repeatedly pausing to stress the word, it became clear that 'Love never faileth' to work ideologically: 'whether there be prophecies, they shall fail; whether there be tongues, they shall cease; whether there be knowledge, it shall vanish away' (1 Corinthians 13, 8).

19 This gap and the revelation of the Other's lack is the turning point in the Lacanian graph of *capitonnage* which marks the failure of the signifier to complete successfully the closure of meaning or to totalize the ideological field. When confronted with the Other's unfathomable question – '*Che vuoi?*' ('What is it that you want from me when you ask me that?') – the subject recognizes the terrifying abyss that is the Other's desire. This is the point, then, at which interpellation necessarily fails (Zizek 1989: 121).

20 Perhaps poetry is appropriate as an epitaph after all: 'Your eyes, lit up like shop windows / And trees illuminated for public celebrations, / With insolence make use of borrowed power' (Charles Baudelaire, *Les Fleurs du Mal*, quoted in Benjamin 1969: 190).

References

Abraham, Nicolas and Torok, Maria (1986) *The Wolf Man's Magic Word: A Cryptonomy*, trans. N. Rand, Minneapolis: University of Minnesota Press.

Abraham, Nicolas and Torok, Maria (1994) *The Shell and the Kernel*, ed. and trans. N. Rand, Chicago: Chicago University Press.

Barthes, Roland (1977) *Image-Music-Text*, ed. and trans. S. Heath, London: Fontana.

Barthes, Roland (1993) *Camera Lucida*, trans. R. Howard, London: Vintage.

Benjamin, Walter (1969) *Illuminations*, ed. H. Arendt, trans. H. Zohn, New York: Schocken Books.

Benjamin, Walter (1985) *The Origin of the German Tragic Drama*, trans. J. Osborne, London: Verso.

Bozovic, Miran (1994) 'The Bond of Love: Lacan and Spinoza', in *Lacan and Love*, ed. Renata Salecl, *New Formations*, no. 23: 69–80.

Butler, Judith (1993) *Bodies that Matter: On the Discursive Limits of 'Sex'*, New York and London: Routledge.

Butler, Judith (1997) *The Psychic Life of Power: Theories in Subjection*, Stanford: Stanford University Press.

Copjec, Joan (ed.) (1996) *Radical Evil*, London: Verso.

Critchley, Simon (1997) 'Di and Dodi Die', *Theory and Event*, vol. 1, no. 4 (Johns Hopkins electronic journal), http://128.220.50.88/journals/theory_&_event/v001/1.4critchley.html

Derrida, Jacques (1986) '*Fors*: The Anglish Words of Nicolas Abraham and Maria Torok', trans. B. Johnson, Foreword to Nicolas Abraham and Maria Torok (1986) *The Wolf Man's Magic Word: A Cryptonymy*, trans. N. Rand, Minneapolis: University of Minnesota Press.

Derrida, Jacques (1994) *Specters of Marx: The State of the Debt, the Work of Mourning and the New International*, trans. P. Kamuf, New York and London: Routledge.

Derrida, Jacques (1995) *The Gift of Death*, trans. D. Wills, Chicago: University of Chicago Press.

Diamond, Elin (1995) 'The Shudder of Catharsis in Twentieth-century Performance', in Andrew Parker and Eve Kosofsky Sedgwick (eds) *Performativity and Performance*, London: Routledge: 152–72.

Diamond, Elin (1997) *Unmaking Mimesis: Essays on Feminism and Theater*, London and New York: Routledge.

Foucault, Michel (1984) 'What is Enlightenment?', trans. C. Potter, in *The Foucault Reader*, ed. Paul Rabinow, London: Penguin: 32–50.

Green, André (1979) *The Tragic Effect: The Oedipus Conflict in Tragedy*, trans. A. Sheridan, Cambridge: Cambridge University Press.

Habermas, Jürgen (1985) 'Modernity: An Incomplete Project', trans. S. Ben-Habib, in Hal Foster (ed.) *Postmodern Culture*, London: Pluto: 3–15.

Habermas, Jürgen (1986) 'Taking Aim at the Heart of the Present', trans. S. Brauner and R. Brown, in David Couzens Hoy (ed.) *Foucault: A Critical Reader*, Oxford: Blackwell: 103–8.

Habermas, Jürgen (1987) *The Philosophical Discourse of Modernity*, trans. F. Lawrence, Cambridge: Polity Press.

Heidegger, Martin (1962) *Being and Time*, trans. J. Macquarrie and E. Robinson, Oxford: Blackwell.

Irigaray, Luce (1985) *Speculum of the Other Woman*, trans. G. C. Gill, Ithaca: Cornell University Press.

Kant, Immanuel (1992) 'An Answer to the Question: What is Enlightenment?', in Patricia Waugh (ed.) *Postmodernism: A Reader*, London: Edward Arnold: 89–95.

Kear, Adrian (1997) 'Eating the Other: Imaging the Fantasy of Incorporation', in Deborah Lynn Steinberg, Debbie Epstein and Richard Johnson (eds) *Border Patrols: Policing the Boundaries of Heterosexuality*, London: Cassell: 253–73.

Kear, Adrian (forthcoming) 'The Body in Pieces: Performance and the Fantasy of Incorporation', in Adrian Kear and Patrick Campbell (eds) *Psychoanalysis and Performance*, London and New York: Routledge.

Lacan, Jacques (1982) 'Desire and the Interpretation of Desire in *Hamlet*', trans. J. Hulbert, in Shoshana Felman (ed.) *Literature and Psychoanalysis: The Question of Reading Otherwise*, Baltimore: Johns Hopkins University Press.

Lacan, Jacques (1992) *The Ethics of Psychoanalysis: The Seminar of Jacques Lacan Book VII*, ed. Jacques-Alain Miller, trans. D. Porter, London: Routledge.

Lacan, Jacques (1993) *The Psychoses: The Seminar of Jacques Lacan Book III*, ed. Jacques-Alain Miller, trans. R. Grigg, London: Routledge.

Lacan, Jacques (1994) *The Four Fundamental Concepts of Psychoanalysis: The Seminar of Jacques Lacan Book XI*, ed. Jacques-Alain Miller, trans. A. Sheridan, Harmondsworth: Penguin.

Laclau, Ernesto and Mouffe, Chantal (1985) *Hegemony and Socialist Strategy: Towards a Radical Democratic Politics*, London: Verso.

Levinas, Emmanuel (1989) *The Levinas Reader*, ed. Seán Hand, Oxford: Blackwell.

Lukacher, Ned (1986) *Primal Scenes: Literature, Philosophy, Psychoanalysis*, Ithaca and London: Cornell University Press.

Lukacher, Ned (1989) 'Anamorphic Stuff: Shakespeare, Catharsis, Lacan', *South Atlantic Quarterly*, vol. 88, no. 4: 863–98.

Mafessoli, Michel (1991) 'The Ethic of Aesthetics', *Theory, Culture, Society*, vol. 8: 7–20.

Murray, Timothy (1997) *Drama Trauma: Specters of Race and Sexuality in Performance, Video, and Art*, New York and London: Routledge.

Nietzsche, Friedrich (1956) *The Birth of Tragedy and The Genealogy of Morals*, trans. F. Golffing, New York: Anchor Books.

Nietzsche, Friedrich (1976) *The Portable Nietzsche*, ed. and trans. Walter Kaufmann, Harmondsworth: Penguin.

Read, Alan (1993) *Theatre and Everyday Life: An Ethics of Performance*, London: Routledge.

Roach, Joseph (1996) *Cities of the Dead: Circum-Atlantic Performance*, New York: Columbia University Press.

Salecl, Renata (1994) 'Love: Providence or Despair', in *Lacan and Love*, ed. Renata Salecl, *New Formations*, no. 23: 13–24.

Sloterdijk, Peter (1988) *Critique of Cynical Reason*, trans. M. Eldred, Minneapolis: University of Minnesota Press.

Sloterdijk, Peter (1989) *Thinker on Stage: Nietzsche's Materialism*, trans. J. O. Daniel, Minneapolis: University of Minnesota Press.

Zizek, Slavoj (1989) *The Sublime Object of Ideology*, London: Verso.

Zizek, Slavoj (1991) *For They Know Not What They Do: Enjoyment as a Political Factor*, London: Verso.

Zizek, Slavoj (1993) *Tarrying with the Negative: Kant, Hegel and the Critique of Ideology*, Durham: Duke University Press.

Zizek, Slavoj (1997) *The Plague of Fantasies*, London: Verso.

13

DOWNLOADING GRIEF

Minority populations mourn Diana

Diana Taylor

We sat on the sofa – my young daughter, Marina, on my lap – lamenting the death of a woman we didn't know. As the coffin slowly made its way towards Westminster Abbey, the commentators reverentially droned on about the silence, the mood, the dramatic demonstration of public emotion. But there were so many publics, it seemed, participating in what looked like one and the same theatre of mourning. The exclusive, well-behaved public of dignitaries and movie stars inside the Abbey, the charged 'popular' audience on the meadows outside, the two billion people watching each other watching around the world. Everywhere the camera rested, people were sobbing silently. The emotion was contagious – the pity for Diana and her boys, the terror of sudden death, the rage at the ungiving queen, the contempt for the unloving husband. As in theatre, emotion gave way to applause. It irrupted outside the Abbey following Earl Spencer's eulogy and pushed its way inside, back to front, uninvited, disrupting the solemnity and reminding the high and mighty that this was, after all, the public's command performance. Then, as the hearse carrying the remains made its way out of London, the public threw its last bouquets at the departing diva. The incessant 'repeats' of the coverage assured us we were watching 'live'. What does 'live' mean, I wondered out loud, watching as we were across the Atlantic? 'It means we're live and she's dead', Marina explains. Then, 'You won't die, will you, Mummy?' punctuated by crying. 'No, darling, no, I promise', suddenly crying too, but embarrassed. Our tears were of a different kind – hers about pity and fear; mine complicated by my determination to resist this kind of identification which I found coercive and humiliating.

What's Diana to me, that I should weep for her? This was an odd mirroring effect – one Diana crying for another.

Once again, I was that awkward, chubby child in Parral, Chihuahua – my hair pulled back in pigtails so tight that my eyes wouldn't shut, my skirt pinned together because I'd popped my button, wearing my cowgirl boots, my fringed suede jacket and my beloved little gold scissors earrings that opened and closed. My Anglo-Canadian grandmother said I looked like a savage. Princess Anne, she reminded me, didn't wear suede jackets, to say nothing of the scissors earrings. I certainly was not her

187

'little princess' and I would never grow up and marry the prince if I didn't shape up and act like a good girl. Every holiday brought a new corrective for my savage condition – a royal calendar, a commemorative teacup. Now, there she was, the other Diana, the one who had been tall and blonde and beautiful, the one who would never be caught dead without a button, the one who would sooner have died than be chubby; the one who had married the prince. And look what happened to her. Here, once more, I was caught in a drama that had unexpectedly become my own. I felt a shudder, sensed the ghost.

Whose fantasy was this, I kept wondering during the weeks following the death and funeral of Diana, Princess of Wales? Or, rather, how did so many disparate fantasies come to converge on this rather ordinary human being? The disparity between the accident-as-incident and the spectacularity of the worldwide reaction demanded reflection. Diana's ghost, I suspected, had more to tell us about international relations than Madeleine Albright. What was the basis of such seemingly widespread identification? Were we watching a hodgepodge of funerary traditions or was this really a case of multicultural mourning styles coalescing before our eyes? What were the politics of such memorializing energy and the mimetic performances of grief being enacted simultaneously in various parts of the world, the synchronized moments of silence, the condolence book signings, the floral shrines? In Argentina, a magazine ran a drawing of Santa Evita and Santa Diana sitting side by side in heaven. There she was, 'the most beloved lady of our time', gracing the stamps of the Togolaise Republic. The Trinidadian carnival featured a number, 'Paparazzi is Hell' as a 'Tribute to the Queen of Hearts'. And there again, on the memorial walls on the Lower East Side of Manhattan, painted by US artists of colour. One mural, by Chico, places her next to other female Latina victims: Selena and Elisa (figs 13.1, 2, 3), both murdered by people close to them. Was this a conspiracy mural? On another, Diana is a saviour, along with Mother Teresa in 'royalty and holiness' (fig. 13.4). And here, in an admonishing mural by A. Charles that covers a synagogue on Houston Street, Diana's death is depicted as media overkill (fig. 13.5) and she's placed next to fallen African-American icons: Tupac Shakur and Mike Tyson, 'Live by the gun, Die by the Gun' (fig. 13.6). The murals made visible the versions of the saint, victim, and media object circulating in the public sphere. How did these global images get downloaded on to these neighbourhood walls? Why would minority populations care about her, when their own icons – from Evita to Selena to Tupac – had fared so poorly in the media? By what mechanism did Diana's popularity get construed as 'the popular'? The world willingly suspended its disbelief as this most aristocratic of women, married to a prince and future king, the mother of princes and future kings, who socialized with billionaires and celebrities, was transformed before our eyes into 'the People's Princess' and 'queen of people's hearts'.

Figs 13.1–3 Murals on East Houston (New York City) by Chico: Diana, Selena, Elisa. Photos by Diana Taylor

Fig. 13.4 Mural on Eleventh Street and Avenue A (New York City) by Chico, 'In Memory of Royalty and Holiness'. Photo by Diana Taylor

Diana's life, death, funeral and after life as quasi-sacred relic on display illuminates the way that multiple, intersecting social dramas play both globally and locally. All sorts of issues, ranging from eating disorders to unhappy marriages, to AIDS, to the workings of the media, to neo-colonialism, to globalization seem magically incarnated in her image. The tragic emplotment of the events surrounding Diana, and the theatricality of the staging, transmitted internationally, create the illusion of a cohesive, 'universal' audience. But is this not perhaps an international spectacle, in the Debordian sense, that 'presents itself simultaneously as all of society, as part of society and as an instrument of unification' as it 'concentrates all gazing and all consciousness' (Debord 1983: 3)? There is a difference between playing to a global audience and claiming that the drama has a universal appeal. By looking at the nature and staging of these social dramas, I'd like to explore, first, how globalization gets cast as 'universality' and, second, how this 'universality' gets downloaded strategically and reconfigured on the local level.

If we follow Victor Turner's model of the 'social drama', a model he claims to be universally valid, we can easily recognize the four phases he identifies: the *breach* (or social rupture and flouting of the norm), *crisis* (in which the breach widens and escalates), *redressive action* (which seeks to contain the spread of the crisis) and the *reintegration* (the reordering of

Figs 13.5–6 Murals on Houston and First Avenue (New York City) by A. Charles: Diana, Tupac Shakur. Photos by Diana Taylor

social norms) (Turner 1974: 37–42). Each of the four stages unfolds in a different dramatic mode, each rivalling the last in pushing the limits of theatricality.

The breach – Diana's divorce from Charles and her estrangement from the royal family – was pure melodrama. Played in the shrill key of interrogatives, declaratives and denunciations, the drama unfolded in explosive, sporadic cries and whispers. Almost everyone could (and apparently did) tune in to the latest episodes featuring the insensitive husband, the other woman, the disapproving mother-in-law. The boundaries of the 'appropriate' were repeatedly emphasized and transgressed. This private drama so publicly enacted situated protagonists and spectators alike on, and often over, the very brink of the admissible. I, like millions of others, lived the traumas of the infidelities and the self-destructive behaviours, eavesdropped on conversations, and shared the thrill of revelations and denials. When she wasn't struggling to hold back the tears, the captions pointed at the evidence of vulnerability. Her pain became the spectacle, played out in a hide-and-seek mode of strategic self-exposure on her part and the unrepentant voyeurism on mine. What made it all so thrilling, of course, was not its originality but its predictability – her story, played out so glamorously in the here and now, was basically the same old story. I, like many, many others, had lived it or seen it all before.

Diana's death – the crisis – was tragic drama. The fateful crash, which I (like those before me) will replay at length later, moved Diana out of the 'same-old' and cast her as the 'one'. We're alive and she's dead – she'd left the anonymity of the 'we' to inhabit the singularity of the 'she'. She crystallized into the original, quintessential, tragic lover, beautiful princess, angel of mercy and doting mother. Her sudden uniqueness, her tragic magnitude, allowed us to forget for a moment that she was also very much the product of a long history of collective imaginings that have normalized heterosexuality, glorified maternity, fetishized youth and femininity, glamorized whiteness, eroticized imperialism and promoted a discourse of volunteerism. Live? Or one more 'repeat' of the 'live'?

The redressive action – the funeral – was a theatrical performance. Following in the tradition of other state funerals, this event was one more repetition, only the latest, but never the first or the last of such spectacles. Eleanor of Castile, apparently, had a sumptuous send-off in 1290. Evita's funeral in 1952 was a magnificent spectacle – as massive, magnificent and stately as Diana's. It was a performance, orchestrated with a beginning, middle and end. The theatricality emanated from the careful choreographing of colour, movement, sound, space and regalia. Theatricality, commonly thought to be an attribute of theatre, clearly precedes and extends beyond it. Communities without 'theatre' (such as non-Western cultures like the Mexica) understood, and were ruled by, theatricality. And issues concerning theatricality lay at the centre of many of the tensions between the Queen and the British population. How much or how little theatricality should the country demand in honouring the passing of their Princess?

The theatricality of the event, as state spectacle, claimed visual power through layering – the addition and augmentation of traditional and non-traditional elements. Diana's funeral, weighed down in splendour, outdid those that had come before. But repetition was not simply a mimetic return to former displays of pomp and circumstance. Rather, it placed the pomp associated with the past in the service of monumentalizing the present. Each *re*-incarnation gains power through accumulation. Citationality, thus, was put to the service of originality, enhancing the 'new,' non-traditional touches, such as Elton John singing his pop hit, 'Candle in the Wind' – in itself recalling an earlier death. Yet, the prescribed, twice-behaved nature of funerals also has another, ritual, function. The formal handling of painful or dangerous transitions, or passings, helps to regulate the expenditure of emotion. Funerals have long served to channel and control grief. But this televised funeral, with its insistence on participation, seemed to provoke the very emotions it was designed to channel. The spectators, as much as the casket and the visible royals, became the spectacle for a global audience brought together, perhaps by grief, but most certainly by television, news-papers, journals and the Web. Unlike these earlier events, the media and communications systems performed the identification they claimed to report, assuring us that the loss, like the princess, was 'ours.'

The phase of reintegration, the period of reordering social norms, is playing itself out in multiple, less cohesive, less centralized, dramas. After the initial phase of virtual participation through frantic memorialization, Diana's ghost has become a site of intense renegotiating among various communities. Will the status quo ruptured by the breach be restored? Will the monarchy be reinvigorated, or permanently outmoded? Is Diana the new face of Tony Blair's kinder, gentler, more modern England? Does the burial site con-structed by her brother emblematize England's 'image in the world [as] a low tech "theme park of royal pageantry"' (Churchill 1998)? Or has she been transformed into a thoroughly non-British relic in a pay-per-view shrine out of Disney? Are the ruptures and divides made visible by her death overcome in this moment of reintegration, or are the divides more starkly visible than before?

Various modalities of expressive culture are made visible through the social drama paradigm outlined by Turner. And he is probably correct in affirming that this four-stage model illuminates all types of social conflict, ranging from office disputes to national conflicts. However, I am less convinced that these dramas play internationally and cross-culturally in any clear-cut way. The 'drama' of Diana's death and the 'theatricality' of her funeral elide rather than clarify the 'trauma' of border crossings as spectres traverse ethnic or national boundaries. What counts as a 'drama' in one context gets demoted to a mere 'incident' elsewhere. The Diana spectre becomes visible and meaningful as it dances within various scopic, political and economic repertoires – and vice versa. England's rose occludes Norma Jean as the new candle dancing in the wind. The dance performs more plays of substitution or, in Joseph Roach's term, surrogation (Roach 1996: 2) – England's rose crowds out Selena, the Rose of Texas; her funeral outdoes Evita's as the most over produced funeral of the century for a woman. The spectre, the spectacle and the spectator are all dancing at this funeral. Maybe because it's so hard to get a handle on *spec-ere* (to see) that phantoms, fantasy and performance have traditionally been placed on the opposite side of the 'real' and 'historical'. The fantasies in play may be linked to so-called universal and eternal anxieties about a glorious life, an unexpected death, and the fall of the great. The iterative and highly stylized nature of this stately display should not suggest that it is not, at the same time, deeply political and historically specific. What conditions allow these fantasies to become visibly incarnated in a woman no one cares much about? Though the spectre may come in and out of time, and though performances make visible the conflicts which otherwise remain diffuse, both spectres and performances are very 'live'. 'Haunting', Derrida notes, 'is historical [. . .] but not dated' (Derrida 1994: 4). The fantasies converging around the figure of Diana, I'll suggest here, require certain conditions of visibility, and bring various histories, ontologies and hauntologies of performance into focus.

In *Unmarked*, Peggy Phelan outlines the 'ontology of performance', stressing the liveness of the performative event, the *now* in which that performance takes place: 'performance's only life is in the present. Performance cannot be saved, recorded, documented, or otherwise participate in the circulation of representations of representation' (Phelan 1993: 146). Events such as Diana's death and funeral, however, also beg us to look at the flip side of performance's 'ontology' – at what Derrida has called its 'hauntology'. Many cultures are grounded on the notion of a second coming – the Mexica, the Christian, the Jewish, the Marxist to name a few. The ghost is, by definition, a repetition, Derrida's *revenant*. This is the moment of post-disappearance, rather than the moment preceding it that Phelan points to. The sumptuousness of the ceremony performs the sacralization of the *remains* – theoretically antithetical to performance. The remains, in this spectacle, take on a life of their own – so much so that one tabloid photo montage has Di looking on at her own funeral from the corner with a bitter-sweet smile – one more witness to an event that has overtaken her. The body that we assume lies in the coffin is all that we have to assure us that Diana was 'real'. It provides the authenticating materiality that sustains the performance of resuscitation. In spirit, she was present at her funeral as perhaps, inversely, we could argue that she was absent from her life. The shrine housing her remains will continue to guarantee the materiality of the global phenomenon that is 'Diana', the massive reappearance of the *revenant*.

Politically and symbolically, we haven't seen the end of her. The caption of a photograph of a London news-stand states that 'one might be forgiven for imagining that Diana never died last August. The Princess of Wales still keeps the presses roaring' (Hoge, *New York Times*, 9 February 1998). A cover of *People* (2 February 1998) depicts Diana as active in death as she was in life: 'In death as in life, she has raised millions for charity.'

My view of performance rests on the notion of ghosting – that visualization that continues to act politically even as it exceeds the 'live'. Like Peggy Phelan's definition, it hinges on the relationship between visibility and invisibility, or appearance and disappearance, but comes at it from a different angle. For Phelan, the defining feature of performance – that which separates it from all other phenomena – is that it is 'live' and 'disappears' without a trace. The way I see it, performance makes visible (for an instant, 'live', 'now') that which is always already there – the ghosts, the tropes, the scenarios that structure our individual and collective life. These spectres, made manifest through performance, alter future phantoms, future fantasies. Diana may have been the product of one way of envisioning royalty, but she has changed the look, style and scope in which royalty will be performed, and desired, in the future. Her enactment left a trace. Every woman running for political office in Argentina today wears the obligatory dyed blonde bun and Dior suit. In one sense, of course, the 'live' performance eludes the 'economy of reproduction' as Phelan puts it (1993: 146); but I would argue that its efficacy, whether as art or as politics, stems from the way performances tap into public fantasies and leave a trace, reproducing and at times altering cultural repertoires. Performance, then, involves more than an object (as in performance art), more than an accomplishment or a carrying through. It constitutes a (quasi-magical) invocational practice. It provokes emotions it claims only to represent, evokes memories and grief that belong to some other body. It conjures up and makes visible not just the 'live' but the powerful army of the always already living. The power of seeing through performance is the recognition that we've seen it all before – the fantasies that shape our sense of self, of community, that organize our scenarios of interaction, conflict and resolution.

What conditions of visibility are needed to conjure up the ghost? Of all the many potential spectres, why do certain ones gain such power? Why Diana and not somebody else? Why, as Michael Taussig asks in *Mimesis and Alterity*, does the spirit (and I would add, the ghost) need embodiment at all? (1993: 10). Evita's corpse, perhaps, can shed some light on the need to give material shape to a political force. Evita, the most politically powerful woman in the world in the early 1950s, has the world's most expensive corpse. It cost $200,000 in the early 1950s to embalm her and three wax copies were produced to trick all the would-be body-snatchers. The copies were so authentic that Dr Ara removed the tip of her little finger to distinguish her 'real' body from its replications. The original, here as elsewhere, is never as whole as its representation. Her body, the most politically charged fetish of the twentieth century, is key because it anchors the 'other Eva', the more powerful one, the one whose ghost continues to dominate Argentine politics (fig 13.7). *Spec-ere*, to see, is possible only through a history of spectacles and ghosts. Performance, be it artistic or political, accomplishes a moment of revisualization. It disappears only to

Fig. 13.7 'La Otra Evita', *Pagina 12*, 22 September 1996, Radar Section, cover. Photo uncredited

hover; it promises or threatens to reappear, albeit in another shape or form.

Performance becomes visible, meaningful, within the context of a phantasmagoric repertoire of 'repeats'. But there is double mechanism at work. On the one hand, we see only what we have been conditioned to see – that which we have seen before. So part of the grief we feel surrounding Diana's death is that she is so familiar to us. She represents the most general, undifferentiated version of the death of the beautiful woman – a trope so powerful, so naturalized, that it underwrites the Western imaginary and seems always to have been there. On the other, the spectacle presents itself as a universal and unifying event. But spectacle, to conjure up Debord, 'is not a collection of images, but a social relation among people, mediated by images' (1983: 4). The spectacle, then, is that which we do *not* see, the invisible that 'appears' only through mediation. Diana's spectre unites the spectators in the fantasy of loving and losing a woman no one really knows even as it hides the social relations among the very people who, theoretically, participate in the fantasy. Diana's death looks more like one more repetition of the same. Her death (singular and sudden) represents both the instant of her passing ('real', not-performative) *and* the reappearance of another death: Evita, Selena, Marilyn Monroe, Mother Teresa. As Elisabeth Bronfen argues:

> the death of a beautiful woman emerges as the requirement for a preservation of existing cultural norms and values [. . .] Over her dead body, cultural norms are reconfirmed or secured, whether because the sacrifice of the virtuous, innocent woman serves a social critique and transformation or because a sacrifice of the dangerous woman reestablishes an order that was momentarily suspended due to her presence.
>
> (Bronfen 1992: 181)

This, seemingly universal, trope elides the politics of cultural transmission. What we don't see, as the world mourns Diana, is that these women (judged innocent or dangerous, and usually both) form part of profoundly different imaginaries, and the borders of these imaginaries are policed. The spectre hides the spectacle. The mourning rituals may be similar; they may even encourage fantasies that they are communicable to different populations. But the politics are untranslatable.

Chicanas and Chicanos, as well as other Latinos, mourned Selena *en masse*, covered her coffin with thousands of roses, gathered tens of thousands of signatures in commemorative books, declared an official Selena Day, and attempted to inscribe her name and face on everything from websites to memorial walls to Coca-Cola bottles. The similarity of the rituals highlights the lack of empathetic reciprocity; theatricality blinds even as it makes visible. The redressive moment of one social drama (Selena's funeral) signals the moment of breach in another. A few hours before her funeral, Howard Stern had already shipped her back to Mexico: 'Selena? Her music is awful. I don't know what Mexicans are into. If you're going to sing about what's going on in Mexico, what can you say? . . . You can't grow crops, you got a cardboard house, your eleven-year-old daughter is a prostitute . . . This is music to perform abortions to!' (Stern quoted in Arraras 1997: 24). According to Stern, this death proves too lowly to constitute a drama. It's reduced to an incident – no drama, no breach. These non-dramas don't travel. How, then, do some ghosts dance over cultural boundaries while others are stopped, stripped searched and denied entry?

The spectre is as visible and powerful as the cultural narratives surrounding them. Stern's 'what can you say' relegates Selena to the ignominity of particularism: poverty, deviance, genocide. Stern sets himself up as the 'migra' of the imaginary, the border police that ensure that certain identifications don't sneak into dominant culture. There are no fictions of the reciprocity that Walter Benjamin ascribes to translation here, no lip service to communication (Benjamin 1955: 72), no invitation to make meaning in this puzzling affair – we don't understand you, what are Mexicans into? Punto. The performance of explicit non-caring performs the breach even as it denies the drama. By refusing to acknowledge a loss, it forecloses the possibility of redressive action and reintegration. The contempt of mourning rite denies the ghost its afterlife – this is about aborting. Diana, on the other hand, is invoked in hushed, reverential terms. She is assured an after life variously as saint, as mother of the future king or as a fundraiser for charities. Guaranteed a visa, her face crosses borders on stamps, calendars, magazines. Her image serves as the occasion for bringing artists together in the service of disenfranchised communities, even as members of those communities are denied the stage. Yet everyone, it seems, is invited to participate and conjecture – to participate by conjecturing. The staging of her death ricochets between twin poles of singularity and universality – Diana's life and death, though utterly unique and one of a kind, none the less sheds light on misery, suffering and stoicism everywhere. The coverage relished each detail, including what she ate for dinner on that fateful night! Yet, it shunned particularism, stressing that this death was also about everything and everyone. Immediately, the death was aestheticized as drama and cast in the most powerful and universalizing paradigm available to meaning-making culture – tragedy.

Diana's death and funeral are the clearest example I have ever witnessed of an Aristotelian tragedy of international magnitude, 'made sensuously attractive . . . enacted by the persons themselves', provoking pity and fear in millions of spectators (Aristotle 1973: 25). True, Aristotle insists that tragedy is the 'imitation' of an action, rather than the 'real' action itself. And in a sense, of course, the distinction between 'art' and 'life' is a vital one. But there is also a way in which life imitates, or is constructed through, art, and not the way around, that allows us to think of life as 'performative' in the early Butlerian usage of the term as 'a stylized repetition of acts' (Butler 1990: 270). The 'Diana' we knew was a performative construct, the product of stylized acts – royal protocol, fairytales, designer styles and Hollywood fantasy – a 'real' princess, a royal model as well as a new model for royalty. Her wedding provided the role and inserted her into script shaped by tradition. She temporarily fitted the bill (a young, aristocratic, malleable, good-looking virgin) the way an actor might be typecast for a role. What, one wonders, is 'real' about this 'live' performance?

Diana's death seemed similarly scripted, not by royal protocol this time but by 'fate' and the media. Everything about it was 'impossibly tragic'. It was significant and of Aristotlean 'magnitude' because of the nobility and beauty (heroic stature) of the woman, the struggle to shape her own destiny, the tricks to ward off fate (the 'real' driver leaving the Ritz as decoy). Diana's *hamartia* (tragic flaw) was so simple, so human according to the media/chorus: she merely wanted to be happy. The *peripeteia*, or reversal of fortune, was abrupt. The inevitability of the *catastrophe* was almost a given, considering the persistent mad chase by the paparazzi and the equally mad attempts at flight. The identification, as always in tragedy, was written into the performance. We don't have to know these great figures in order to weep for them.

And the timing couldn't be more tragically ironic. Just as she was starting her new life, which she had attained against all odds, she died on the very night he gave her 'the ring'. Not only that, she died with her lover – the latest version of the 'star-crossed lovers' as one tabloid called them. Even the names played into the tragedy as 'Dodi', meaning 'my beloved' and 'Di' raced off to their 'destiny' (as the accident is repeatedly alluded to by the tabloids). It was already written – not just in Aristotle but in the Song of Songs: *Dodí li va-aní lo* (my beloved is mine and I am his). Others find her death already coded in Genesis. The spectacle of the death elicits the spectres of the already there. We're moved because we already know the story – the dark tunnel, the frantic chase, Diana the huntress hunted down. The paparazzi, who dedicated their lives to 'doing Di', to banging, blitzing, hosing, ripping, smudging and whacking her (all words, we learn, for taking pictures rapidly), finally got their prey (Lyall, *New York Times*, 10 September 1997). The pace of the drama was fast, the tunnel tomblike in its dark enclosure; the plot revolved around sex and love; the reversal from supreme happiness to sudden death was precipitous; the end unexpected, shocking. And there was even a whiff of conspiracy about this end to a life that was otherwise so transparent, so devoid of mystery. Was the thought of Diana marrying an Egyptian playboy with a purportedly mafioso background too much for the royal family? The innocent woman had little by little become the dangerous woman – the woman whose bulimia, suicide attempts and infidelities threatened the image of the royal body, and now, its ethnic purity and exclusivity. Or was her accident contrived by the royal family to elicit popular support for itself? Project INTERFLORA, too, has seen it all before and warns its audience, 'REMEMBER! Awaken!!!!' It reads the 'Di thing' as a way of assuring the 'continuance of the Monarchy'. The floral tributes are an example of 'Flower Power . . . an M15 mind control program aimed at mass manipulation of the hearts and minds of the people of Britain [. . .] These floral tributes are NOT spontaneous!' Even Aristotle could not have envisioned a more perfectly crafted plot. While one tabloid headline screams out 'She didn't have to die!' (*Globe*, 16 September 1997), the way that the media 'made sense' of her death stressed the tragic inevitability of 'the love she died for' (*Globe*, 16 September 1997: 22). Anyone who has grown up with *Romeo and Juliet* or *West Side Story* – not to mention Agatha Christie and the Old Testament – might find something to relate to in this drama.

Diana's death precipitated a process of transformation and resolution on multiple levels. Diana, the dangerous and transgressive woman, 'died a lover'.[1] However, she was buried a mother, an innocent victim, a model of humanitarianism, a quasi-saintly do-gooder, and a member of the royal family. Once again, her image was transposed from one economy to another – the fairytale princess in the heavy gown of the wedding photos and the formally attired, motherly wife of the early years had already given way to the casual, lightly clad, jet-setting image of her final ones. Her death weighted her down again with the heavy brocade of the royal colours. She was back in the fold, centre-stage in the state's (polyvalent) self-imaging. After her wedding to Dodi, a sumptuous state funeral would have been unthinkable. Even as it was, the Queen initially demanded that 'Diana's body should not be placed in any of the royal palaces and should be taken to a private mortuary' (Ahmed, *Guardian (International Edition)*, 9 September 1997). The body, now saturated with the sacred/ abject power of the transgressor, had to be kept away from the 'royal'. It was 'private' now, exiled to the mundane sphere of the ordinary. But the non-royals wouldn't have it, not for 'their' princess. It was the Queen's turn to undergo public shaming. The 'people' forced her to perform her emotions, whether she felt them or not. 'Show Us You Care,' demanded *The Express*; 'Your People are Suffering: SPEAK TO US MA'AM,' *The Mirror* shouted from the stands. 'Where is Our Queen? Where is Her Flag,' *The Sun* wanted to know. 'Let the Flag Fly at Half Mast,' the *Daily Mail* insisted, giving the Queen her own little lesson in protocol.

The funeral was equally dramatic, though in a different way. This was imperial 'theatre', theoretically brokered by the 'people' and elaborately negotiated by all parties. The behind-the-scenes bickering of how much or how little (whether in terms of spectacle, emotion, viewers) was suspended by the splendour of the affair. The lavishness of the funeral made visible that the feuding, like the body, could be laid to rest; now that Diana was dead, rivalries and contentions could be forgotten. The country was once more 'united' in tragedy, and the overwhelming sensual experience (the smell of the flowers, the echoing sound of the horses' hooves, the trembling bodies of sobbing spectators) rekindled the erotic, though ambivalent, attraction to the state. So the funeral was an act of national conflict and resolution, an act of remembering one Diana by forgetting the others, of celebrating a life and transcending (obscuring) it with claims to a higher purpose and sanctity it never had. The transgressive, casual Diana was now thoroughly snuffed out, in part, by the very people who claimed to love her.

The funeral, as imperial theatre, was the opposite of the death, as drama. As in theatre, a word that refers both to the physical, institutional frame and the intentional action that takes place within its limits, the theatricality of the funeral elided issues of Diana's relationship to the monarchy by normalizing the rite of passage within the demarcations of historical tradition. Tensions disappeared behind the sensuousness, the ceremony of it all. The route, the lines of spectators, the choreography of the funeral party: this was a deliberate staging of the restoration of order, carefully modelled on previous, orderly funerals. It was about the 'again', 'now' and the 'as always' of royal self-representation. It disappears only to reappear. The achingly slow procession signalled the seemingly eternal and stable quality of a royal order now so openly up for grabs. The monarchy on show was very different from the one that waved at the world during the wedding. But the physical staging was also an act of restoration; it bracketed and emplotted the event, the first and last act of the 'Princess of Wales'. After the abrupt crisis caused by the crash, the funeral provided aesthetic closure and emotional resolution. As in ritual, this final stage promised to be deeply conservative. The restitution of the social order, disrupted but probably not profoundly altered by the crisis, meant that Diana once more returned to the official body she tried so hard to elude. As Charles, the two young princes, Prince Philip and Earl Spencer followed the coffin on foot, it was clear that the procession was as much about possession and control as about emotion and empathy.

What do 'the people' have to do with this imperial theatre, with the struggles between the Queen and the Prince, the Windsors and the Spencers, the Tories and Tony Blair's Labour Party? Que vela tenemos nosotros en este entierro? How do 'the people' get constructed? The 'staging of the popular,' as Nestor Garcia Canclini argues in *Hybrid Cultures*, 'has been a mix of participation and simulacrum' (1995: 191). Newspapers around the world ran the same article, extending the reach of the 'we' as it extended its audience. The same picture of Diana would appear, often with the same text, reporting on 'our' reaction to the devastating turn of events. One website instructed the user to 'send your feelings, condolences, or memorial regarding Princess Diana by *clicking here*. The 'Princess Diana fax poll' (set up by *The Post*) asked people to define what she meant to them (*New York Post* 4 September 1997).

In England, the event was interpreted as a 'revolution' (of sorts) because it showed 'the people' their new power. *The New York Times* reports the 'remarkable confrontation between the British people and Buckingham Palace and [. . .] an even more remarkable royal retreat' (Hoge, *New York Times*, 9 September 1997). 'The people' won their show-down with the Queen. They had demanded the pomp and ceremony of empire self-fashioning. The ritual, traditional to the extreme, could be read as a subversive reversal, for it was the public, not the Crown, who ordered it. Now, Tony Blair would have us believe, the old aristocratic ways vanished in one more act of surrogation: The Queen is dead; Long live Diana, the Queen of the people's hearts. Diana was the new face of the new England – stylish, youthful and compassionate. Hegemony now enjoyed a more casual, photogenic look. Diana, like England, was coming out of a depression. She would be the good will ambassador, the kinder, gentler, post-Thatcher face of England. Instead of politics, style. Instead of bitter ideological divides, consensus and national unity. 'The people' were featured as actors, rather than spectators, in the national drama.

The drama, then, is not just about Diana's tragic death, her regal funeral or the current political situation in England. The event, commentators insist, is performative – it is about changing structures of feeling. It changed the way the English performed their emotions – *out* with stiff upper lips and mean-spirited politics; in with touching, smiling and generous public displays of spontaneity. Diana touching AIDS patients, or dying children, signalled a new mode of being (British).

Loss. A ghost is about loss, loss made manifest, the vision of that which is no longer there. But what, I wonder, has been lost? Diana's candles, like Evita's and Mother Teresa's, provided the thousand points of light that corporate governments no longer feel compelled to provide. Lost, too, were both a working-class and a feminist agenda. Unlike Evita, who came from a working-class background and wielded unprecedented political power in Argentina, Diana and Mother Teresa had no political aspirations. Evita's popularity, channelled into a formidable populism, exceeded her death to the point that her ghost is still the most politically powerful player in Argentine politics today. This world is not ready for another Evita. The female powerhouse of the 1940s becomes the apolitical, unthreatening sophisticate of the 1990s. Evita too is denied a visa. When she was resuscitated in the movie *Evita*, Madonna was a style, a 'look'. The passionate public of political actors who maintained Evita in power melted into teary-eyed spectators and consumers. Evita's prophecy of her *revenance*, 'I will return, and I will be millions', seemed ironically fulfilled. For here she was, incarnated by Madonna of all people. Even the walls cried out in protest:

'Out Madonna, Evita lives.' Evita lives, but only in Argentina. In the USA, she is a lipstick, a fascist, a whore and an oddity. What next, Frank Rich asks? Maybe 'Barbie-like Evita dolls laid out in little clear plastic caskets' (Rich, *Journal, New York Times*, 11 December 1997). The conjuring act accomplishes one more disappearance by repetition – one face for another, one name for another, Evita dissolves in Madonna, while Madonna gains visibility through Evita (fig. 13.8).

So the choices were not, and never could be, between Diana and Evita, but about Diana and Mother Teresa (fig. 13.9). The way of the empire and the way of the Church–each take their ambassadors on the clearly one-way journey across borders, unsolicited yet living proof that the First World cares. In the language of 'love' rather than power, these women claim to relinquish their enormous political, economic and symbolic capital to the

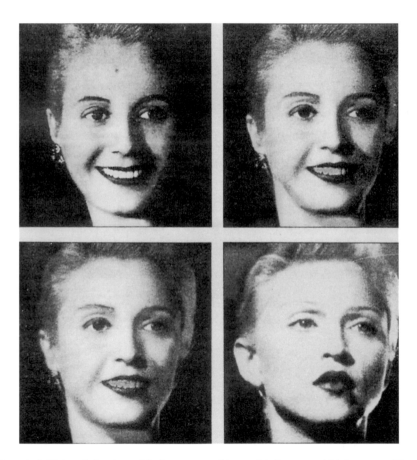

Fig. 13.8 Evita fades into Madonna. *La Maga*, 31 January 1996, cover. Photo uncredited

Fig. 13.9 Cartoon from *The New Yorker*. c. 1998 *The New Yorker* collection, Frank
Cotham from cartoonbank.com. All rights reserved.

have-nots. As with all overloaded icons, these women looked so transparent.
It's all so simple, this love talk. One could love Diana and love Mother
Teresa and hate still politics – as if the naturalized act of charitable giving
had nothing to do with the expansionism of imperialism, Catholicism and
late capitalism.

Lost, too, perhaps is the colonial nostalgia for the royal love. For viewers
in the former colonies, Diana also embodied a love–hate relationship with
empire and imperialism which she simultaneously represented and transcended. Her estrangement from the royals allowed for the ambiguous
positioning, the 'nepantla' of Latin American post-colonialism, or the
'ambivalence' stemming from what Homi Bhabha refers to as the 'double
articulation' (the like, but not quite) of the colonial predicament (Bhabha
1994). What options do colonials have but to juggle the complicated play
of identification and disindentification? She was living proof that the royal
love had failed. Yet the love of the royal could continue through 'our' love of
her. And our love for her led us to the possibility of transcending the racism
at the heart of colonialism through her new romantic attachment to Dodi.
This dark, sexy, playboy 'other', the ultimate consumer, was the antithesis
of Charles – the ultimate, old-fashioned, nerdy 'one of them'. It made her,
supposedly, 'one of us' – one of those left out or betrayed by an atrociously
uptight establishment. Okay, Dodi was a billionaire jet-setter, maybe not

quite one of us, and in our heart of hearts we wonder if they would have been happy, but the beauty of fairytales depends precisely, on the suddenness and untimeliness of their endings.

In another way, of course, Diana's death was about the loss of another form of materiality. Her image gave a 'universal' face to the disembodied globalism facilitated by satellites and the worldwide web. A product of intercommunication systems, the 'Diana' we saw was never and always 'live'. Never 'live' because, as one publication put it, 'No Pix, No Di' (Frankel, *New York Times Magazine*, 21 September 1997). Her liveness was a product of mediation. Susan Stewart, in *TV Guide*, writes: 'I know for a fact that Diana existed apart from television: I once shook her hand. It was exciting – she was already an international icon – but almost meaningless. All I remember is a blur of blond hair, a purr of a greeting. There are at least a dozen film clips of Diana more vivid in my mind than our actual off-screen meeting' (Stewart, 20 September 1997). Her physical existence, even redundant in life, served merely to authenticate her more complete, 'real' and ubiquitous image that continues to defy the limits of space and time.

Thus, she was never (but is always) 'live' and 'here' everywhere, haunting our present. A Virtual Di, her image will outlive her death – the signifier has no need of the signified, except as authenticating remains. She existed; that's enough to hang our dramas on. The web asks us to light a candle for her, expanding the simulacrum of participation. She is a fetish, a sacred image whose meaning emanates not from within but is assigned to it from without. As a fetish (whether in psychoanalytic terms or as commodity fetishism), her success stems both from the facility with which anxieties and fears are displaced on to her and the process of disavowal whereby the public can admire the image while ignoring the violence that contributed to its making. Her vulnerability, unhappiness and physical distress only contributed to her popularity, for, as someone noted, the unhappier she was, the better she looked. After her death, a new (and improved) generation of commodities circulate with her image on them – commemorative stamps, plates and dolls. The music and books she's inspired have reached the top of the charts and grossed millions of dollars. Her name is invoked in the war against drunken driving, landmines, AIDS, bulimia and other assorted social ills. A new army of designers will take charge of dressing and tutoring the ghost. Sightings have already been reported. New performances, political, artistic or entrepreneurial, will rise out of these archival remains. Other women will dance in that space of impossibility made visible by her performance.

But after the orgy of promiscuous identification has passed, do communities feel the abandonment and exploitation of the one-night stand? When we look in that colonial mirror, does her reflection look back at us, or do we see ourselves – complete with pigtails and popped buttons? The murals, as spaces of communal, public mourning, show signs of ongoing debate. Rather than simply reiterate the 'universal' show of love and loss, the murals make the events local, bringing them right into the heart of the community. 'Why do we care about Diana?' they seem to ask. By honouring her untimely death, the memorial walls situate her squarely in the long, unacknowledged history of untimely deaths in these neighbourhoods. They call attention to the gang and police violence in New York City that people prefer to overlook. But the walls also manifest the anger of the unrequited – 'why should we care about her when no one cares about us?' The Latino murals to 'Princess Di' now have 'Die' written all over them. Someone has written 'NO MORE SPECTACLES AT ALL, LADY DIE' in yellow paint on the admonishing mural that had warned about 'media overkill'. The mural that had declared its love for Diana, announcing that she would be missed worldwide, now has a consciously post-colonial message on it: 'We spent years of toil to break from the tyranny of British rule. NO SAINTS, NO SINNERS.' The Holiness and Royalty mural featuring Diana and Mother Teresa not only screams 'DIE! DIE! DIE!' (figs 13.10, 11, 12) but it participates in another form of circulation. This photograph (fig. 13.13) shows more than the displaced images of transnational globalization. It captures, too, the flip-side of that same economy that leaves people out in the cold – the displaced people, poverty, and homelessness that volunteerism does not dissipate on the Lower East Side.

Diana's ghost keeps dancing, tracing the convergence of pre-existing phantoms and the latest crisis – always a rewriting, an updating, a making actual, of something that is already. Because we are all caught in transnational economic and iconographic systems, we have no choice, it seems, but to participate in the circulation of capital, symbolic as well as economic. How we download these images and engage with them, however, reflects the power of the local community in framing the terms of the debates. On one level, of course, Diana's death and funeral constitutes a global drama of mass appeal. It has all the ingredients of a successful tear-jerker: the death of a noble, beautiful and misunderstood princess. Thus it is both a first and a repetition, a ghosting, a performative reappearance. In this particular staging, 'the people' are not only the consumers but also the constructed of this death. The spectacle of the spectre makes the spectator. Instead of mourning, the undifferentiated multitudes consume grief – the recipients, not the agents, of an emotion that is not their own.

'The people' light imaginary candles for Diana on the web in a virtual act of identification. But, on another level, the event has also staged the need for active participation. Is it so strange that we may want to act in a drama that we know full well is not our own? If we must engage, as it seems we must, these muralists show that people will establish the terms of conversation. Rather than constitute one more space for a downloading of the global, it opens one more strategic site for the negotiation of the local. Maybe it's not

Fig. 13.10 'No More Spectacles', Murals on Houston and First Avenue (New York City) by A. Charles. Photo by Diana Taylor

Fig. 13.11 'No Saints, No Sinners', mural on East Houston (New York City) by Chico. Photo by Diana Taylor

Figs. 13.12–13 'In Memory of Royalty and Holiness' by Chico (Fig. 13.4), with later additions. Photo by Diana Taylor

so odd that we, like the artists of the memorial walls, may wish to insert our own version of events by placing her next to our victims, next to other icons of caring, knowing full well that the gesture will never be reciprocated. But as always, there is the ambivalent push–pull of the imperial fantasy. The 'DI' erupts in 'DIE'. These rituals of passing insist that we should forget that we don't belong, even as we make clear that we remember.

Acknowledgements

This chapter is dedicated to Marina, BKG, and my students at NYU, all kindrid hauntologists.

Notes

1 I have drawn this insight from Barbara Kirshenblatt-Gimblett, 'Issues and Methods' class, Performance Studies, New York University, September 1997.

References

Ahmed, Kamal (1997) 'Charles and the Queen at War over Diana', *Guardian (International Edition)*, 9 September: 1.

Aristotle (1973) *The Poetics*, trans. G. Else, Ann Arbor: University of Michigan Press.

Arraras, Maria Celeste (1997) *Selena's Secret*, New York: Simon and Schuster.

Benjamin, Walter (1955) *Illuminations: Essays and Reflections*, New York: Harcourt, Brace and World Inc.

Bhabha, Homi K. (1994) *The Location of Culture*, New York and London: Routledge.

Bronfen, Elisabeth (1992) *Over Her Dead Body: Death, Femininity and the Aesthetic*, Manchester and New York. Manchester University Press and Routledge.

Butler, Judith (1990) 'Performative Acts and Gender Constitution: An Essay in Phenomenology and Feminist Theory', in Sue-Ellen Case (ed.) *Performing Feminisms: Feminist Critical Theory and Theatre*, Baltimore: Johns Hopkins University Press.

Canclini, Nestor Garcia (1995) *Hybrid Cultures*, Minnesota: University of Minnesota Press.

Churchill, Winston S. (1998) 'Modernizing Britain, the Tony Blair Way', *New York Times*, 2 January: A17.

Debord, Guy (1983) *Society of the Spectacle*, Detroit: Black and Red.

Derrida, Jacques (1994) *Specters of Marx: The State of the Debt, the Work of Mourning, and the New International*, trans. P. Kamuf, New York and London: Routledge.

Frankel, Max (1997) 'No Pix, No Di', *New York Times Magazine*, 21 September: 53.

Globe (1997a) 'She Didn't Have to Die', 16 September (cover).

Globe (1997b) 'The Love She Died For', 16 September: 22.

Hodge, Warren (1997) 'Flower Power', *New York Times*, 9 September: A1.

Hodge, Warren (1998) 'Diana's Hereafter, an Eternity of Newsstand Life', *New York Times*, 9 February: A4.

Lyall, Sarah (1997) 'Daina's Hunters: How Quarry was Stalked', *New York Times*, 10 September: A1.

New York Post (1997) 'Princess Diana Fax Poll', 4 September: 5.

People Weekly (1998), 2 February.

Phelan, Peggy (1993) *Unmarked: The Politics of Performance*, New York: Routledge.

Rich, Frank (1996) '101 Evitas', *Journal, New York Times*, 11 December: A27.

Roach, Joseph (1996) *Cities of the Dead: Circum-Atlantic Performance*, New York: Columbia University Press.

Stewart, Susan (1997) *TV Guide*, New York, 20 September: 24.

Taussig, Michael (1993) *Mimesis and Alterity*, New York: Routledge.

Turner, Victor (1974) *Dramas, Fields, and Metaphors: Symbolic Action in Human Society*, Ithaca and London: Cornell University Press.

NOTES ON CONTRIBUTORS

Jean Duruz teaches cultural studies at the University of South Australia and writes in the field of cultures of everyday life, with a particular interest in constructions of femininity, theories of consumption and the culture of food.

Susanne Greenhalgh lectures in drama and theatre studies at Roehampton Institute London. She has published on a wide range of subjects, including women and terrorism in contemporary drama, growing up female, televizing theatre, and children's books and the media. Forthcoming publications include essays on contemporary productions of medieval drama and children's audiotapes. She is currently writing a book on war in Western theatre.

Valerie Hey is a researcher in gender and education at the Institute of Education, University of London. She has written widely on educational politics and social policy, and is currently working on the analysis of the impact of New Labour politics. She is presently co-directing a study of gender and learning in primary schools and has recently published *The Company She Keeps: An Ethnography of Girls' Friendship*.

Carol Johnson teaches in the Politics Department at the University of Adelaide and has written extensively on various aspects of Australian political discourse, most recently on the discourse of the Howard liberal government and the race/gender politics of Pauline Hanson.

Richard Johnson is a professor of cultural studies at Nottingham Trent University, where he teaches research practice and cultural theory to PhD and MA students. From 1974 to 1993 he taught at the Centre for Contemporary Cultural Studies, University of Birmingham. Recent publications include: *Schooling Sexualities* (with Debbie Epstein); *Border Patrols: Policing the Boundaries of Heterosexuality* (co-edited with Deborah Lynn Steinberg and Debbie Epstein) and articles on collective research and authorship; sexuality politics; narrative and public and private grieving.

Adrian Kear lectures in drama and theatre studies at Roehampton Institute London. He is the author of several articles investigating the relationships between critical theory, cultural politics, performance and ethics. He is a contributor to the academic journals *Contemporary Theatre Review*, *Performance Research*, and *JPCS*. Adrian is currently co-editing another book for Routledge, *Psychoanalysis and Performance*. He also makes theatre work and undertakes performance research.

Joe Kelleher lectures in drama and theatre studies at Roehampton Institute London. He is the author of a monograph, *Tony Harrison*, and recent essays on children in film, writing and performance, and psychoanalysis and performance. His texts for the theatre include *The Wolfman*, *Mrs Freud and Mrs Jung*, and *The Clouded Eye*. He is a member of the London-based theatre company Theatre PUR.

Mica Nava is Professor of cultural studies at the University of East London. She is author of *Changing Cultures: Feminism, Youth and Consumerism* and co-editor of *Modern Times: Reflections on a Century of English Modernity* and *Buy This Book: Studies in Advertising and Consumption*.

Arvind Rajagopal is an associate professor in media studies at New York University and a member at the School of Social Science in the Institute for Advanced Study, Princeton for 1998–99. He is the author of the forthcoming *Politics After Television: Hindu Nationalism and the Reshaping of the Indian Public*.

William J. Spurlin is currently visiting scholar at Columbia University. His books include *The New Criticism and Contemporary Literary Theory: Connections and Continuities* and *Reclaiming the Heartland: Lesbian and Gay Voices from the Midwest*. He is currently editing a collection, *Lesbian and Gay Studies and the Teaching of English: Positions, Pedagogies, and Cultural Politics*, and he is also writing another book, tentatively entitled, *Imperialism within the Margins: Queer Identities and Cultural Practices in Post Colonial Contexts*. Professor Spurlin is the author of numerous essays on queer theory, American cultural studies and critical theory.

Deborah Lynn Steinberg teaches feminist, media and cultural theory at the University of Warwick and is an associate lecturer in women's studies for the Open University. Recent publications include *Border Patrols: Policing the Boundaries of Heterosexuality* (co-edited with Debbie Epstein and Richard Johnson) and *Bodies in Glass, Genetics, Eugenics, Embryo Ethics*. She has also written extensively on scientific and popular cultures of the gene, eugenics, sexuality and the body, and (with Debbie Epstein) on televisual cultures and the chat-show genre.

Diana Taylor is Professor and Chair of Performance Studies at NYU. She is the author of *Theatre of Crisis: Drama and Politics in Latin America*, and of

Disappearing Acts: Spectacles of Gender and Nationalism in Argentina's 'Dirty War'. She co-edited *Negotiating Performance in Latin/o America: Gender, Sexuality and Theatricality*, and *The Politics of Motherhood: Activists from Left to Right*. Professor Taylor has also edited three volumes of critical essays on Latin American, Latino and Spanish playwrights. Her articles on Latin American and Latino performance have appeared in *The Drama Review*, *Theatre Journal*, *Performing Arts Journal*, *Latin American Theatre Review*, *Estreno*, *Gestos* and other scholarly journals. She has also directed and participated in staging Latin American and Latino theatre in Mexico and the United States.

Jatinder Verma is the co-founder and artistic director of Tara Arts, London. He has directed, written and adapted most of Tara's productions, which have ranged from contemporary plays to the classics of the world stage. These have been staged at a variety of major theatres in Britain. His production of Molière's *Tartuffe*, with an all-Asian cast, at the Royal National Theatre in 1991 was followed by his staging of an eighth century Sanskrit play, *The Little Clay Cart* – the first time the Royal National Theatre had produced a non-European text. Jatinder is frequently called upon as a specialist cultural commentator by the media; he regularly addresses arts conferences around the world and has contributed to a number of academic publications.

Valerie Walkerdine is currently foundation professor of critical psychology and head of critical psychology at the University of Western Sydney, Nepean, Sydney, Australia. Her latest book is *Daddy's Girl: Young Girls and Popular Culture*. She is currently finishing two books to be published by Macmillan: *Mass Hysteria: Critical Psychology and Media Studies* (with Lisa Blackman) and *Growing Up Girl* (working title) with Helen Lucey and June Melody, a study of class and gender transformation in contemporary Britain.

INDEX

Note: the letter 'n' following a page number indicates a reference in the notes.